Mud Between Your Toes

A Rhodesian Farm

PETER WOOD

The events in *Mud Between Your Toes* are portrayed according to the author's best memory. While all the stories are true, the conversations in the book come from the author's recollections and are not written to represent word-for-word transcripts, rather they have been retold in a way that evokes the feeling and meaning of what was said and in all instances the essence of the dialogue is accurate.

First published in the United States of America in 2016.

Library of Congress Catalogue Number: 2015918050

ISBN: 1518830730

ISBN-13: 978-1518830730

*For my mum, Libby,
who loved the whole
damned lot of us*

MAP OF ZIMBABWE

Zambezi Valley

ZAMBIA

M'sitwe Farm

HARARE

ZIMBABWE

MOZAMBIQUE

Beira

Bulawayo

BOTSWANA

Beitbridge

SOUTH
AFRICA

CONTENTS

ACKNOWLEDGEMENTS

Writing *Mud Between Your Toes* has been an extremely uplifting experience, digging deep into the psyche of the numerous people from my past, and unearthing stories that might have been lost in the mists of time. It has been several years in the making, mainly because I had to steal time during my weekends in order to write. I am therefore incredibly fortunate to be working for the French news agency Agence France-Presse, where I have been surrounded by people who make words a part of their everyday life. I learned much from them and the care and guidance of these people cannot be underestimated.

First and foremost, I would like to thank Alison Holloway, who not only believed in me but also had the unenviable job of taking my rambling and oft-incoherent 150,000 words and honing them down to a more readable 80,000. Were it not for Alison this book would not exist.

I have been lucky to know Lachlan Colquhoun, a great friend and a man of many talents, journalism being one of them. Lachlan had been to M'sitwe Farm before it was taken by Mugabe's war veterans, had seen the farm in its prime and had met the complex character who is my father. Lachlan leapt at the chance to become my second editor, developing the chapters and castigating me for my appalling paragraphing. Many a happy hour was spent discussing the book over a glass of claret our time illuminated by Lachlan's wit and wisdom.

Mark Presley from Insight Productions in Hong Kong offered his expertise and camera equipment to shoot my interviews with Lachlan, which can be found at *www.facebook.com/ MudBetweenYourToes*. His direction and eye for detail have been essential in promoting this book. I would also like to thank Jack Colquhoun, Lachlan's son, who has taken time out from the Australian Film, Television and Radio School in Sydney to edit the video clips.

A sea of red ink covered the pages after Tim Pratt from the *South China Morning Post* and James Hossack from AFP were tasked with proofing the book. Both did a sterling job, suggesting improvements along the way. A final edit and the design of the inside pages by Simon Wait of Asiawide Media set the book in motion. Jason Fisher-Jones created the beautiful cover with the help of little Jack Chicken who kindly modelled his toes.

On occasion I have had to resort to the more colourful language of Mozambique Portuguese. Huge thanks go to Filipa De Paiva Raposo and Prof Teresa Cruz for their translation of my Beira trench talk.

This book is a memoir, and while it is a true story my memory can be scatty at the best of times. So it goes without saying that I thank everyone in my family who gave honest advice, encouragement, reason, humour and, of course, their side of the stories that have been retold herein. They were kind enough to read and provide detailed comments on many of the tales. These include my brother and sister Duncan and Mandy, my cousins Mark and Madeleine Olden, Lady Montagu of Beaulieu and not forgetting my mum, Libby, who wracked her brain and dredged up the past with absolute gusto. Her rich, fertile imagination made this journey as cathartic to her as it was to me.

Finally, I would like to thank the people of the Victory Block and Umvukwes who unwittingly gave me so much inspiration and content for *Mud Between Your Toes*. I do hope I have done them justice.

Peter Wood, September 2015

FOREWORD

Within minutes of meeting Pete Wood I was captivated by his storytelling.

It was 1998 and I had just moved to Hong Kong. A photographer friend had thrown a party for my birthday as a way of introducing me to the local media crowd. Of all of them, Pete Wood was the one I connected with.

His seemingly inexhaustible supply of priceless stories, delivered with a wicked but self-deprecating humour, had me enthralled as he held court, magnificently.

Most of the tales, of course, were about his native Zimbabwe, the former Rhodesia, and vividly re-created a world of rampant wildlife and adventure, but in the context of a vicious civil war in which life was continuing with an admirable stoicism and a stiff upper lip.

As we were born in the same year, the contrasts between our own experiences fascinated me. Mine was safe, suburban 1970s Australia, while Pete grew up and came of age in the midst of a deadly conflict and world-changing events.

The morality of my world was clear-cut and uncomplicated, while Pete had grown up a member of a community ostracised and outcast by the majority of the English-speaking world. And yet when I visited his family and stayed on the family farm I understood that these were generous people with a deep connection to their home, but wrong-footed by history.

Later, I was privileged to read the diaries Pete kept in these years, from 1975 to 1979. In strong detail he recorded amazing first-hand experiences of living through the Rhodesian Bush War, while at the same time recording the innermost thoughts of a young man growing up and bravely coming to terms with his own identity in volatile circumstances.

The diaries were unique documents and had a unique voice and perspective which demanded a wider audience.

With the publication of *Mud Between Your Toes*, I am delighted that Pete is releasing his own story into the world.

It is an invitation to a remarkable insider's view of a tumultuous period. But it is not only history, it is a personal journey told with sensitivity, compassion and, of course, with Pete's trademark humour which makes it a rollicking read, and well worth the time spent.

Lachlan Colquhoun, October 2015

I am an African

*I owe my being to the hills and
the valleys, the mountains
and the glades, the rivers, the deserts,
the trees, the flowers, the seas
and the ever-changing seasons that
define the face of our native land*

Thabo Mbeki
Cape Town, 8 May 1996

INTRODUCTION

I am an African

Standing on either side of me, hands gripped firmly on my shoulders, the two well-built South African immigration officers pulled me from the queue to the side of the room.

'What are you?' one of them asked.

The question took me by surprise. I looked up at them, hoping my face showed a mixture of confusion and innocence. They did not smile.

'What am I?'

It was not a question that readily springs to mind. I paused. 'I'm not sure I understand. I don't think I follow you, officer.'

I was beginning to stammer. His large hand weighed like a Virginia ham on my shoulder. His fingers tightened. It was not a friendly gesture.

They had singled me out from all the other passengers. Bugger, I thought. A lifetime of being treated like a two-headed alien, a pariah at border posts the world over, had made me rather twitchy.

The queues of tired, irritable, passengers across the room suddenly felt very distant, my escape route through immigration now appeared less than certain. I caught the eye of a woman I recognised from the flight. She looked pale, ashen under the harsh strip lights. Quickly she dropped her gaze.

The ham on my shoulder tightened its grip further. I pondered his question. What the fuck am I?

Male. Middle-aged. Gay. Caucasian. Chinese. Trying to find my African roots. Trying to rediscover my identity. They were losing their patience.

'But of course you understand,' one growled. 'What. Are. You?'

'Well, yes. Yes of course. You see...' I looked around me as if it were perfectly obvious, 'I am Chinese. Look, it says it there on the passport. Well, not so much Chinese,' I shrugged, 'but more HongKongese.'

I smiled. A weak, rather pointless smile. They stared. They shook their heads. Somehow the tiny gesture made the movement seem almost sinister. Like a leopard twitching its tail just before pouncing. This was not looking good.

'Chinese? Impossible!' the other man said. 'You are white. And look right there ... it clearly says you were born in Zimbabwe.'

The first man wagged a stumpy finger at me and pursed his lips.

'So, I will say this one more time...'

He leaned down until his face was inches from mine. I could smell his morning brew on his breath.

'What are you?'

Biting my lip to hold my tongue, I watched as the officer held up my passport, like he was handling a soiled handkerchief.

'It says nationality *Chinese*.' He looked me up and down. 'But you are not Chinese. So tell me, what are you?'

'Yes, well...' I answered, stifling a groan. I shrugged my shoulders. 'Look, it's complicated.' Invariably this would result in a rolling of the eyes, a shake of the head and a deep sigh. 'How complicated? Please humour me – I have all day Mr Wood. Or is that Mr Wu?' He peered at the passport photo in astonishment. 'You don't look very Chinese, if I must say so.'

It became apparent that as soon as I set foot in a foreign country, some form of explanation was required.

The Australian immigration, in their own inimitable way, would simply laugh and pass the document down the line to show their colleagues. 'Nathan, Shawna, look at this. The bloke is Chinese!' They would guffaw and look across at me as if I were a monkey with an accordion.

Unfortunately, not everyone was quite as friendly.

To prevent any further confusion, perhaps I should pause right here and introduce myself.

What am I?

I am an African.

I am a white African four generations strong. But I am also, rather confusingly, a first generation white Chinese. I chose to renounce my Zimbabwean citizenship and take out Chinese nationality, mainly for the Hong Kong passport.

But as I was soon to find out, in order to become a lawful Hongkonger one must first become Chinese. A Chinese national to be precise.

Of course, there was another very good reason to ditch the passport of my birth.

The Zimbabwe passport was virtually worthless. Travel restrictions made that green and gold document somewhat redundant and travelling around the world became a major pain in the backside. The old Zimbabwe document required a visa for every conceivable country (except Malaysia where president Mugabe and the first lady spent their summer holidays, in Langkawi).

I was pissed off at having to ditch the passport of my birth, but I felt I had little option.

The trouble really all began when the Zimbabwe currency went into free-fall. We should have seen it coming. After all, hyperinflation began back in the late 1990s and should have set alarm bells ringing.

The real crash happened in 2008 and by then it had become impossible to even measure. Zimbabweans began talking about millions, which soon turned into billions, then trillions. By the end of that year, inflation was loosely estimated at 76.6 billion per cent. No one knew what the extra zeros on the bank notes even meant. Gazillions? Katrillions? The US$ was now equivalent to 2,621,984,228 Zim dollars and counting.

People shuffled around the empty supermarkets dazed and confused like zombies from *The Walking Dead*. Little old ladies would lug an expandable Samsonite full of banknotes into a store and come away triumphant with a loaf of bread. Lavatory paper became more valuable than money, adding to the expression 'not worth the paper it's printed on'. Silver and copper coins disappeared overnight and even the bank notes became obsolete, having been replaced by worthless Bearer cheques or Agro-cheques.

Passport pages became rather rare once the country had run out of money to buy passport paper. Well, to be fair, the country had run out of money to buy anything at all. So with every page in my passport filled to the brim with exit, entry and visa stamps, I decided to return home in 2006 to get a new one on the black market, at a cost of US$120, or its equivalent at the time of Z$2,500,000, all in crisp bank notes stuffed into a cardboard box and pushed surreptitiously under the table to a rather dodgy-looking character.

The gentleman behind the desk knew immediately that we had the right amount of money. There was no counting of notes back then, they were into weighing their bank notes in 'bricks'. He placed the carton on a set of scales, nodded briefly and slid it back beneath the desk. Job done. A man appeared and ushered us downstairs to our car. He slipped quietly into the back seat and ordered us to drive.

Before long, we were being navigated down roads I had never dared travel on in the past. We drove through the newly blossoming shanty towns and past old run-down suburbs I had never ventured into before. Harare became a blip on the horizon. The fuel gauge was edging towards a quarter of a tank. My palms began to sweat. The dark man in the back seat, shades on and mobile phone stuck to his ear, never spoke to me once, merely gesturing for us to go 'left, right or straight'.

'Christ,' I whispered to my mother who was sitting quietly next to me in the car, 'we might be taken away and raped.'

Glancing at me, she rolled her eyes. 'No such luck at my age,' she mumbled.

Finally, we reached an abandoned school that was buzzing with people, policemen, chickens, goats, piles of over-ripe guavas and paw paws for sale, and long queues. My heart sank when I saw the long lines but thankfully Z$2.5 million, back then, still had some clout. I hate pushing in, it just seems so unfair. Still,

I was secretly delighted to have our broody, undemonstrative gentleman friend at my side.

People parted as we were led straight to the front of the queue, where to my astonishment we were confronted by the most enormous, pristine, whirring machine spitting out Zimbabwe ID cards and passports like an automatic poker dealer. Who was I to question this gift from the Tel Aviv Dizengoff diamond traders to our dear country? A jolly, overweight man scanned my fingers, thumbs and face – and god knows what else – and after a few minutes I went away, having been prodded and probed, as the proud owner of not one, but two Zim ID cards. 'In case you lose one,' the cheery operator said with a wink.

The next day our shady dealer, mobile phone still stuck to his head, took me to the ominously pitch-black passport office near Harare Park. No electricity meant that old Imperial typewriters could be heard clicking and clacking away in the candlelit gloom. Lines of bored people leaned against the walls, fanning themselves in the heat. If the fetid body odour didn't knock you out, the low-hanging fixtures certainly would. But within hours, I miraculously skipped away with a shiny green Republic of Zimbabwe passport. Not bad for two days work and two-and-a-half million dollars.

Soon afterwards, when working for the French news agency AFP, I went on a business trip to Tokyo. The Japanese immigration insisted that my document was false. Despite my protestations, not to mention my business visa stamp, they promptly put me into a room full of Nigerian and Ghanaian traders. Everyone seemed larger than life with deep baritone voices and brightly patterned garments.

It was like being committed to an asylum full of African Demis Roussos lookalikes. I was the only man in a suit. The rest were attired in a colourful riot of tie-dyed Ghanaian *fugus*, kaftans and the obligatory sunglasses. Yet these loud, confident Africans treated me as an African, and I loved it. Oddly, I felt part of something much bigger. Something that ran much deeper than mere skin colour.

When I lived in what was then Rhodesia, I always felt strongly that my roots were firmly planted in Africa. I saw myself as African. I saw myself as Zimbabwean. Robert Mugabe, on the other hand, felt otherwise. Every white person became persona non grata.

And so, reluctantly, I decided to apply to become a Chinese national. I felt cheated by Mugabe. Angry. My birthright was at stake. Still, it seemed better to be part of a very rich corrupt regime rather than a very poor corrupt regime.

Feeling somewhat deflated, I marched into the Hong Kong Immigration office demanding a Hong Kong passport. *Demanding?* I could not ever imagine demanding anything in Zimbabwe.

'Sir, you will just have to wait,' invariably would be the response back in Africa. There is no hurry in Africa.

'I have been here for 15 years. I deserve a passport,' I hollered at the officer. The young, handsome and immaculately uniformed man behind the counter simply laughed.

'But Mr Wood,' he said with utter bemusement, 'you are not ethnic Chinese. You do not stand a hope in hell of being accepted.'

'ETHNIC Chinese. *ETHNIC CHINESE?*' I barked, 'I want to be a Hongkie. Not a Chinese. What does being *ethnic* Chinese have to do with it?'

Having had my African ethnicity questioned constantly back home, indeed rammed down my throat on a daily basis, I was rather tired of the whole ethnic issue by now.

'Well, you see,' said the very patient man, 'now that Hong Kong is part of China you need to become a Chinese national before you can even apply for a Hong Kong passport. And of course you cannot become a Chinese national unless you are, well, an ethnic Chinese. Besides,' he continued, 'you need to conduct a second interview in a Chinese language of your own choice – I get the feeling THAT might be a problem?' He sat back in his chair and smiled.

I peered at his serenely handsome face. I took in his immaculate uniform, the pips on his shoulders, the manicured nails, and then slowly, as if in a dream, I slid my hand across the desk beneath the glass divider and touched his hand, summoning all my powers of seduction. Staring into his fathomless eyes, I told him straight out, 'Did you know that you have a beautiful uniform?'

The poor man fell apart. 'Well, Mr Wood, we can but try.'

He was mine.

'Oh, and Mr Wood,' he called through the glass partition at my retreating form. 'Would you like to have lunch sometime?'

YES! I thought. I had won.

Ten days later, an officious letter stamped with the red star arrived from the Motherland congratulating me on becoming a Chinese national. No second interview ever took place. My less than rudimentary knowledge of Mandarin was never to be questioned. The handsome man never called me back. Oh, and my new Chinese name was Mr Wu.

And so, there you have it. I grew up as a minority. I am still a minority. Indeed, throw in the gender factor and you get a minority-within-a-minority. A gay, white African. No, let's call me a gay, white, Afro-Chinese. The mind boggles. So in reality, I am a gay, white Chinese who used to be a gay, white African. Fucked-up or what?

Yet, I was always a minority, even growing up in Rhodesia. Back then, I simply could not cope with life in the country as a (closeted) gay, white minority-within-a-majority. I needed space to breathe. I had to discover myself. I moved to London and became a part of the (largely) white majority-within-a-majority. Briefly. Then I came out of the closet and once again became a minority-within-a-majority, finally moving to Hong Kong and becoming a minority-within-a-minority. I guess life would be frightfully dull were it not so complicated.

Yet the story of my journey to Zimbabwe from Hong Kong began way before that with some diaries, the embossed gilded dates 1975 to 1979 still barely visible along the spines. Tatty, with old Sellotaped cuttings and photos peeling away, many had onion skin pages slipping from their bindings. Dried flowers from the farm and dog-eared tickets to a Lena Zavaroni[1] or 5000 Volts[2] concert would slip out and float to the floor. Languishing in a cardboard box aptly named 'Pete Wood's Life' they had more air miles than I could ever hope to earn.

My old school friend had just completed 22 years as a Reuters war correspondent. For reasons lost in the mists of time, Foxy had acquired this small, hermetically sealed box for safekeeping. Every time he decamped to a new bureau, the box travelled with

---

[1] Lena Hilda Zavaroni was a Scottish child singer. With her album *Ma! (He's Making Eyes At Me)* at ten years of age, she became the youngest person in history to have an album in the Top 10 of the UK charts.

[2] 5000 Volts was a British disco act popular in Europe in the 1970s.

him: Hong Kong, London, Brussels, Nairobi, Singapore, Jakarta, and now finally back to Hong Kong, by which time Foxy had scribbled on the label 'Pete Wood's *diminishing* Life'.

Around this time I read an amusing yet poignant article written by Kenyan journalist Aidan Hartley for *The Spectator* titled *Back in the Trenches.*

How ironic that their legacy is a British diaspora across the Commonwealth of people who are rather confused about who they are. In Kenya I am a 'mzungu'. My family has been here since the 1920s but I am still what the Afrikaners call a 'salt dick' – with one foot in Africa, one foot in Europe and my tackle hanging down in the sea between.

God only knew where my tackle was hanging, but I needed to find out.

And so, crown jewels tucked between my legs and Hong Kong passport in hand, I flew back to Africa and it was with this thought in my mind that I stepped off the aircraft and walked across the hot tarmac, rippling in the mid-afternoon haze to the brand-new, unpaid-for, state-of-the-art North Korean-built Harare International Airport terminal. A hideous parody of the Great Zimbabwe ruins, the air traffic control tower, loosely built to resemble the 15th century stone tower. Harare International Airport: a building even a mother couldn't love.

The power was out. The conveyor belts at a standstill. I sighed with satisfaction.

I was home.

1

The Old House

When my brother Duncan was born at Lady Chancellor Hospital in 1959, my father and his best friend Gerry von Memerty turned up rather late, and a little worse for wear. They found the corridor barred by a stern-looking matron, hands upon her broad hips and starched cornette perched upon her head.

'Only husbands or fathers beyond here,' she growled, one eyebrow raised, double chins aquiver. As quick as a flash, Gerry responded, 'Well HE'S the husband and I'M the father.'

She found this so amusing that she let them pass, giggling like two naughty schoolboys caught bunking out. My father crossed the darkened ward and congratulated my mum by handing her a stick of half-eaten beef biltong. My mother, recovering from a Caesarean, was the only patient without flowers and many of the white dames in the ward must have thought she was a fallen woman.

By the time I arrived in 1962, it was my mother's third C-section in as many years. Complications arising from my being seven weeks premature meant that my father was asked to choose to save the mother or the child if things took a turn. My father chose the mother.

Somewhat typical of my mother's spooky side of the family, she told us that during the birth she had undergone an autoscopic or out-of-body experience, where she found herself levitating above her own body. She watched with morbid fascination while the surgeon cut into her and removed this tiny baby. She claims that she could hear the doctors discussing clear as day whether she was going to live or die. Naturally this *expérience de mort imminente* or *silver thread* as it is commonly known, had a profound effect on her relationship with her baby boy.

And so began my life on a southern African farm.

It was a childhood of great freedom beneath the enormous Lomagundi skies, but at the same time constricted by decades of rigid colonial norms and a brutal, very personal civil war. To the north the sluggish Hunyani River ran towards the Zambezi. To the east the deep Umsengedzi River, or Musengezi as it is now known, wound its way to Mozambique, and to the south flowed the green M'sitwe River from which our farm took its name. Like a scar through the heart of the country ran the Great Dyke, known in our district as the Umvukwe Range, and to the west the smoky blue Ayrshire Hills of Raffingora.

Nestled in a peaceful valley among these features was M'sitwe Farm.

More than four decades after my birth I find myself again passing through the Umvukwes village, once neat with crocodiles of uniformed schoolchildren in khaki shorts or green gingham dresses with felt cloche hats pulled down over the brow.

The clipped hedgerows and tidy mown lawns that grew right to the edge of the road have now been replaced by litter. Food wrappers and pages from the *Zimbabwe Herald* flutter against chain-link fences, broken flip-flops made in China, known locally as ching-chongs and the ubiquitous plastic bags – the scourge of Africa – lie scattered at the Matambanadzo bus stop. Flap, flap, flap.

My brother navigates the Land Rover around a pothole big enough to break the axle. Still, I am surprised how well maintained the roads are in the village. In the back, my 76-year-old mother sits quietly, an occasional gasp or 'oh god, look at that' punctuating the cabin. I question whether I should have bullied her into coming. I thought it might prove cathartic, but now I have my reservations. Certain landmarks spur her into humorous stories or dreary reminiscences. Others make her go silent and broody. My brother occasionally glances across at me and raises his eyebrows in a manner that suggests 'I told you so'.

'It'll do her good,' I mumble.

'I heard that!' my mother says. 'I'm not dead yet you know.'

A Zimbabwe flag still flies proudly at the post office, the colours rather faded. Fred Youngman's, the butcher, is now closed and shuttered. The gas station without fuel.

'I'll give you the grand tour,' Duncan says. 'It'll take about three minutes.' His deep laugh booms through the cabin.

We drive past the Umvukwes clinic teeming with people, women with toddlers balanced on their hips or babies tied on their backs, some with both. A clinic that offers hope but is now dark without power and without *muti*[3]. In the gloom the indomitable Doctor Sithole and his nurses soldier on despite the cut-backs – not even a bottle of aspirin on their empty shelves.

'I had to take a woman there last week,' my brother says, gesturing as we drive past.

'Inside the corridors of the clinic it was so dark you could only see people when they laughed or opened their eyes. The place looked like the setting for *Hotel Rwanda*.' Another roar of laughter.

---

[3] Shona word meaning 'medicine'.

The Spa store was open with people lounging on its steps talking loudly into mobile phones. *M'bira Chimurenga*[4] could be heard coming from the store, booming from old battery-operated ghetto blasters. It is very strange driving through a village that has no power but still resonates with activity. People come and go as usual, but the darkness inside the shops is troubling.

Umvukwes had never been a picturesque village. It was like any frontier farming town. But now as plastic bags sweep across the road one gets a sense that the old world lay buried beneath the litter, not too deep but out of sight. If you scratched the surface you might find something from the past. Fragments of a time gone by, shattered like a mirror but still barely visible.

I notice the occasional SUV or farm pick-up covered in dust, possibly from one of the few remaining farmers eking out a living in nearby Forester Estate. An elderly white man hobbling on a cane near the Malvern House Home for the Elderly gives Dunc a wave as we drive past. Dunc toots the horn. 'Christ he's aged,' Duncan says. 'Poor bugger.'

Umvukwes and indeed Zimbabwe, tatty as it may be, has largely escaped the urban scribble of American graffiti. If any, the graffiti is political: a few for the MDC (open hand) but largely ZANU-PF[5] (closed fist). The stencils or imprints of flat open palms plastered against walls, rocks and trees imply that the opposition party, the MDC, was still alive, albeit underground.

'This is a ZANU-PF stronghold,' Duncan explains. 'Few people in the village would dare give the MDC salute.'

---

[4]Zimbabwean Chimurenga music was popularised by Thomas Mapfumo and has its roots in traditional Shona music which used *ngoma* drums and *m'bira* (a thumb-piano). The Shona word *chimurenga* means 'liberation' or 'rebellion' and entered common usage during the Rhodesian Bush War.

[5]Robert Mugabe's ruling party, the Zimbabwe African National Union – Patriotic Front.

The Farmer's Co-op, renamed The Farm & City, bustles with shoppers. The place still worked. Just. The post office is, as always, painted in its government colours of jade green and cream. Indestructible *police camp flowers*[6] struggle to survive along the pathway lined with whitewashed rocks.

The Zim postal service is still the best lifeline to the rest of the world. Incredibly, despite all the difficulties in Zimbabwe, this service actually works in a place where all other government organisations seemed to be riddled with corruption and incompetence. If you were patient, you might even call the postal service efficient.

Children and family members who had *taken the gap*[7] to the UK, USA and South Africa still sent back parcels and hampers of goods from Walmart, M&S, Asda and Sainsbury's. Goodies such as candles and matches, vacuum-packed rice, canned goods such as sardines or tuna – basic stuff to live on – not the old kind of hampers from Fortnum's that were stuffed full of Quality Streets and cashmere jerseys and long ghastly scarves knitted lovingly by some maiden aunt. Nowadays airmail took three or four weeks, but the mail always got through in the end. Umvukwes, just like the country itself, ticked over, albeit haphazardly.

ZANU-PF posters hang on fences flapping in the wind, the bespectacled face of President Mugabe peering out behind his characteristic spectacles more like a school teacher than a dictator. A pair of bush doves roosting above the posters left a series of white splatters across his face hiding those intense, beady eyes. We drive past the grain depot, now empty apart from a few lonely sacks of unidentified grain used by some NGO hoping to make a difference or at the very least make

---

[6] Madagascar peonies.

[7] 'Run away abroad'.

some 'philanthropic' billionaire sleep better at night because he had given something back. One of the biggest grain depots in the country now reduced to a few sacks of mealies[8]. We are through the village in minutes and back on the road to the V block, short for Victory Block.

'Shouldn't we be turning right?' I ask my brother.

'Nah,' he says, 'that road through the Birkdale Pass is buggered – washed away in the last rainy season. We have to go around via Mutorashanga – it's a pain in the arse but safer. You get the scenic route today! The Road Council hasn't been paid in over six months so all repairs are done by us.'

I am disappointed. That journey through the Birkdale Pass was ingrained in my memory. We drive on in silence past so many farms that used to belong to friends, now mostly derelict and empty. There is a beauty to the countryside that is hard to pinpoint. Where the agriculture has vanished, the bush has crept back in to reclaim what once belonged to it. The Umvukwes countryside is breathtaking. I imagine that it is the old Umvukwes from before white men arrived. Before we ploughed up the land to plant our foreign seeds and tore at the hillsides for minerals and ores. All along the drive the stunning range known as the Great Dyke rises above the plateau, and continues unbroken to the horizon.

Once through the Dyke we drive fast through the Mutorashanga mining town with its row upon row of tin huts, identical except each street is painted a different pastel colour. Like beach huts in Brighton, I think to myself. Row upon row. Pinks and baby blues and lavender and lemon. The mine roads are still good owing to the Chinese influence. For miles we can see alluvial mining on either side of the road, huge tracts of land where the

---

[8] Maize or corn.

topsoil has been removed and sifted for rare earth minerals. Sadly, the land never recovers and very little ever grows in the barren earth. Along the Dyke, deep red scars from dozens of prospectors can be seen. The hills look as if they are bleeding.

'I thought this had been banned in the seventies?' I ask Duncan.

'So did I. But I reckon the Chinese money talks around here,' he says, gesturing towards a corrugated iron hoarding with the words Sinosteel Corporation | 中国中钢集团公司. 'One of yours?' he asks with a wry grin.

We pass a massive truck emblazoned with the same Chinese characters and loaded down with soil, the huge wheels barely fitting on the narrow tar road.

'See that?' Dunc continues, 'they just take all the soil as is and ship the whole bloody lot back to China in giant containers. Nothing is left. Even Africa is getting shipped away. Truck-load by truck-load.'

After the mining town the going gets more picturesque, but also much harder and slower. The roads become dirt, rocky. In places they are washed away entirely. We change into 4WD. What once might have taken 20 minutes now takes nearly an hour to cover, the gears and wheels grinding against the surface. This is the Sipolilo Loop Road and it was the main artery adjoining the two massive farming areas of Raffingora and Umvukwes. It seems time has stood still.

All along the way things are familiar from when we used to travel this road almost daily. Every corner, every farm, every African store were part of our everyday lives. Here and there the tarmac peeps shyly through the gravel, reminding us what the road used to be like. It was never particularly good at the best of times, but now it is a series of gullies and exposed rocks.

The Girdlestones farmhouse. Burned to the ground.

Dave Dolphin's store. Roofless and dark.

Cyril Hall's farm. Deserted.

My heart begins to pound as we near the M'sitwe Halt. And there it is, across the valley to my left, the farm I grew up on. A sea of green trees and granite *kopjes*[9], the Bald Kopje forming the centrepiece. The beauty is breathtaking.

'Good Lord, just look at that. I had quite forgotten how staggering it really was,' my mother says.

She speaks in the past tense. This part of her life is finished. We stop briefly to survey the landscape. No one speaks for a while. A line of young women, colourful in their sarongs, baskets and enamel dishes balanced upon their heads, file past. They smile as if seeing a 4WD down these parts is quite normal. Beyond the valley the tall rock edifice of Matimba, the tallest peak in the V Block, and then in the distance the extraordinary rhino shaped *kopje* of Bugaziwa on Kelston Ranch tower out of the grey bushveld. My mother is leaning back in the seat, her usual chatter gone.

We drive on and ten minutes later arrive at the barns of M'sitwe, our farm. It looks like a war zone. All the corrugated iron roofing has gone from the sheds. Walls have caved in in places. Pigweed and blackjacks have taken hold in unruly bunches along the edge of the walls and across the yard. The old fuel shed with its ancient spoke-wheel window stands alone – all the other walls having crumbled around it. Perhaps what is most disturbing is the silence. Only the crunch of our wheels on the gravel. No chickens. No women carrying babies.

---

[9] *Kopje* is an Afrikaans word for a small granite hill.

No tractors. No hammering or singing or cursing. No noise at all. Nothing. No one.

We engage first gear and head up the hill. The final stretch before the old house. As soon as Duncan switches off the car engine, I am immediately and overwhelmingly engulfed by the silence. Utter silence. Something I have not experienced for a long time. Somehow the ticking of the engine as it cools seems to make the silence even more palpable. I sit back in the car, my sweaty back sticking to the seat, and quietly take in my surroundings. Not a cricket nor a bush dove breaks the solitude. Midday on the African savannah and the world is asleep.

Duncan looks across at me. 'Shit, man. I told you we should not have come here.'

My eyes move slowly over the flat-topped flamboyant trees, a few bright red blooms dried and scorched on the dirt. A spiny dead jacaranda, listing to one side has fallen into the remains of a security fence. No one has bothered to move it, it lies like a skeleton across the chain-link. Ahead a burst of colour from a lilac bougainvillea clawing its way over the tumbling wrought-iron gate, uprooting and twisting the rusted support beams in their path. There is no grass to speak of, just the hard arid earth and a few sad patches of what used to be a lush, irrigated lawn. A small dust devil gathers up a few leaves and eddies across the baked earth before petering out, the leaves floating back down to the dirt. This is the dry season and it seems that the entire country just holds its breath for those first quenching, exhilarating drops of rain. Above, the endless, eternal, azure blue sky, cloudless.

I look up towards the house, hidden behind some overgrown creepers; a mess of morning glory and some periwinkle blue plumbago blossoms peep out from the weeds. Remnants of a once fragrant garden. I stare for what seems like several minutes, both horrified and fascinated. And then I see the woman. The car must have woken her. I doubt if many visitors pass this way, if ever. She steps across a gap in a half wall and walks to the gate. A bright polyester *jongwe*[10] headscarf and a shiny sarong bound tightly around her waist. I suppose I expect or wish that she would look as poverty stricken as her home. She stands for a second beyond the twisted gate. Obviously someone has driven into it and no one had bothered to make any repairs. She adjusts the child on her back, observing me. There is no animosity, just a slight surprise to be receiving a visitor at this time of day.

'You are on your own now *boet*[11]. Just go in. You don't have to ask permission. This is our home anyway,' mumbles Duncan.

My mum remains in the car, in the darkness. The woman says nothing. Just stands there adjusting the strap carrying the baby on her back. I open the car door and approach the gate.

'Hello. How are you?' I say, rather pointlessly. I look up towards the house. 'I used to live here. This...' I say, waving my hands around me, 'was my home. I was just wondering if I could look around...'

She cuts me short by peering over my shoulder at my mother and brother in the Land Rover. A vague recognition passes over her face. Maybe a memory of when they fought for possession of this place.

'Where have you come from?' she asks.

'I am from Hong Kong. But I used to live here many...'

'Yes, I know,' she cuts in. 'You have told me already.'

---

[10] Shona word meaning 'rooster', which is the symbol of ZANU-PF.

[11] Afrikaans word meaning 'brother'.

She is looking me over. Her face gives nothing away. She emits an almost inaudible sigh then shrugs in an African way that might mean anything from resignation to annoyance.

'Alright then. Come.'

Her accent is thick but clearly educated. She turns to leave, walking back behind the house to where the servants used to sit out, gesturing me to go via the front and have a look.

My stomach is in knots. No longer am I so sure that this was a good plan. As if in a dream, I glide towards the gate, my hand touching the rusted metal handle. Sliding it across, just enough force and a slight lift of the gate with my foot gets the latch gliding across without grating. That much I remember. I had done it countless times, particularly late at night when we wanted to sneak in after a drinking session at the club. Silly really because everyone would have heard the car coming up the hill.

M'sitwe.

I take in a deep breath. What an amazing house. I had almost forgotten. Across from me the lawns have been dug up and planted with sweet potatoes in neat ridges, a few pumpkins creeping between the furrows. The view is shielded by a patch of tall mealies. I step on to the veranda. It seems huge now that it is devoid of furniture or pot plants or hunting trophies. A giant pink-and-white bougainvillea has pulled down half the ceiling near where I am standing. I look up into the cavernous roof, half expecting to see the little family of civets that used to reside there.

The ceiling boards in this part of the house are decayed, falling down or rotted away. An old rusted tractor has been backed on to the veranda. Across the top of the support beams my mum's fancy *broekie*[12] lace wrought-iron borders now hang down at odd angles. These once-treasured pieces of colonial Rhodesiana now impractical, unloved and unwanted. Footpaths criss-cross between the furrows of crops towards various parts of the garden, disappearing over the lip of the hill into an impenetrable mass of weeds and creepers where our water garden once trickled and gurgled down to deep green ponds full of bream and large mutant goldfish – also long since gone, taken by greedy garden centres in Harare. Towards one side of the house stands the cottage. Washing hangs limply outside. A massive blue *Petrea volubilis* once adorned the front of that cottage; Africa's version of the wisteria. Now the building appears uninviting and dark. Several window panes are smashed. Yet it seems more inhabited than the main house. Perhaps this is where the woman lives. A shadow passes across the threshold. It is a young child, no more than five or six years old, his naked tummy protruding from a pair of tatty khaki shorts.

'Do you live here?' I ask. He points to the small cottage.

'This house is too big. I don't like,' he says.

I smile at him and walk off the veranda towards the swimming pool and I am disturbed to see the empty mosaic kidney-shaped pool, now a stinking shallow puddle of brackish water. Grecian pillars have fallen among creepers, a peeling granite dolphin, its mouth agape never again to trickle bubbling water into the sparkling blue pool. Mealies are growing right up to the edge of the pool. It shocks me.

Swimming pools. They are one of the things that seemed to incite the liberal press overseas, I think wryly. The thought of wealthy landowners sunbathing beside their pools, gin eternally clasped in manicured hands. A tray of Mazoe Orange, ice and

<hr>

[12] Afrikaans word meaning 'panties' or 'knickers'.

refreshments under the cool gazebo. Sliced lemons in a saucer and the fizz of tonic in one's nose. The aroma of meat roasting on the nearby *braai*[13], the smell of the water as it splashed from the garden boy's hose on to the flower beds. The garden boy, always hovering, wanting to cop a look at the girls sunbathing in their bikinis.

I shake my head in an attempt to kick-start the memories. It is like discovering some sad and forgotten Roman ruin. More than anything else this upsets me the most. The way the bush and poor agriculture has replaced the verdant lawns, the borders of flowers, the hanging baskets, and the laughter of children.

I am startled by the child who approaches me silently from behind. He giggles and gestures for me to follow him into the house. He has no political view. He sees me as an odd, hopefully exciting stranger in his home. I quickly look about me. There appear to be no adults around so I follow him into my old bedroom. I find myself shivering despite the mid-day heat. It surprises me that the bedroom is so neat and tidy, someone's clothes folded better than I ever did, the rickety beds neatly made, and the floors clean and well swept apart from ugly black stains up the walls from burning paraffin heaters.

I walk to the back window and peer out. A group of adults sit around the old boiler chatting amiably. The child tugs my sleeve. He wants me to see more. Quickly I walk through the corridor to my parents' room. This room is uninhabited. I am shocked by the emptiness. With no pictures on the walls, my eyes fall on the small neat hole in the plaster above the space where my mother's dressing table used to be, a hole made by a bullet from my rifle. I had nearly killed her that day with an

---

[13] Afrikaans word meaning 'grill' or 'barbecue'.

accidental discharge[14]. The doors to my mother's closet have been torn off, possibly used for firewood. Again the deep dark roof soars above me, the ceiling boards having fallen in and never been replaced, exposing the superb timber structure of the steep roof, built by my father.

I make my way back to the sitting room at the end of the long L-shaped veranda. My hand lightly touching the cool cement of a half wall. We used to have a blue floral cushion here. This is where we had our afternoon tea and evening drinks. My eyes dart from place to place, not wanting to miss anything, searching for clues, memories, visions. The slate floor, swept but unpolished.

I silently walk into the sitting room. I don't remember it being so large and cavernous. Surprisingly, the ceiling in this room is intact and still looks magnificent. Antique moulded tin taken from The Grand Hotel in Salisbury after it had been pulled down. Although too young to know The Grand, I had seen an old poster dated 1940 advertising *'100 modern rooms. You experience REAL COMFORT when you stay at The GRAND. Grand Hotel Grill Room – only one of its kind in Rhodesia'.* The poster also featured a wonderful proud three-storey structure with elaborate cornices, wrought-iron balconies and a spire.

The woman returns. I feel I need to say something so I point to the ceiling and tell her about its history. I am pleasantly surprised when she asks questions: 'Which Grand? Bulawayo or Salisbury?' How would she know that, I wonder? 'Aah, Salisbury was it? Such a nice hotel.' I look at her, wanting to hate her. She tilts her head to one side like a knowing great-aunt. 'My son is at Wits University,' she says absently while running a finger across a shelf looking for dust, then lovingly touching a framed photo. She points to the picture of a proud young man in an ill-fitting

---

[14] The unintentional firing of a gun.

suit. Then she looks at me and simply raises her eyebrows. I know what she was getting at. Don't take me as a fool is what she really means. She is not being judgemental.

'Sorry?' I say, 'but I did not catch your name.'

'Kanga Chepe,' she says. 'Mrs Kanga Chepe.'

Kanga Chepe, the bitch who had made my mother's life hell. Looking at her now, she seems anything but a bitch. For some reason, and despite everything, I do not blame her. Too much time has passed. Did she know my mother was in the car? I quickly move on.

My feet have left dust marks along the parquet flooring, now lying uncared for and unwaxed, yet still all in place. How often I had heard the sound of bare feet running across that surface. The laughter of children as they scampered to the dining room to get some sweets from the silver dish, or maybe a peach if they were in season. I imagine the sound of a dog barking and the splash of water as someone dives into the cooling aquamarine of the swimming pool. My mind is running wild.

Light streams through the bay windows at the far end of the room, dust motes caught in the afternoon rays. One pane is covered now with a yellow fertiliser bag. A fan above my head, now covered in cobwebs, useless without electricity. Geckos scuttle across the walls hunting for food. I search for the huge piebald territorial male gecko that used to rule the roost on these walls. The largest I have ever seen at almost nine inches long, he was like a baby croc. His huge eyes would flicker at us as he tried to squeeze beneath a picture on the wall. But of course he was long gone, pushed from his perch by more agile young guns. I smile at the thought of my mum constantly going around straightening the pictures. 'Bloody gecko,' she would moan.

Someone has sticky-taped tourist posters to the walls, *Visit Canada and the Rockies.* Another with some azure lake in Switzerland fringed with snowy peaks. On the far wall my eye rests upon a shape and I take a breath when I realise that it was where the old leopard skin had been, the outline of the cat clearly visible against the pale cream of the wall. An old picture of me when I was four or five shows me standing next to the dead beast, its head resting against my left leg, my right arm holding a rifle taller than me. That leopard had been culled because it had become a cattle killer, and it had adorned our wall for as long as I can remember.

I look up towards the long passageway that leads from the dining room to the kitchen, half expecting the sound of clatter and chatter coming from Fred or Konda, the clip of my mother's shoes on the black-and-white lino, or the tinkle of the bell summoning Konda to bring the main course. I move back on to the veranda, choked with memories.

The doorway from the veranda to the sleeping area is just a wooden frame, the door nowhere to be seen. I can still see the yellow paint speckled around the edge of the door frame and the faded notches made with a Bowie knife labelled Mandy, Dunc, Pete. I glance back towards my old room, as if seeing a ghost and without thinking, turn and stride out across the veranda, over the dry lawn, to the waiting vehicle. I did not thank Kanga Chepe. She did not care. She had already disappeared around the back of the house to the servants' quarters.

It is getting late and we don't want to be on the road after dusk. Without asking Dunc takes off, skirting around the gaping hole that was once a cattle grid, past the space where our stables stood, and accelerates down the road. Tears well up in my eyes, blurring my vision.

'Please stop,' my mother quietly commands from the back.

Duncan slams on the brakes, dust engulfing the vehicle, and waits while we gather ourselves. For me this trip has been educational, selfish, a way of putting something to bed, if an entire lifetime can simply be *put to bed*. For mum it is catastrophic. Emotional at the best of times, now she is traumatised.

'You okay, Lib?' I ask. She looks across at me and squeezes my shoulder. It should be me comforting her. Her eyes are shielded by dark sunglasses, her neck taut, her hand across her chest as if she is trying to slow down her heartbeat. She gasps and points.

'God, look at that!' I follow her gaze. Ahead is a stretch of arable land, now a field overgrown with insidious pink pigweed and scrubby thorn trees, and then there on the horizon stands the majestic, impossible beauty of the Bald Kopje, jutting above the smaller granite hills like a monument to eternity. And from behind the Bald Kopje rises the most breathtaking blood moon, sometimes known as a hunter's moon, created by lunar eclipses in another hemisphere: rare, extraordinary and biblical.

'The sun will be turned to darkness, and the moon to blood before the great and dreadful day of the Lord comes,' mum says.

For several minutes we sit in absolute silence watching the gorgeous phenomena, casting its light across the landscape.

'D'you know something, Duncan?' I say, letting out a deep breath, 'that house is not our home. What I saw back there was just bricks.' Duncan raises his eyebrows and rolls his eyes but says nothing. I glance back towards the old house, now hidden behind the creaking bamboos and leafless *mufuti* trees. The African bush seems to have swallowed it up. Gone like one of those early morning dreams you can almost put your finger on but by breakfast has faded into a distant memory.

'Okay,' I say. 'Let's go.'

2

Woody

'Light me a fag, Pete,' my dad said. I was sitting in the Land Rover with him about to head out to see the tobacco grading. Reaching across the cab I picked up his packet of 555s and put a cigarette into my mouth. Fumbling with the Lion matches I just managed to light the cigarette, trying my best not to inhale. I was only five and being asked to light his fag seemed incredibly grown-up. I enjoyed this daily ritual of going down to the sheds to check on the farm work. The day always began with the cigarette lighting ceremony. My father glanced across at me, a grin on his face. 'You're getting better at it, careful you don't burn your fingers.' I inhaled a lungful and immediately coughed. He reached across and took the cigarette from my hand and had a good puff to get it going.

The acrid blue smoke tumbled from his nostrils and permeated the cab of the Land Rover. The old vehicle was rolling down the hill from the house in neutral. As we gathered pace my father engaged second gear and let out the clutch. The engine growled, sending a brood of chickens dashing into the bush, wheels sliding over the red gravel of the drive, a fart of blue smoke belched from the rear. Then we were off, heading down to the sheds and tobacco barns. The cab now deliciously hazy with tobacco and diesel fumes.

This need to save a drop of petrol on hill starts got some people into hot water. Local farmer Sunny Townsend once free-wheeled quietly back to his house only to find his cook boy of many years lying on HIS bed, in HIS pyjamas and HIS dressing gown, reading the *Rhodesia Herald* wearing HIS reading glasses, smoking HIS pipe and being served tea by HIS maid. He had no idea whether to laugh or cry. 'I wanted to feed the cheeky bugger to my pet crocs, but the look on the cook's face was just priceless,' Sunny would often joke. 'I simply cracked up laughing.' He was never content with a mere dog as a pet. In his garden he had a large walled enclosure full of giant crocodiles. The enclosure was landscaped with palm trees and waterfalls and sandy banks festooned with tumbling nasturtiums and ivy. It was beautiful and at the same time ghastly. Close to the croc enclosure was a staggeringly beautiful swimming pool built into the granite rock face, made to look like a natural rock pool. Dark, deep and green. The reptiles had escaped once and ended up in the pool.

The Land Rover was now nearing the sheds.

'You're a tough little bugger aren't you?' my dad said. He gave my knee a tight squeeze and then a tickle under my arm. I wriggled free and laughed.

'Of course I'm tough! I'm tough like Frikkie Du Preez.' I shadow boxed the air and pretended to pass a rugby ball. I knew that this would please my father who was an avid rugby fan and I was desperate to please him.

'Do you know who Frikkie is then?' he asked.

'Ja. He's the best rugger player Northern Transvaal has ever had.'

'Clever. Actually, he's the best damn player the Springboks have ever had. Maybe one day you will grow up to be a rugby player like Frik?' He ruffled my hair.

'Maybe,' I answered. I wasn't too convinced.

My father definitely had his quirks. Love him or loathe him, you had to admire him. J.A.C. Wood Esq. John Alexander Charles. Such a grand name and in his own words 'what a bloody beaut!' I adored my dad but I was also terrified of him. Woody, as he was known to his pals, or John to us three kids, was one of those chaps who was the life of the party and the death of the wife. Privately a tortured soul and publicly one of the guys, one of the real men, or as they say in Southern Africa, one of the *ouens*[15]. Of course, we often felt he did not love us, and he certainly did seem happier away from his family on hunting trips or on police reserve duty. I expect he was simply a man who hid his feelings, believing that it was sissy to show any kind of emotion. 'I think he just hates women,' my mum would say after one of their epic rows. I might have thrown children into that equation, too.

By now we had pulled into the space between the towering red brick tobacco barns. Built for curing the green leaf using flues of hot air, these massive structures stood sentinel either side of the grading shed. The Rhodesian Virginia tobacco farm was a very special kind of place. Unlike most farms that might have a barn for hay or for milking cows, the Rhodesian farm was generally laid out with two or three very tall, very long, red brick (or sometimes whitewashed) curing sheds. These could be as tall as a three-storey house and 170 feet long. The sheds are always laid out facing each other with a large low-roofed grading shed bang in the centre for sorting the leaf, baling it and storing it until the tobacco sales begin at the end of the season. All the red bricks on the farm were home-made in kilns. Each curing shed had a furnace connected to large tin curing flues that heat up the space. These furnaces were carefully monitored by an ancient *madala*[16]. Of course, my father always tried to diversify, once even growing geraniums for their essential oils. It was an unmitigated disaster, the dealer in South Africa taking them all for a ride and disappearing with the profits. On

---

[15] Afrikaans word meaning 'bloke' or 'chap'.

[16] Shona word meaning 'old man'.

other occasions it might be cotton or coffee, or citrus or pimentos, but this part of the world was tobacco country and the golden leaf reigned supreme.

'Come and have a look at the grading Pete,' said John. 'Bloody good crop this year, the rains came just at the right time, but I can't see us making much money with these damn sanctions. Goddamn Poms and liberals.'

I wasn't entirely sure what sanctions were. Grown-ups talked about them all the time. But I knew what a Pommie was. Most of our relatives were Poms but that didn't stop John holding a grudge.

Woody was born during the Great Depression in 1928 at Shangani, that eerie haunted place where just three decades earlier, 34 brave but ill-advised British South Africa Company troops, led by the 21-year-old Alan Wilson, perished at the hands of three thousand of Lobengula's finest *assegai*[17]-wielding warriors. The rumour goes that John's mother suckled him until he was nearly five years old, to save money on food. A typical tough Scots lassie. Granny Wood could shoot a double-barrelled shotgun as well as any man. She was stout and square with a no-nonsense Aberdeenshire disposition, practical hairstyle, strong legs and a twinkle in her fabulous blue eyes. As a granny she was wonderful in that baked cookie type of way, but I suspect she felt much more comfy down at the dip counting the *mombe*[18].

My dad said the Scots weren't real Poms. Only the English. Actually, only people south of Leeds were considered Poms. I suspect this was all aimed at my mum's relatives. Scottish-ness ran deep in our roots and mum's side of the family was bracketed into those queer, arty English types according to my father.

---

[17] An iron-tipped hardwood spear used chiefly by southern African peoples.

[18] Shona word meaning 'cow' or 'cattle'.

Never got their bloody hands dirty in their lives, or so John thought. He could be extremely narrow-minded and irritating at times. Ironically, my mother's side was equally, if not more Scottish than my dad's, but that did not seem to matter.

My grandfather Walter Wood died the year I was born so I never knew him. Walter was the seventh son of a seventh son, a sign of fantastical good luck in folklore. The holder of such honour wields great powers, so they say. Walter fled the hardships of post-war Europe for the big skies of Matabeleland, bringing with him his dour Scots way of life, much of which had rubbed off on Woody.

Back in the vehicle, John slowed to watch a trailer trundle by loaded with cords of wood. These tough woodsmen would chop and chop all day, their axes echoing across the farm at certain times of the year from daybreak to dusk. Each woodcutter would be paid per cord, which measured four-by-four-by-eight feet. So much of farming is about routine and common sense. In the beginning, all the tobacco was cured using wood-fired furnaces. Later coal became the fuel of choice. But John always had stacks and stacks of cords cut as a back-up. He also believed that the wood gave the tobacco a much more fragrant aroma, and I think this makes perfect sense. We had a plaque in our sitting room that read 'Tobacco Loves Wood'.

Although John owned the farm, the district was still under some archaic colonial or federation ruling, which meant that the mines could come and prospect at anytime, anywhere on the farm. We lived with the horror that should they ever find any minerals of value within our borders they would be allowed to build and excavate as they saw fit. Being so close to the mineral rich Great Dyke, this was not such a specious notion. The mere idea of some noisy mining company building on our pristine land was unimaginable. It also meant that as heavily wooded as the area was (after all, its African name was *Matimba*

– the place of wood) the hewing of timber was forbidden unless it was for mining use. Of course, Woody totally disregarded this, or at the very least would pretend he was stumping[19] the land for agricultural use, which was permitted. In truth, most of the stumped land would become virgin bush after only a few short years.

I enjoyed the woodcutting, you could hear them chopping from miles away, and you could smell them before you could see them. That heady odour of tree sap, not the nasal cleansing sharpness of fir trees or pine, but a sweeter acacia smell more like cinnamon and honey. The cords could be found dotted around the landscape revealing their cream outer core and deep mahogany inner. After a few days, a tractor would come along to collect the cords and the men would be paid accordingly. They must have been tough men. No chainsaws were ever used, only a good old-fashioned home-made axe, commonly known as a *demo*.

My father was no stranger to hard graft. When granddad and granny Wood left Scotland and settled in Matabeleland they had never been off the farm, let alone out of Scotland, and must have found the rough pioneering life quite daunting, to say the least. So, at the advice of friends, they decided to move to the cooler Mashonaland Plateau, finally settling in the beautiful soft blue hills of the Mazoe Valley, naming the farm Kincardine after their beloved Scottish home.

For most of my childhood, Kincardine was the seat of the family. A place that we drove past every time we went to town. Craning our necks out of the car window, we would always gaze up at the wonderful long avenue of jacaranda trees, so large they met in the middle like a canopy in a Gainsborough painting. The jacaranda avenue stretched all the way to the huge house on

---

[19] Clearing the fields of tree stumps for agricultural use.

the hill and is one of my most enduring memories, particularly when in full bloom, casting their mauve blossoms on to the rich red earth like a blanket of purple snow. Kincardine always smelled of oranges. The famous Mazoe Orange plantations spread out all around the hill in every direction, acre upon acre, row after row, and in the spring the scent was intoxicating. Even the architecture of Kincardine was different. Colonial. Imposing. A rich red corrugated-iron roof shaded by vast, red oxide verandas enclosed with wire mesh and dotted with fabulously comfy cowhide *rimpi*[20] chairs and misshapen deep soft armchairs.

I jumped out of the Land Rover and walked across the yard to the large grading shed. We pushed open the swing doors and walked into a scene that could have come from the American deep south before independence. Clouds of steam forced through pipes from the furnace rolled across the ceiling. The steam was used to soften the brittle tobacco leaf before it could be graded for size and colour, then baled before going to auction.

I loved the smell in here. The surprisingly sweet smell from the tobacco almost choking you as you entered, but within a few minutes you got used to it. It was believed, possibly incorrectly, that this nicotine steam bath prevented people from getting many illnesses such as flu, colds or asthma. The African women of all ages, from young unmarried *mufazi*[21] to elderly crones sitting on the floor surrounded by huge piles of leaf ready for grading might have thought otherwise. The gaggle of voices, singing what in retrospect I suspect were *chimurenga* songs, would greet you as you entered the large room. Snotty babies neatly tied to their backs in slings of colourful cloth would take one look at us white ghosts and bawl their eyes out.

---

[20] Strips of animal hide.

[21] Shona word meaning 'young woman'.

Many had never set eyes on a *murungu*[22] before. Most women, unless very young, wore *doeks*[23] – a brightly-patterned headscarf bound around their heads and tied at the nape of the neck. The women always did the grading. The men did the loading, carting, steaming and baling of the leaf. Climbing high up into the rafters of the barns and hauling down *mateppe*[24] hung with golden brown leaf. The steam made it very humid and hot so most men were shirtless, their dark brown skins shining in the glow of the neon strips. The scene could have been taken from *Uncle Tom's Cabin*. And I loved it. To my naive white mind, this happy pastoral scene was a place of safety, security, built on solid foundations. Something that was here forever.

How hideously wrong we all were. We were not to know that by the 1970s civil war would grip the country for a generation.

Farming was in my father's blood. I admired him for having such vision. His first school was the Salisbury Convent with only four other boys, a sinister dark Dickensian kind of place. Red-brick institutional buildings surrounded by tall prison-like walls and patrolled by nuns who had no compunction to spare the child. Lacking in love or bodily comfort, like a foundling hospital, they stripped the children of all reference to family or home. John always claimed that the nuns deliberately starved him to the point of having to cadge food off the other lads who were Catholics and therefore received more grub. He had the skinniest legs in the country, something he always blamed on those nuns.

When John finally left school he was sent to relatives in Scotland for two years to learn all about farming under extreme post-war conditions. It might seem a strange thing to do, but the lessons

---

[22] Shona word meaning 'white man'.

[23] Afrikaans word meaning 'cloth'.

[24] A straight pole used for hanging hands of tobacco.

my father learned on those cold bracken-covered Scottish braes stayed with him all his life, and indeed my brother Duncan still benefits from many of his farming techniques.

Woody arrived in the UK during the coldest winter on record wearing flannels and a sports coat, together with an icicle attached to the end of his nose. It was 1945. When the rest of the world was trying to get out of Europe my father was sent back. Work in Scotland was hard by any stretch of the imagination, let alone for a young man who had grown up in Africa's warm climate. Faced with biting winds, hail, snowstorms the like of which many a Scotsmen had not seen, and miles of wet scratchy heather on the east coast of Scotland near a village called Auchenblae, Woody cut his teeth. During lambing season, John came rushing into the house to anxiously tell his uncle that one of the lambs had been born without a bumhole. Looking John up and down, his dour uncle said, 'Then don't just stand there, laddie! G'out and make a bloody hole!' Which of course John did using a sharp pike, and the lamb lived to see another day.

John never forgot the hardships of Britain, the poverty of war, the ghastly weather, the grey skies hanging overhead like a pall, the pallid, haunted faces of the people returning from hell. But he also left with a lasting love of this wild, godforsaken country and its hard-working folk. After a short sojourn in Europe, he saved up the cost of his fare home to Rhodesia and never left Africa again.

Always an adventurous spirit, my dad made his way into the untamed bush 120 miles north of Salisbury and opened up M'sitwe Farm in the Victory Block, Umvukwes, with neighbours Tim Harington, Alon Crouch and Martin Chance. It was a lonely life for Woody with rarely a visitor, roads being largely unnavigable back then.

This fabulous, wild land had many hazards. Least of all were the leopards that roamed right up to the bottom of the garden, even when I was a child. On one occasion, John's vehicle broke down at night on the way back from a neighbouring farm and he was followed all the way home by a hungry male. John recalled how each time the moon came out from behind a cloud, he could see the yellow shape of the animal slinking along in the shadows a few yards away. One moment it was there. Then it was gone into the shadows only to return again a few minutes later. The whole way back that leopard tracked him. Woody loved every minute of it, the danger, the excitement, the adrenaline. His love for the wildlife possibly surpassed his love of the farm. Woody carved that farm out of nothing. Mile upon mile of rough rocky woodland. M'sitwe Farm was his life, all 13,000 acres of it. He knew every crevice, every hill, every undulation and every brook. He was selfish about it. Protective of it, even. You could see this passion in his eyes.

My father crossed the grading shed and walked into his office to check the books while I wandered around the shed trying to act interested and making sure not to stand on any of the searingly hot steel pipes that snaked across the floor. I rarely wore shoes on the farm, particularly as a child.

Some staff nodded or greeted me in Chilapalapa.

'Kunjun, piccanin bwana?'[25]

'Kunjun, Joel,'[26] I would reply. It was always the men who greeted you. Never the women, who might giggle behind their hands like shy geishas, no doubt saying something sarcastic to their companions, the whole group bursting into uncontrolled laughter. We were none the wiser since neither John nor I spoke Shona.

---

[25] 'Hello, little master'.

[26] 'Hello, Joel'.

Chilapalapa is a pidgin form of Shona, Swahili and English with a smattering of Afrikaans and a tiny bit of French thrown in, possibly from the days of the Huguenots in South Africa. It came to be loathed later as it represented all that was colonial. Shona was an easy language yet we chose not to learn it at school. Back then, it simply did not cross our minds to learn and, I suppose, Chilapalapa was conveniently understood across the board with all tribes.

John emerged from his small, dusty office which was really a glorified corner housing a rickety rattan chair and a three-legged table, the fourth leg a pile of bricks. His office at the house was not much better and was situated at the end of the long veranda behind a stable door. Inside, a pile of elephant tusks were piled untidily beneath a chest of drawers built from African teak by my great-grandfather.

On the wall, Woody had pinned a large aerial photo of the farm. This black-and-white image detailed every minute detail of the 13,000 acres, the tiny dirt road between the two sections winding lonely and thread-like between *kopjes* and dark gullies and ravines through the middle of the land mass. The largest area on the map was Matimba, just a massive grey expanse of woodland and bush. And, of course, the pin-prick of the house, so small, so insignificant, surrounded by dense, dark woodland. Our life reduced to numbers and tram lines in a ratio of 50,000:1. My father's office never had glass in the window, just a metal grill, drafty in winter and damp in the wet season. Little wonder granddad's chest of drawers had warped. My father was a hands-on farmer and he spent as little time as possible writing cheques or poring over invoices. Perhaps his Scottish ancestry made him allergic to the cheque book.

'Okay, it's teatime, let's go.' Jumping back into the Land Rover, John pressed the start button and the engine grumbled into life. There was no hill start down here at the sheds. No saving of fuel by free-wheeling down the hill. But incredibly the ancient vehicle soldiered on.

Life here was dominated by second-hand goods, cheap Rhodesian-made products, spare parts repurposed over the years, chocolate that separates and goes white after a few weeks. Fuel coupons were issued with the meanness of a typical colonial bean counter. With sanctions imposed on the country, fuel was tightly rationed and many vehicles, such as the Land Rover, ran on an evil blend of diesel and paraffin. Many other petrol-based vehicles ran on a mix of petrol and ethanol. This innocuously named 'blend' could be purchased from most fuel stations if you had coupons.

The paraffin mix, on the other hand, was my father's ingenious invention, which we all accepted despite the very real possibility that it might explode at any moment. With tubes and pipes leading from a wobbly jerry can stuck behind the driver's seat, this vehicle was definitely a health hazard. We fed a pipe from a can of paraffin in the back through the cab to the petrol tank. It was innovative, dangerous, and light on fuel. No one thought not to smoke. Everyone smoked back then.

The faithful jeep, as old as the farm itself, boasted a bent frame, was re-wired, re-engined, re-mufflered and had a strong head that pulled to the side like a horse. The water pump was shot, the camshaft bearings and seals were gone, the alternator was fried, the worn clutch-plate was in dire need of realigning, the fuel line was clogged and normally required weekly cleaning by a farm mechanic who blew out the crap, the steering gear assembly was wrecked, oh, and it had a fucked diff. But once going nothing could stop that bastard of a thing. Literally. The brakes were also buggered and required frantic pumping to get the hydraulic fluid flowing.

About that steering assembly, another major hazard. You could literally rotate it 360 degrees without any noticeable movement from the wheels. After three or maybe four full rotations the sluggish vehicle would start to turn. It was like manoeuvring the Queen Mary into dry dock. I learned to drive in this old rust bucket. The result of wrenching at that steering wheel remained with me when I used to drive a Morris Minor in London, grinding the gears and almost tearing the wheel from the shaft. Passengers used to look at me like I was a maniac.

John lit another fag and we drove around the sheds, stopping to have a word with Sixpence the cattle boy and Solomon the mechanic, who was hammering away at a spare part in the 'garage', basically a gum pole and corrugated-iron lean-to, oily black from years of sumps being drained from tractors.

'Christ,' muttered John to himself. 'They always have to be so bloody rough. Look at him just pounding away at that spare part.' Mind you, the whole set-up was all a bit Heath Robinson those days. Tractors were held together with wire and rubber bands. Nuts and bolts soaked in kerosene were ready to be reused again and again. An old orange Nuffield tractor covered in bird crap and rusted to hell, pigweed and a stunted wild cherry growing through the frame, wasn't done for. In fact, with a bit of hammering and greasing, who knows what life we could get out of the old bugger.

The Wood family was never exactly renowned for its mechanical expertise. Those posh farms over the Great Dyke boasted teams of highly skilled mechanics attired in bright blue clean overalls and gumboots, while our born-and-bred M'sitwe lads were clad in stained trousers torn at the knee and patched at the backside. My father, it could be said, had a deep understanding of recycling, or at least never throwing away anything that might come in handy next week, year or decade.

Also in the yard were remnants of a bygone age, skeletons of vintage cars that were ancient even when Woody was a kid. God knows where they came from. I don't think my father owned them, but I suspect they came from his mad car-collector friend Norrie Spicer. We never ventured into that scrap heap, largely because cobras and mambas lived among the rusty axles and tangled blackjack bushes.

Across from the garage a small brick hut belched out fluffy white puffs of powder. This was the 'poop' shed. Poop, of course was not the faecal variety but the word used for ground maize, or mealie-meal. A rhythmic thumping could be heard from inside as the rickety mill, attached to a tractor by a fan belt, did its magic, grinding the home-grown corn into a fine powder.

Poop, beans and dried fish were doled out weekly by the boss boy to all the men and women who worked on the farm. He would stand waist-deep covered head-to-toe in the white powder scooping large ladles of the meal into eagerly waiting chipped enamel buckets. Occasionally he would laugh out loud at a joke, his teeth whiter than white, his eyes shining, his skin and curly hair powdered like an 18th century aristocrat or mad professor. Sometimes he would shout at a worker who had been skiving off or had not done his share that week, scolding him and telling him in Shona to bugger off, although I suspect that was all for show when my father was around. No one went hungry.

We would always stop off at the feed pens. John was a cattle man, first and foremost. Tobacco paid the bills, but cattle was his love. Many farmers kept pure-breeds, but for general hardiness and quality of meat, hybrid vigour was the order of the day. In our case it was a cross between the Hereford for the meat, and the Brahman or Afrikaner for the hardiness. Other farmers who had pedigree herds, such as Bill Francis, with his magnificent white herd of Charolais, or Selby Chance, and his stout caramel Sussex, often ribbed John for his cross-breeds. Pedigree herds meant problems during calving or in breeding, although artificial insemination soon fixed that. The offspring of the M'sitwe cattle often ended up with the beautiful white fluffy faces of the Hereford and the heavy set rumps of the Afrikaner with their large humped neck.

Sheep on the other hand were Dorpers. A cross between the Dorset Horn and the Blackhead Persian. The Persian side providing resistance to drought, the Dorset offering the best lamb and mutton on the market. Separately these breeds offered little. Yet when mixed they produced succulent meat in a harsh environment. My mother and I adored breeding sheep. She purchased the first batch of ewes and a ram from Martin and Mary Malan in Raffingora. The Malans were one of the country's top Dorper breeders and would later take me on as an assistant, teaching me everything I ever needed to know about rearing Dorpers, from castrating to dosing, to foot-rot and lambing, and finally to using a lethal electric saw when cutting up the meat into chops, loins, legs and fillets. I loved it. My father hated sheep. Sheep and all their problems were simply dismissed as a waste of time. I could see his point. Sheep could be needy. I suspect his dislike for sheep stemmed from those days back in Scotland when he had to run over the hills looking for wild Scottish Blackface.

Before I went to boarding school my relationship with my dad was close. My siblings had been shipped off to Umvukwes School, so with no friends around, these trips down to the sheds were to become one of our daily highlights. Once I went to school we became more distant. Sometimes when he was angry he would blame my mum, saying that she had turned me against him. Of course, this was absolute rubbish. As I grew up I became more aware of his temper and his fights with my mother and these had a profound effect on me, certainly into my late teens. My strained relationship with my father often meant that I was scared shitless to try and make an effort with him. He could be extremely intimidating.

Returning from boarding school I would rack my brains trying to think of a question that would not make him snort or think me an idiot. Inevitably, my asinine conversation with my father would tend to be all about the rainy season, or how did the dipping go? I was not capable of saying, 'John – tell me why you think that beast will fetch more at the market than the other? Why did you choose that bull rather than the other? What are the merits of feeding the cattle with urea and at what stage does urea become toxic to a ruminant?' I have absolutely no doubt he would have loved to answer these questions, but I never gave him the chance.

Like farmers the world over, my father kept to a strict routine. Mornings on the farm always began at 'sparrow fart' as he liked to call it. Everyone in the household would be woken by great hacking coughs coming from my parents' room. Huge, retching, phlegmy barks that rumbled through the slumbering home. It sounded like the bugger would be dead before Konda had laid the breakfast table. Those 'Country Club' cheroots were finally taking their toll on his lungs and would continue to plague him until his death some 30 years later.

'Jesus, John,' my mother would moan as she reached for the Teasmade, 'you'll wake the bloody dead.'

'Is that what you want, woman?' he would retort as he made his way along the veranda to down his one and only Coke of the day, always followed by a loud burp.

'Damn good,' he would remark to himself. 'The only way to get rid of a hangover.'

Then he would be off to the 'other section', which required driving some distance every day. The other section was about five miles from the homestead over stunning countryside. His day would often begin with this lonely drive on his own through the farm to check on the work along the way. Like the main section, the other section was built almost identically. Rows of tobacco barns with a grading shed in the middle. The compound on the other section was larger owing to there being more arable land and therefore more hands needed to work it. The manager's house at the time was an ugly square structure built atop a granite rock overlooking the valley towards the Great Dyke, another bit of architecture designed on the back of a fag packet.

I could never describe M'sitwe as attractive, although at certain times of the year, like in spring, it did have its pretty side. Mostly it was inspiring. Grey-blue leafless trees in the dry season stretching to the horizon like a Chinese ink sketch, the *kopjes* emerging from the grey wash like sugarloaf mountains. In late October, early November the grey would suddenly burst like magic into a whole spectrum of reds and greens as the new leaves broke free from the tough bark of lifeless trees. In the summer, you were surrounded by a universe of deep sea green right up to the roadside, often surprising browsing antelope such as kudu, duiker, impala and, if you were really lucky, the majestic yet shy sable.

His daily drive each morning would have greeted him with sights that must, even for a tough old bugger like Woody, have taken his breath away. Above the dawn mist the peaks of Matimba and the Bald Kopje rose like islands, momentarily bright, lit by the early morning sun. Around him and in the uninhabited Mazindarindi Valley to his right it was often like sitting on the shore of a sea of swirling white vapour, as waves of light from the distant Dyke washed the sides of the rocky granite hills. The few times I got up early enough I would witness this sight. It was enchanting and if ever one was to believe in god, ghosts, faeries or sprites, this was the time.

Not one for fancy words, Woody might just shake his head at

breakfast and say, 'Jesus, Lib. What a sunrise today,' then go back to his porridge. He may not have had the words to express himself, but his love of this land was profound.

Woody never varied his routine, even during the bush war. Despite the imminent danger from landmines and terrorist ambush, John always came home safe. It was often said that the terrorists used the farm as a base camp and were not about to shit on their own doorstep. I have no doubt in my mind that they knew his every move, day-in and day-out. And I am certain John was very aware of this too as he revved the engine between gullies and fords that frothed aquamarine from the minerals washed down from the Great Dyke.

In the rainy season the small rivers would become torrents, washing away the road in places. Creeping along in four-wheel drive, the tyres sliding in the red mud, John must have thought he was a sitting duck. All along the way the road wound between the balancing rocks, the dense bush, the massive *dwalas*, veering around the cattle grid which had several loose cross-bars, past the old dip with its sagging thatched roof, a brief stop at the cattle lick to throw off a block of salt and then through to the other section, a journey that might take half an hour. After a cuppa with the manager, John would be back in the Land Rover checking on whatever seasonal job needed seeing to, from ploughing and harrowing, to sowing the tobacco seed beds or topping the flowers off the young plants. There was always something to do and someone to yell at or instruct or shake his head at and growl about how this damn farm was just a bloody money pit. And then the same journey back the way he came to the main farm in time for tea.

I don't think he ever hugged me or ever picked me up as a child, but he had other ways of showing his love. His tales of the bush and wildlife were like adventures straight out of story books. His unwavering love of Rhodesia, his constant disappointment with England and his hatred and disgust of what he referred to as that 'insipid' Harold Wilson government kept us constantly amused.

Sometimes he would take us out on to the lawn at night and lie down staring at the Milky Way and point out the constellations, in particular his own star sign, Scorpio, snaking across the universe with its curved tail ready to strike. More than any constellation, Scorpius, resembles its namesake. If you live in the northern hemisphere, Scorpius crawls across the southern sky, close to the horizon. But if you live in the southern hemisphere, it passes high in the sky. The bright star Antares marks the heart of the arachnid, and its long curving tail trails to the south. The scorpion once had claws, but they were cut off by Julius Caesar to form the constellation Libra. The scorpion also holds an infamous place in Greek mythology as the slayer of Orion. One story tells that Orion fled the scorpion by swimming the sea to the island of Delos to see his lover, Artemis. Apollo, seeking to punish Artemis, joined her and challenged her hunting skills, daring her to shoot the black dot that approached in the water. Artemis won the challenge, unknowingly killing her lover by doing so. A story of daring, betrayal and courage and of hunting, so typical of my father.

The Southern Cross was a favourite and he taught us how to find magnetic south by following the pointer stars and bisecting them straight down the middle. These lessons were both practical and fabulously interesting, and rather rare. John had a gentleness which could be seen when using a needle to remove a thorn from our foot or blowing an egg or sticking together a delicate model of a ship. It surprised me to find I carried none of these genes. I have little patience for this kind of thing. My attempts at crafts, origami or model-making ended with tons of glue all over the place, lots of crumpled paper on the floor and a hideously ugly clay ashtray that was quite unusable.

John encouraged us to take up hobbies. His idea of a hobby generally involved the great outdoors. He taught us to blow bird eggs by pricking a tiny hole in the end and puffing through a straw or just your mouth until all the contents had dribbled out. He was finicky in that sort of way. I generally broke the egg. But he was an expert. He had an extensive collection which he had started when he was a kid: gently and safely packed in cotton wool in neat boxes separated by delicate compartments, each containing one egg, protected and coveted like a curator for the Darwin collection at the Natural History Museum, each egg neatly labelled with a number and a name. These collections had been carefully carried over bumpy roads and rocky ground from farm to farm until they came to rest in the top of my cupboard. There were delicate blue eggs and large green speckled eggs. Brown and beige, and one tiny egg that was almost aubergine in colour. The rarest egg he had was possibly the least interesting, belonging to the Verreaux's eagle (*Aquila verreauxii*), also known as the black eagle. The elongated chalky white egg looked more like that of a bantam. But to get to it, John had to climb the sheer cliff of a granite *kopje* to reach the eerie, explaining that he only ever took one egg to ensure that the birds could keep reproducing.

All my young life a pair of black eagles soared hypnotically above our farm and despite their vast range, the pair would always come home to M'sitwe to roost. Sadly, typical of kids, we did not look after the egg collection and by the time I was a teenager most of them had been broken, the entire box finally getting chucked out one day.

Woody insisted on punctuality, far beyond what was necessary. If we were five minutes late he would yell at us, yet he himself never owned a watch, was never late and always rose with the sparrows. Decades later I still found myself arriving at dinner parties absolutely on the dot, often finding my hosts half-dressed and in a total flap.

John had a canny way of being able to see into a person. He either liked you or did not like you. It was as simple as that. Impatient, utterly intolerant, easily irritated, fastidious to an obsessive degree (he could not bear the idea of men wearing cologne or 'smellies' as he called them, other than Vitalis for his hair), yet incredibly courageous and possessed of great charm and old-world manners. If ever we had dull or boring guests he was quick to grumble, 'Have these people no bloody homes to go to?'

Back at the barns John would make a final scan of the yard then away we went, labouring up the hill past the servants' compound, a mist of blue smoke creeping through the thatch of the conical huts, swerving to miss the M'sitwe Wanderers Football Club's ball made out of rolled-up plastic bags as we went. The M'sitwe Wanderers were well known to be rough players. They practised on a pitch that sloped at a 35-degree angle and had a large ant hill right in the middle. When the Wanderers won the inter-farms championship one year, we bought them all boots and jerseys. These lasted about a week until my father found the entire team wearing the boots and jerseys while working in the fields. He confiscated the lot.

We rounded the corner past some giant poinsettias that had grown so large they reached across the road like a canopy, and on to the front lawn under the shade of the magnificent *Cassia fistula*, its luscious blooms drooping down in bunches and carpeting the floor of the lawn in canary yellow.

The gate to the security fence was open and the dogs dashed out barking and snapping at the wheels. Jumping up and slobbering all over me, we moved en masse into the main garden.

'Konda!' called John. 'Bwesa tea[27].'

---

[27] Chilapalapa phrase meaning 'bring tea'.

3

Alec

My siblings Duncan and Mandy are both older than me and spent their early years doing correspondence school. But by the age of six they were sent off to Umvukwes boarding school some 26 miles away, leaving me to fumble my own way through life back on the farm. My first attempts at correspondence school ended in a fiasco when I swallowed the tiny white 'Cuisenaire rod', the coloured wood blocks of varied sizes used to teach children numbers and sums. Without them, lessons soon ground to halt.

After shadowing me all day like a Marabou stork, my mother finally pounced when I needed to do a pooh under the guava tree, and with two sticks picked the rather grisly offending article out of my turd, a bit like choosing a choice piece of veggie from a stir fry. Lessons were never the same after that and an alternative plan was drastically required. I had to go to a real school despite being only five. I had never worn shoes in my life, let alone learned to tie laces. I had never made a bed nor slept a single night away from my mother.

There was, however, another more pressing problem that was beginning to worry my parents. Unless nipped in the bud early, this might cause no end of trouble for them and me, or so they believed. Rhodesia in 1967 was a segregated country and white people simply did not mix with blacks. Countries to the north had already thrown off the shackles of colonialism and declared independence from Britain. This rather terrified the white community in southern Africa and Rhodesia had chosen to take another path entirely by declaring UDI or a Unilateral

Declaration of Independence[28] without a formal agreement with the UK. The last country to have had the nerve to do this was the United States in 1776.

As a five-year-old kid alone on a 13,000-acre farm in the middle of white-ruled Africa, one whose life was completely bound by servants, nannies, a loving, if slightly flighty, hipsterish mother, and a stern father, I was, to say the least, lonely. My brother and sister away for weeks at boarding school meant I had no company other than my adoring nanny. But nanny had a plan.

After lunch every day, my mum and dad had a kip. During these siestas, nanny would tie me in a *doek* on her back and walk down to the compound – something even today that suggests exciting and forbidden fruits. The compound! I was told never to go down there under any circumstances, This was where the servants lived. There were *skellums*[29] like ringworm that could crawl into my skin, diseases, bad *munts*[30] who might hurt me, filthy overflowing PKs (short for *piccaninny kias*[31]) and of course rabies from the dogs that skulked around the perimeter bushes eating shit. It is no wonder white kids grew up with a massive distrust of their black servants. Yet despite all these obstacles, nanny and I knew it was worth it. Because down in the compound there was Alec.

Alec was my age. He was Fred and nanny's first-born son, and he was my first real friend. For an hour every afternoon Alec and I would have the freedom of the compound and the surrounding bush. We would explore the balancing rocks,

---

[28] Unilateral Declaration of Independence – an assertion of the independence of an aspiring state or states. In particular, Rhodesia's Unilateral Declaration of Independence in November 1965 and the United States in 1776.

[29] Rogue. From the Dutch/Old High German word *skelmo* meaning 'devil'.

[30] A black African. From the Zulu word *umuntu* meaning 'person'.

[31] Toilet. Piccaninny means 'child' or 'small'; *kia* means 'house'.

chase eccentric-looking blue-headed lizards across the yard, use a catapult to try to shoot down doves high up in the branches of the *mazhanje* trees, climb into nearby caves to stare and wonder at the shapes and animals painted on the rock faces hundreds of years ago, quite possibly by Alec's early ancestors. There were kudu with their curled horns, elephants, warthogs, crocodiles, fat-bellied men with bows and arrows, women with large protruding breasts. The intricate and beautifully rendered paintings fascinated us.

Occasionally we would even find a shard of pottery, which we always carefully placed back where we found it in case we upset the spirits of the long-dead San bushmen.

This was an education far better than anything Cuisenaire or Montessori could ever offer. Later when the sun dipped slightly in the sky and the shadows began to lengthen across the cleanly swept yard, people would emerge from their mud huts to go back to work. Women would stir the pots of *sadza*[32] on the embers of the fire built in front of the mud *kias* or put the tin pots on their heads and walk elegantly down to the nearby river to scrub the enamelware with sand to remove the remnants of the lunchtime meal. Men would roll up a piece of newspaper with tobacco scrap and squat down next to the fire or in the shade of their small *stoep*[33] and have a smoke. The acrid, blue tobacco smoke smelt so much more exotic than the shop-bought cigarettes the Europeans smoked.

Nanny or one of the other women, often with a wailing baby on their back, would roll up a small piece of sadza in their hand and feed it to me, occasionally with the delicious green relish they made from wild vegetables and blue-green rape. Dust streaked our faces, blackjacks and 'wait-a-bit' thorns stuck to our clothes

---

[32] Ground maize known as mealie-meal.

[33] Afrikaans word meaning 'veranda'.

and hair. Dry mud caked between our toes. Then the highlight of the day would begin.

Nanny would take an old zinc tub, place it on a concrete slab that served as their bathroom, the only privacy being the flimsy grass fence. She would fill the tub with warm water, strip the two of us kids and in we would jump, splashing and cavorting in the deliciously warm water. Nothing in our own avocado-green bathroom could ever compare to those afternoon washes in the compound shaded by the *mufuti*[34] and mountain acacia trees and surrounded by the life of the villagers.

African women have a remarkably tender, yet rough way of dealing with children. They might firmly hold you up dangling like a monkey by your arm while they lathered your legs and tummy using the huge green bars of soap available in roadside stores. Alec hated this and he would scream, wriggle and wail, but for me it was bliss. Perhaps I knew deep down that being the child of the Nkosi, any kind of bawling or screaming could have major repercussions, certainly it would have made the other people in the compound very uncomfortable having the piccanin bwana crying. After all, they were the servants and they all knew my presence in the compound could bring down the wrath of my father.

Eventually, this daily sojourn would come to an end at the sound of the gong being struck – either Fred or Konda banging a *simbe*[35] against an old plough disk up the hill outside the kitchen. This acted as an alarm clock and could be heard for miles around, alerting all the farm workers that siesta was over and it was time to get back to the fields and workshops. It

---

[34] *Brachystegia boehmii* is a flat-topped tree with a spreading crown that is native to eastern and southern Africa. Common names are *mufuti* (Zimbabwe) and Prince of Wales feathers.

[35] A metal pipe.

also marked the time for me to sneak back up the hill, in time for milky tea on the veranda with my mum and dad, and the world's thinnest cucumber sandwiches. I often wonder if they ever noticed my squeaky clean shiny pink skin, fresh from being scrubbed raw by nanny. Only Konda serving the tea would have a twinkle in his eye.

For the most part, my parents were clueless about this despite on occasion seeing me playing with Alec at the back of the house where the servants hung out. It might have worried them had they known how often this happened. It was time I made 'proper' friends with white kids from the district. So a plan was set in motion that would change everything. As with the young calves down in the paddock, this was a time of weaning.

One day early in January, shortly after Dunc and Mandy had gone back to school, mum popped me in the old Rambler car and drove off towards Raffingora, some 20 miles away along rocky and corrugated dirt roads.

'Where are we going, mum?' I asked excitedly.

'We are off to see Norma and Lofty Standage, and Gillian. You remember Gillian, don't you? She's your age. She is someone you can play with.'

I felt excited to see Gillian although I did not remember having met her before. It was rare to see other white kids. Getting around was not easy like it is today. Norma and Lofty were also farmers, living near the village of Raffingora. A few weeks previously their home on the hill had spectacularly burned to the ground after a lightning strike. Nothing remained of the old thatched farmhouse except the corrugated-iron kitchen, which like many farmhouses was built apart from the main house, not for practical purposes, but to keep the cook out of your hair. To my astonishment, the old house was literally a charred pile of ash still slightly smoking, the odd whitewashed wall from one of the rooms still stood crumbling and now blackened with soot. A hundred yards away, nestled under a mountain acacia, stood a single white, thatched *rondavel*[36]. This was where Granny Standage lived.

Mum and I, led by Lofty, Norma and Gillian all piled into the small, cramped *rondavel* for tea and the most delicious home-made date cake I had ever tasted. Thank goodness the kitchen still stood, I thought.

Gillian and I chatted and played while the adults looked over at us with more interest than we really deserved. Then Gillian took me down a rocky pathway dotted with mauve aloes and Christ's Thorn to the red-brick tobacco sheds and barns. 'This is where we live now,' she gestured, showing me into a gloomy windowless interior with four old brass beds separated only by a flimsy curtain. 'It's all we could get out of the house before it burned down,' she explained.

The place smelt pungently of tobacco scrap. A nail was hammered into the wall next to each bed, where a sponge bag hung rather incongruously. My curiosity getting the better of me, I asked where they washed and bathed. 'Oh, we managed to pull the old bathtub down the hill and we've made a wash area outside on a piece of flat concrete. I hate it. It's just like the *muntus* have.' I wanted to tell her that I loved washing in a tub outdoors, but explaining this would require giving up too many secrets and I knew Alec would be furious.

I heard the car starting up near the *rondavel*. 'I have to go!' I shouted to Gillian and ran outside. But already the car was a hundred or so yards down the hill, dust gathering in its wake.

---

[36] A *rondavel* (from the Afrikaans word *rondawel*) is a Westernised version of an African-style hut.

I ran after it shouting for my mum to stop. But the vehicle just kept going. On and on I ran, tears streaking down my now dusty face. How could she? How could she just forget me? 'Mum, don't leave me! Come back!' I shouted one last time as the car finally turned the bend and disappeared from sight. Slowly the dust settled and I stared at the empty road, willing the car to turn around and come back for me.

'Pete,' said a kindly voice behind me. It was Norma. 'Didn't your mum tell you? You are staying with us now. You have to start going to school in Raffingora with Gillian and the other white kids. You're a big boy now. Don't worry, you'll love it. So many people to play with. And so many adventures.'

But I already had people to play with, I thought. I already had adventures. And I had Alec. I had never been away from my mum and I simply didn't understand. Mandy and Duncan never had to do this. They went to a proper school. They didn't have to sleep in a barn surrounded by strange people. They didn't have to eat in a *rondavel* cluttered with a piano, piles of furniture and an old woman with white hair. Why me?

To my little mind this was treachery and the first day at school I decided to cry non-stop all day. Even 40 years later I loathe and detest the story of Peter Rabbit. I blamed the end of my baby days on Beatrix Potter and that spiteful rabbit. I wasn't to know that mum had left without saying goodbye because she did not want me to see the tears rolling down her cheeks.

Routine and distance blurred the boundaries. I suppose I began to have fun. I loved my teacher Lorraine. And I learned that I had a talent. I could draw well. Also on the plus side I adored Gillian. Norma and Granny Standage taught us about food. There were cakes, scones, flapjacks and we were always allowed to lick the bowl. Beautiful aromas constantly wafted from that tiny, tin kitchen. My own mum rarely cooked and never baked cakes. Lofty slowly became like a surrogate father. And living in a barn taught me for the first time that to be different was not necessarily a bad thing. Life once again was an adventure.

The folks from Raffingora were different to those in Umvukwes. The Raff crowd were not quite so snooty, they were more artistic and liberal minded and not so set in their ways. I was not too surprised to learn later in life that this is where the writer Doris Lessing spent many years living in a simple thatched house overlooking the beautiful Ayrshire hills (although perhaps not quite as happy as one might imagine – she did abandon her husband and kids all in the name of art). Some of her greatest collected works, such as *This Was The Old Chief's Country* and *The Sun Between Their Feet*, were written just up the road.

Many whites across the country naturally felt that Lessing was a typical liberal sell-out. Some were simply 'disappointed' that she left her poor children behind. The Raffingora crowd felt otherwise. Her short story called *Old John's Place* tells of the farmers in Raffingora as 'people of the district, mostly solidly established farmers who intended to live and die on their land'. She foretold a time when Africa would take back what belonged to it. In her own words, 'Africa gives you the knowledge that man is a small creature, among other creatures, in a large landscape.' How fitting.

At first I was a weekday boarder. Back at home on Saturday afternoons I would still sneak down to the compound to play with Alec. But something intangible had changed and would stay changed forever. That age of innocence was gone. As I met other kids my own age and skin colour, as I began to learn drawing, sums and crafts, I started to see a world outside the confines of the farm, and my feelings for Alec shifted. Alec saw this too and he slowly began drawing further and further away. Nanny stopped wrapping me in her *doek* and taking me down to the compound.

'Besides,' she said, 'you are getting too *makulu*[37].'

Within a year I would not even look at Alec. I seemed hardly to notice him when we drove past the compound in the back of the Land Rover, laughing with my brother and sister and maybe one or two of my new-found friends. Occasionally I would glance at Alec among a group of other African kids as we drove by. I rarely acknowledged his wave or his smile. All he got was the dust from the vehicle and a bitching from one of the *madala* women for nearly getting run over. No longer would cast-off clothes be delivered to the hut, warm from the iron and smelling of Omo washing powder. Sometimes there would be food, after all Fred was the cookboy. But a distance had developed between the two of us boys.

When I naively asked nanny why Alec never came up to the back of the house to play, she gently explained, 'It's not good, piccanin boss. You are a man now and you must not play with the African kids. The *nkosi*[38] will get angry and fire me.' She was kind, but firm. Our friendship was finished.

Sunday afternoons were hell. While I screamed and fought as mum carried me squirming to the car to take me back to the Standages, Alec would pick up his textbooks and walk the five miles across the bush to the small school on the neighbouring farm. He was a clever kid and learned well, according to his parents. At first, I took an interest in his education. I was surprised at how clever he was. Better than me, I thought. Alec's formal education ended when he was ten. Deep down I knew this was the order of things. This was what was expected. This was my new life now.

Slowly but inevitably Alec drew further and further away

---

[37] Chilapalapa word meaning 'big'.

[38] South African term of address for a superior, master, chief.

until one day he disappeared from my life altogether. My very first friend. A boy I had played with and shared dreams and aspirations with. Laughed at the sound of the go-away bird[39], burned our bare feet on the flat rock as we chased geckos and cried as the soap suds stung our eyes when nanny washed us. Yet my early days were always quite different to those of Alec. Even when our friendship was at its zenith my life was always different to his. At the sound of the gong I would be whisked back to the sanctuary of the big house, the plush Axminster carpets, the cool slate verandas, the soft-sprung beds and silky, cotton sheets. Back to the framed prints of Degas and Pissarro, the delicate Wedgwood porcelain figurines on the mantelpiece and the routine of family life in a middle-class colonial home. Alec went back to the hut he shared with his mother, father and siblings. He was sent to fetch wood for the fire or water for the *sadza*. There were many chores to do before bedtime.

Years later, during the liberation war, Alec became an active *mujiba*. These were teenage boys who acted as runners and messengers for the guerrillas. *Mujiba* were so endemic in the war that it is arguable they played a major part in the victory for Mugabe. When home for the holidays I would hear snippets of conversation about Alec. How he had turned feral. How he had gone against his parents' wishes. On hearing about Alec's fall from grace, I was furious. Also a little scared. It came as a shock to me when I found out that he was quite likely a *mujiba*. We often spoke about these go-betweens and how we were surprised at their bravery, their unbending faith in the freedom fighters, and their knowledge that the police or army would rarely torture children. After all, to the *murungu* they were just bloody piccaninnies running around having fun.

---

[39] Turacos make up the bird family *Musophagidae* (literally 'banana-eaters') which includes plantain-eaters and go-away-birds. In southern Africa both turacos and go-away-birds are commonly known as Louries.

'Do you know,' my mum often said during the war; 'if I were black, I would be a *mujiba*.'

'Jesus, mum, they are no better than bloody terrorists. How can you even think like that?' we would chorus. This kind of talk genuinely scared us.

'Yes, I realise THAT,' she would say with a dramatic shrug and roll of the eyes, 'but look what they have. They have nothing. Can you just imagine if you lived the life they live? Down there in the compound. In the heat and dust and flies. Well, I don't know about you, but as for me I would want to strive to get more.' Naively, she would react with horror if we asked her if she were black would she become a terrorist.

'God, no! They are nothing but murderers. How can you say such a thing?'

Mujiba seemed less evil than terrorists. Less dangerous. More benign. And perhaps slightly romantic. They had a dream of freedom and one man, one vote, but they were underaged and bore no arms, and therefore escaped the same fate as the adult freedom fighters.

It's notable that many *mujiba* were fairly well educated, at least up to grade four. They wanted more than their parents and even grew to despise their elders. Alec, thanks to my friendship and his intimate knowledge of life in the big house up the hill, was almost certainly to blame for the theft of several elephant tusks among other things priceless only to us, and quite valueless elsewhere. I often wonder what he did with them. My father banished Alec from the farm, like a feudal landlord.

'Never trusted that little shit,' he would say. Like a coward, I hid in my father's shadow trying to forget that Alec and I had been best friends.

Alec returned to the farm occasionally. Once during the height of the war it was believed he was responsible for luring our dogs away and locking them up so that they would not bark when a group of guerrillas, led by an infamous man named 'Mao', wanted to attack our house. Our dogs only trusted family, and Alec was most certainly a family member. On this occasion the guerrillas preferred to remain incognito and the dogs returned one day, well fed and tails wagging. That Alec might have been instrumental in our deaths was uncomfortable to say the least, particularly for his father Fred. The second time was at the end, in those awful last few weeks of 2001, when my parents were being thrown off the farm. Alec most certainly led the troupe who sat outside my parents' bedroom window, night after night, slowly drumming on the tom-toms, like a scene from *Zulu Dawn*. Tormenting. Torturing. Tap, tap, tapping, night after night right outside their window.

By then Alec was a leader and he hated us all with a passion quite horrifying to us at the time. All his life his parents had given themselves to us, to this one family, yet Alec had nothing. Oh, perhaps the odd cast-off item of clothing. And then the final insult, to be banished from the farm. The farm he grew up on. The very place where his mother and father served as cook and nanny to the white people in the big house on the hill. Naturally he was bitter and wanted revenge. So bitter he never even came to his father's funeral, as he regarded Fred a sell-out. Getting my parents thrown off their land must have been sweet revenge.

For a brief period Alec must have felt he was, at long last, the winner. But squabbling and greed soon laid waste to all of that. Like a recurring nightmare, Alec ended up with nothing. Within months of my parents leaving M'sitwe, the graves of the dogs still fresh in the ground, all the money had gone. The country had crashed and burned. The currency valueless. The big house on the hill began to crumble. The sparkling blue swimming pool became a dark viscous pond of rotting vegetation, frog spawn and dead bugs. The lawns and gardens were overtaken by weeds and creepers and nettles and snakes. The shade trees – ancient jacarandas, Parkinsonia and flamboyants – were felled for firewood.

Not for the first time poor Alec became a shadow and drifted away. Some say he went slightly mad. There was nothing left to keep him there. Perhaps that was his final prize. His last vindictive act of vengeance. Everything my father had, had now reverted back to the bush. The white colonial masters banished just like Alec to wander aimlessly for the rest of their days.

But return, he did, many years later. This time to my brother's farm, he came armed with a head full of demons and a body ravaged by poverty. With an axe he hacked up one of my brother's cows. What he hoped to achieve is anyone's guess. But taking pity on him, Duncan allowed him to stay on the farm in a small hut at the end of the compound. Alone, like so often in his past. Many of the farm workers remembered Alec from their own childhood and kept clear of him, avoiding those sunken angry eyes, the hollow cheeks and his ranting, tortured mind.

Alec Chimbata died of a stroke on 23 July 2014. He was 52. It was my birthday. He was buried on the farm, quietly and without ceremony. Fate deals many cards and Alec, that funny gifted child who was my first friend, was dealt a rotten hand.

4

Back to School

It was the dogs that really began the whole sulky thing. They always knew. As soon as those battered ugly black tin trunks were hauled out, the dogs started to sulk. Once the dogs started, then we kids started. It was contagious. The hols were over and in a few days the freedom we had enjoyed would be gone.

Mum was also feeling it and generally managed to keep herself busy, lovingly sewing our name tags on to every piece of clothing, from undies to blazers and riding helmets. Even the cricket bats had our names stencilled on them, and the inside of our garters with a black marker pen. List after list of required clothing was bought from McCullagh & Bothwell in Salisbury, from a wizened old salesman with dreadful halitosis, a Dickensian apparition.

We tried hard, but were always different from the other families. At the end of term it was always the Wood kids left alone sitting on their tin trunks while all the other kids had been collected and gone home. It did not bother us, we kept telling ourselves. As the dust settled from the departing cars filled with excited, chattering children, there beneath the fir trees, sitting calmly on their trunks, were the three Wood kids. This was part and parcel of being a Wood.

Having an older brother and sister at the same school did help a bit. But only marginally. But Mandy was in the girls' hostel at the other end of the school grounds. Duncan was at an age where looking after the little brother was frowned upon. I remember spending the first week sneaking off to play games under the fir trees with my sister and her best friend, Peggy Strong. But this came to an end when the older boys accused me of having 'pink fleas'. Running around, brushing their clothes and jumping as if they were being bitten was enough to send me confused and shamefaced back to the hostel. Those damn pink fleas were rather persistent and would come back to haunt me later in life.

Everything was strange, new, regimented by the clanging of the bell, six of the best with a cane for any wrongdoing, a clip across the ear for lack of concentration, and rules. They kept giving me those simple two-word instructions such as 'stand here' or 'go there' or 'don't talk' and reminding me with relish what was going to happen to me if I got it wrong. 'AND DO YOU UNDERSTAND?' they would bellow, as if I was stone deaf. Even the uniform had me scratching my head in puzzlement.

Having grown up without shoes and only ever having owned a pair of faded red shorts, my first experiences of school were a rapid learning curve. I now had to learn to tie laces, knot a tie, use garters for my socks, not to mention having to make a bed with hospital corners, and then try and sleep in that bed at night to the snuffling sounds of a dozen kids crying into their pillows.

Like all schools, there were those teachers who were kind and sweet and lovable. My first teacher in KG2 was Miss Blueitt. Pretty, vivacious and endowed with fabulously large breasts. Few boys could resist her sex appeal. There was the sporty, handsome Mr Benson who ran Standard 4, drove a blue Alfasud and went out with Miss McCarthy who had the Standard 1 class. Miss McCarthy was the archetypal '60s-'70s flower child with long, straight hair, fabulous eye shadow and fashionable clobber.

I was slightly in love with Miss McCarthy and one day kept walking past her classroom pulling funny faces – back and forth like someone released from an institution. Eventually she came out, gripped me tightly by my ear lobe, and in front of everyone loudly said, 'Are you going to apologise?' Apologise? Am I going to *what*? The word sounded positively dangerous. I let the strange word with odd syllables swirl about in my brain for a bit. Then responded with a 'No'. I was quite emphatic about that. After an initial silence she looked at me with those perfectly raised eyebrows and gently asked 'do you know what *apologise* means?' Ashamed, I answered, 'Er … no.' I was released on bail much to the laughter of the senior boys.

The housemaster at the boys' hostel, and possibly the man who kept the whole show on the road, was Mr Nightingale. His acerbic tongue and love of the cane was legendary. *Don't cry unless there's blood* was his motto (stolen from local housewife Isabel Simons, who employed the tenet on her two kids, Peta and William, every time they grazed a knee or fell out of a tree). He ran the top class, Standard 5. Few, if any, boys were immune to his acid barbs and his stinging rattan. Had he not been an excellent teacher, he would have been loathed. However, despite his bouts of anger and daily whipping sessions in his office, he was strangely adored. Perhaps this was an early form of Stockholm syndrome. It was not uncommon to hear Mr Nightingale remark to some unruly children, 'For god's sake – go and play in the traffic,' or his favourite, 'Would somebody PLEASE go and drown that child.' He loved labels and would call us Wood Major, Wood Minor and Wood Minimus, with the youngest member of the family often bent over his desk receiving four of the best.

If junior school was a shock, high school as a boarder 150 miles from home was the Royal Flush of Royal Flushes. According to many, my high school, Prince Edward, was the best school in the country by far. But with that in mind, I will be the first to admit that PE, as it was affectionately known, was a disappointment. Everyone who grew up in that milieu will gasp and disagree with me. But what you learn at school is often only made apparent later in life and I have always felt PE lacked in so many ways it beggars belief. Kids who went to the top private schools – St George's, Falcon and Peterhouse, three of the best private schools south of the equator – were often imbued with a sense of determination, knowledge, ambition and, more importantly, a feeling of belonging that I felt I lacked.

Prince Edward was established in 1898, making it the second oldest school in the country after sporting rivals St George's College. The architecture was beautiful, designed by Sir Herbert Baker who also designed Groote Schuur, the stunning Dutch gabled home of Cecil John Rhodes in Cape Town. The ancient Syringa tree-lined fields and avenues of massive old jacarandas were incredible. The school badge was a crown and three ostrich feathers, granted to it by Prince Edward (later King Edward VIII) in the 1920s. The school colours were maroon and dark green and the uniforms were, rather bizarrely considering the intense African heat, straw boaters, blazers and grey flannel trousers. The school motto, *Tot facienda parum factum* ('So much to do, so little done') is attributed as Cecil John Rhodes' last words. The school war cry was somewhat less sophisticated.

Shhhhh!
Slaba Madoda
Whaaa!
Slaba Madoda
Whaaa!
Bomalaka, Bomalaka, Whaaa, Whaaa, Whaaa
Bomalaka, Bomalaka, Chaa, Chaa, Chaa
Shhhhh!
Who are we?
We are, we are, can't you see
We are, we are, can't you guess
We are, we are PES
Hi Zika Zumba Rugby Tigers
PES!
Waaghhhaaaaaa! (boaters in the air ...)

My scant knowledge of Shona/Ndebele/Afrikaans always left me believing the words meant:

Shhhhh! (used by Matabele warriors before going into battle to unnerve their foe)

Hit the boy!

Whaaa!

Hit the boy!

Whaaa!

There we are, there we are, whaaa, whaaa, whaaa.

In fact, rather annoyingly, I was more recently informed that it is more likely to be Ndebele and not Shona and the words actually meant 'we are men' and not 'hit the boy'. But I prefer my version.

Either way, the first verse ends with 'chaa, chaa, chaa' (hit, hit, hit). Not exactly high poetry.

Our headmaster at the time, Raymond Suttle, was a rather ineffectual man living within the shadows of the school. I doubt if he had much control over the kids. Yet there was always someone out there to keep control, to give us that clip across the ear. And that was the teacher we called Wart. Dear old Wart. His nickname wasn't that much better than his real name: Mr Cock.

With a large, well-rounded profile, much like that of Churchill or Hitchcock, old Wart ruled Selous House (and, indeed, many felt ruled Prince Edward) in an autocratic, domineering fashion. A confirmed bachelor, they say old Wart was as gay as a year on

Saturn is long. While none of those rumours were founded on anything, this extraordinary man never got married and gave his life to the school and not to a human of either sex (as far as I know).

Wart did have taste. In abundance. His flat, attached to Selous House, was furnished lavishly, hung with beautiful paintings and the walls covered in flocked paper. His garden was immaculate, as was his attire, if not slightly outdated and staid. All that was lacking was a carnation in his buttonhole and a silver-tipped cane. He was also a great lover of the arts and encouraged us to do drama and choir practice.

Yet for all his artsy traits, he was tough. He had to be to have stuck it out at that job for nigh on 30 years. He was slow on his feet and as fast a viper with the cane – how many times had I pulled down my *broek* and lent over that wonderfully polished Rhodesian *mukwa* table to receive three or four or even six of the best. Rubbing our backsides with methylated spirits beforehand sometimes helped, but rarely did stuffing a newspaper or magazine down the back of our undies ever work.

Old Wart was not dumb. He knew all the tricks in the book. 'And for that …' he would grunt, 'you get one more!' Crack! Hearing the smack of the cane on some poor kid's arse was a warning to all and sundry that Mr Cock meant business. Unlike many teachers who thought the harder you struck, the better, Wart was adept with his cane, employing a wrist action that only a learned expert could ever understand, having had many years' practice. The bendy rod would always find its mark – always on your bum and always leaving the most fabulous blue-black bruises across lily-white skin. Other less adept teachers missed the mark, lashing the legs or worse, flicking the cane around until it struck the groin.

Six of the best was thankfully the most one could inflict on a student, but in truth rarely was a kid dished out the full quota. I believe I was given this accolade twice at Selous House. To my delight, one year I made top marks – by that I mean, I came first in Selous House for having been given the most *dooks* or canings in a term. Mr Cock actually had a written record, comprising the time, date, name, age, crime, punishment, and even the type of cane used.

*The **10mm nursery cane** or **junior cane**: sometimes substituted for the lightest cane, as it would be used for kids under school age.*

*The **senior cane**: a heavier type (about 10mm thick, 75-80cm long) and frequently used for older children (except for the lightest offences); may be synonymous with the **adult cane**.*

*The **reformatory cane**: reserved for the worst, '(otherwise) incorrigible' juveniles. About 12mm thick and 90-120cm long, often used for older inmates in severe cases; similar to the **borstal cane** (mistakenly named after the borstal, a Commonwealth-era reformatory; in fact, caning was never officially permitted in borstals).*

Cock would summon me to his office and show me the large, well-worn ledger of 'Canings, Selous House – 1975' and almost in a doting manner, inform me that I was this year's winner, having had the most number of lashes. One could not help sensing a certain amount of pride in Wart's voice. My credibility at school went up threefold. My chances of ever becoming a prefect diminished into an atomic-sized dot. Somehow those teachers did not see the importance of this in the same way we kids did. Sadly, Mr Cock retired to Johannesburg where he was to be murdered in his bed. An ignoble end to an extraordinary man who nurtured many a child through to adulthood. Mr Cock, I salute you, or in the Matabele tradition: *Bayete!*[40]

---

[40] A traditional Zulu royal salute.

Teachers were the only ones allowed to cane kids, but prefects were given permission, without argument, to thrash kids with any other object that came to hand, such as trainers, rolled up magazines, garrotting wire, fishing twine or the back of the hand. So long as it was not a cane. Again, I managed to break the record. Why?

The first two years at high school, juniors had to be a skivvy (or 'fag' in the British public school parlance). Generally, you were a fag to a prefect, but I, lucky bugger, was fag to the head of house, Alan. As fate should have it, Alan was going out with my sister at the time and for reasons that utterly baffled most people, he thought it was best to give me a hiding every single day. I like to think he was worried that people might assume he was favouring me over other kids since he was, for want of a better word, my brother-in-law.

I would love to be able to say that I used Alan to my advantage because he went out with Mandy. The truth was far more humdrum. Alan did not have the nickname of 'Idi' (as in Idi Amin) for nothing. He was, to put it mildly, unreasonably tough on me. Good looking, great at sport, and let's not forget, like so many bullies, utterly charming and endearing to those above him. But to me, he was hell. I tried to love him. Indeed, I had a schoolboy crush on him – perhaps a knee-jerk reaction to having been beaten every day. It made no difference. At roll call each day at lunchtime, I would wait. 'Shepperd, Southey, Tate, Thackwray, Oosthuizen, Van Huystein, Wyrley-Birch, *WOOD – SEE ME AFTER LUNCH*' (collective groan down the ranks).

I got used to it in the end. Every day he found something wrong, some reason to beat me. I had not rolled his socks correctly, or ironed his shirt properly, or made his toast at breakfast in the manner he preferred – on and on. I might stop here to point out that my skivvy skills were not THAT bad. I was not sloppy, nor was I forgetful or any of the things he accused me of day after day. And my punishment? Two or three really hard, stinging clouts across the backside with one of his sneakers – generally taken at a run for maximum impact.

While I can safely say that I was getting used to these thrashings, one day I was just too exhausted and could not bear the thought of yet another perfectly shaped shoe mark over my buttocks (the Adidas logo beautifully imprinted back-to-front on my bottom), so I offered Alan a bribe – my apple from lunch. Alan graciously took the apple and then promptly gave me an extra hiding for bribery. I never did understand this attitude, yet I was not always the only one being punished. 'Idi' would frequently, and for little reason, put the entire house on detention over a weekend, making every kid from 13-17 years old weed the lawn or plant flowers or do some crappy thing under the guise of 'Beautification of Selous House'. Perhaps he saw himself as an empire builder. He needed to leave his mark – and not just on my bum. I believe in the end he was avoided by both the juniors and the seniors and in many ways this helped my credibility in the house.

Despite all the canings and the detentions and the character-building exercises, Prince Edward was possibly the top government school in the country, oozing with tradition and a list of alumni as long and as powerful as anything else on the continent. Typical of that kind of institution, art was shunned, shoved to an outhouse run by some daft liberal third-grade teacher armed with a few tins of powder paint and some clay for making useless ashtrays or wobbly coffee mugs. Theatre, despite the efforts of the extraordinarily talented John Haig, was largely neglected. Music was non-existent. My mum with her am-dram ideas decided to send me to elocution lessons at a nearby girls' school.

The big annual Christmas semester event was always centred

around Gilbert and Sullivan productions. Despite Haig's efforts in educating us in the finer side of English drama, these absurd operettas, directed by Wart, always came top of the annual arts calendar. The format remained the same year after year. The seniors always played the men, be they pirates, sailors, samurai or whatever, and the juniors played the women, maidens, damsels, geishas and stuff. I had the pleasure of playing one of the maidens in *The Pirates of Penzance*. My 'male' pirate partner was none other than Alan.

Even in a fantasy world of faeries and stardust, Alan's presence could be felt breathing over me. He stood behind me, pinching me so hard it caused bruises on my arms. He constantly tested me to see if I would yelp out at an inopportune moment. Initially, it began as just a bit of humour. Like some masochist, I quite enjoyed the attention. Just getting his undivided attention was enough – at first. I was a Wood and was made of sterner stuff and simply endured this minor torture. After all, in the words of many a great actor, the fucking show must go on! To Alan it was just fun and games.

Of course, my drama career was in full swing (or so I thought). I would rush between eisteddfods having just performed in Shakespeare's very bloody King John, Act IV.

> *Hubert, if you will, cut out my tongue, so I might keep mine eyes; O, spare mine eyes!*

Now, clutching my first-class certificate, straight on to the stage at PE to play some fluttering doe-eyed maiden in distress. Too often, my mother would make me up in the car turning me into some Egyptian princess rather than the required Gilbert and Sullivan tart. As we built up to the grand finale, belting out our last number, Alan would be standing right behind me jabbing me or twisting my arm in a stinging Chinese bangle. But with a dignity and professionalism that might have raised an eyebrow at The Old Vic, I soldiered on until the final curtain call.

Initially, elocution meant the joy of getting out of dreary homework in the evenings. It also allowed me to spread my wings and fly. For once I could just be me. During those many elocution lessons I no longer had to be rugged or masculine or tough. But the price of elocution meant a life of torment back in the dorm. Getting As in an eisteddfod is one thing, but toughing it out in a tough school in a tough country going through a tough war was another thing entirely. Being an outsider at any boarding school could spell disaster. Having a Pommie accent at a time when Harold Wilson's England was hardly flavour of the month was not such a good idea.

It was a brave move but my need to be heard in the farthest reaches of the gods, my craving to tread the boards, my desire to pull on a pair of my mum's tights, velvet tunic and a feathered cap coursed hotly through my veins. Here was a country where the rougher your *yaapie*[41] accent, the more of a man you were. Having the elocution lessons at the Girls' High School, GHS, generated even more ridicule until I told the boys that there were plenty of hot chicks at elocution lessons all vying for my attention. Ironically, I ended up deliberately cultivating a Rhodesian accent, ultimately cancelling out any good work my poor, long-suffering elocution teacher managed to achieve.

I also loved painting and sketching, and so I began having extra lessons at the Salisbury School of Art run by the wonderfully eccentric and incredibly talented Peter Birch. Once a week, I would leave after dinner and walk across town, down the stunning jacaranda-lined avenues to his home and studio in Greenwood Park. Birch's art lessons were mixed – adults

---

[41] *Yaapie* or *Jaapie* is Afrikaans for 'boer', and comes from the Dutch nickname for men named Jaap.

and students, boys and girls. His classes were fun, irreverent, fascinating, sophisticated and often very heated, many sessions lasting late into the night. If he thought you were not putting enough oomph into a painting, he would tear it from your easel and rip it apart in front of a gobsmacked group, once even going so far as to claw at my paper, shredding it up in a rage, his lip curled up like a lion. Wonderful stuff. You never made the same mistake twice.

One vivacious student, Barbrie-Anne Meaker, took the brunt of it, often in the form of Peter Birch's finger prodding her ample boobs. 'The best thing in the world,' he would say, raising his extraordinary Spock eyebrows in an obvious challenge, 'are fabulous large nipples poking through a T-shirt.' Of course he once went too far and ended up with a sound clout across the face. That was the last we saw of him that day. Sometimes Birch would simply walk out of a lesson and disappear upstairs not to be seen again all evening, although one could not ignore the carnal grunting that resonated through the floorboards. We simply put it down to an artistic temperament. I think Peter may have had bisexual tendencies. While I was too naive to even know what 'bisexual' was, I certainly understood the charged atmosphere when he was nearby. My diary from the period clearly states as much – albeit misguided.

Went to art. Had a big row with Peter Birch about art – the usual stuff. He divorced his wife because he was caught in bed with a reporter – whether it was a male or female I don't know?!

In many ways, Peter Birch reminded me of my uncle Andrew. Not the sexual thing, the bohemian thing. Andrew and my aunt Susie had both been successful on the West End and Broadway back in the late 1950s, and in my eyes they were the most sophisticated people I knew. Andrew was well travelled and often brought me marvellous curios from far-off places. Birch reminded me of Andrew. Birch's home was draped in spoils from Kathmandu and Benares. Sets of jewel-encrusted Kukri knives on the walls, stained-glass Moroccan lamps hanging from the ceilings, large, comfy couches draped in mirrored and beaded cloths from Afghanistan. He offered a window to another world, which I jumped through as soon as I was allowed to leave school. Birch taught me the meaning of cool.

One of the greatest crimes for an Anglo-Saxon male was to be too much of a teacher's pet – too much of a brainbox – too well read. At our school, if you were a Cohen or a Landau or a Schwab, being a teacher's pet was cool – indeed de rigueur. Being too bookish for an Anglo-Saxon was frowned upon like a verruca or Doby's itch and would often lead to something worse: the next biggest crime – having unacceptable mates. The two went hand in hand. And talking about hand in hand – being a poofter was the biggest crime of all.

There were hundreds of ways of 'being gay' at school. Funnily enough, Thursdays were always 'Gay Day', or as we called it 'Morf Day'. While it was primarily a joke, I just wonder what would have happened should two lads walk down the avenue on Thursday holding hands? I doubt if they would have made it past the first jacaranda before they would have been 'ball-brushed' with Kiwi shoe polish. Yet, at boarding school, 'gay' could mean anything from being sensitive, compassionate, crying (at any time regardless of the injury or pain), the love of art, theatre or dance, being in the choir (god we made sure our balls dropped quickly) and, finally, reading books written about ALL of the above. NOT being gay (ie, being rugged and butch) ironically meant wanking contests, gripping the prop or hooker tightly by the balls, studying at close quarters each boy's newly grown pubes, skinny dipping at midnight, boisterousness in the shower, sticking your finger up your arse and then shoving it under some unsuspecting person's nose: no wonder poofters grow up confused.

In the face of such childhood adversity, my brother Duncan taught me to always respond with a smile, no matter what.

'Now, *boet*,' he would lecture me when I was just 12 years old. 'When you go to PE you will have to do initiation and I just want you to laugh your way through it. DON'T CRY – WHATEVER YOU DO, DON'T CRY!'

So I smiled my way through three weeks of initiation. I smiled my way through 'rat races' under the bed pushing a penny with my nose until it bled and I smiled when getting thumped with duffel bags as we ran the gauntlet. I smiled when the spittle from an incensed senior drizzled over my face because I had forgotten his name. I smiled after I had run to the tuck shop seven times in one afternoon, each trip just to get a single Penny Kool. I smiled and smiled, like an idiot. And it worked. One day they just stopped. They decided that if they were not going to get the desired reaction, then what was the point? I quickly learned that to survive you had to be tough. So I became tough. I became a rebel. I swore. I smoked. I bunked out at night and got drunk. After a while I became known as a bit of a hell-raiser and party animal, once even setting light to a five-acre field of dry elephant grass near Prince's Field while smoking with my pal David Fox – the sirens of the fire engines could be heard all afternoon from across the school grounds as an ominous pall of grey smoke filled the sky. David and I cowered in the coal shed for fear of our lives.

My diary on a Sunday night says it all:

After a good chapel service, Foxy, Richard, Oosthuizen, Johan, Bloodnut and I went down town. We first went to SS then to the Terracskane – got pissed (very pissed) then to Clubbies – quite nice there and then to the Coq d'Or – closed, so we went to an all-night cafe and ordered a hamburger. We revved the bugger by saying: 'You call this a burger? It's more like a piece of shit between two bricks.' And he told us to fuck off or else he would call the police. Foxy broke the window with his hand by mistake and we tore the canvass canopy and ran off. We slept on Jubilee Field for a while then went to the YMCA (why?). When we got back at half-past midnight Gus Haasbroek was in my bed so I slept on the floor.

Again the following Thursday:

In the evening we (Rich, Foxy, Oosy and I) went and drank a bottle of Twee Jonge Gezellen and a bottle of Fleur du Cap. It was chuffed. We then went to Clubbies but we had to pay to get in and so we went to cause shit with the Indian owner of the all-nighter. He brought out a flick-knife and wanted to kill us (not surprisingly) and threatened to call the cops. After that we ran back to school – a bit of a waste of an evening really.

I formulated a rule of thumb to get me through boarding school:

Brain: find someone who is so damn clever that not even the brawniest bullies will bother him. A guy with a tongue that can lash them and make them feel like absolute plonkers and dickheads. Enter stage right: David Fox, aka Foxy.

Brawn – without the brawn, your brain can't really function. Besides, the brawn gives you status and elevates you to an untouchable level. Enter stage left: Andrew Cockburn, aka Spike.

I found both those traits in my two pals Foxy and Spike. And with them came a group of people who remained loyal to me all my school days. Luckily, Spike also had brains, but his boxing skills, Irish background and small-guy cockiness ticked nearly every box. Noël Coward once said: 'Never trust a short man. His head is too close to his bottom.' I disagree entirely and without these two guys I doubt if I could have managed. One entry in my diary simply states: *Hey Foxy – did you read my diary last night? If you did, don't get the impression I can't stand your guts because really you are the only true friend I've got, but it's just that sometimes you really get on my tits.*

Despite my protective gang, I was bullied. To be honest, I have no idea why. Oddly, it did not happen in the first two years of high school, perhaps because I had my big brother there. It slowly crept up on me and notwithstanding the first three weeks of initiation and then Idi's daily beatings, the real bullying only got going after I turned 15. Yet I was by no means a wimp. I gave as much as I got. I was a champion cross-country runner, always barefoot. Zola Budd had nothing on me. And I had even managed to get into the under-15 rugby first team. Admittedly, when I proudly told my father this news over breakfast, all he said was, 'Really? The standards must have gone down,' and went back to his porridge. His humour was lost on me.

Away from all the balls, I fared a lot better. I was in the cross-country A-team. Foxy, my side-kick brainbox, was not a great runner. Where I failed in the classroom, he succeeded. But watching poor Foxy struggle against nature on an eight-mile run was a lesson in pure, unadulterated torture and determination. Mrs Ball (what with all the Balls and Cocks in the staff room, one's mind boggles) was our coach. She was also our secret weapon. You see, Mrs Ball was sassy, crass, sexy as fuck, fun, cheeky – need I go on – oh yes, and she was married and middle-aged. It seemed insane that a school with a reputation for athletic excellence chose a woman (with perfect bow-shaped scarlet lips, Bardot eyeliner, pouffed hair and the sharpest stilettos I have ever seen) as coach of the cross-country team.

Mrs Ball was adored in the classroom, employing a teaching method that was simply wonderful. She could turn a story, or a famous person or event into a work of art, twisting a dull history class into something bursting with colour and scandal, and love.

Her *pièce de résistance* involved giving us the most descriptive lesson on sex education, going as far as to describe an orgasm in such detail that when I did finally watch *When Harry Met Sally* many years later, the orgasm scene took me straight back to Mrs Ball. Having gained our respect, she proceeded to make us run. So here was this wonderful, exotic woman, draped in a cape, shoes in her hands, running in her stockings alongside her team yelling for us to push harder. 'Go on, you can do it! Run, dammit, run!'

And run we did, winning nearly every race that year, and if memory serves, making history as the best cross-country team the school had ever had. I am blessed with rather long prehensile toes, which allowed me to run for miles at a fast pace. My father always said at least I had a good grip on Africa. Running also gave me leverage. It gave me a strength, a kind of power that shielded those other feelings, those other thoughts that were so derided by everyone else at school.

Good old Mrs Ball knew just how to put those toes into action. Her irreverence was the very thing that made us love her. One evening, Mrs Ball pulled out a *Playboy* and flicked it open to the double-page spread. 'Tonight children,' she commanded, her eyes peering over her stylish 1950s glasses, her manicured hands daintily holding the corner of the magazine to reveal a woman spread-eagled for all the world to see, 'WE TALK ABOUT SEX!' The room erupted into a riot with tables turning over as kids scrambled to tear a page from that most sought-after publication. At that moment Mrs Ball's husband, a rather dour farmer, decided to walk in the door. His anger was palpable as his face turned a blood-red puce. His lips trembled, his hands shook, then he bellowed ... he roared ... he went absolutely ape-shit, tearing the magazine from his wife's hand, grabbing her by the scruff of the neck, and marched our dear, fabulous Mrs Ball out of the pavilion and into obscurity. History and biology were never the same again.

It was hard to forget that there was a war going on. During an exceptionally cold mid-winter on 6 August 1977, several bombs rocked Salisbury, killing scores of innocent people. The first went off at a Woolworths. The second at a train station. The third in the Parkade near the town centre. These bombs became a fact of life for the next year or so – on one notorious day seven post-box bombs exploding across the town, culminating in the biggest bang of all on 12 December 1978, when the main fuel tank that supplied the city with petrol was blown up, darkening the sky with Armageddon-like noxious black smoke for several days. The thundering of the explosions could be heard across the cricket and rugby fields. It may well have been a coincidence, but with the war finally reaching the city, the bullying began in earnest. Violence begets violence. Boys needed to vent their anger. Testosterone levels rose. Young lads, normally quiet and soft spoken, became aggressive. The daily roll call of deaths on TV or at Sunday chapel service became routine.

Monday, 8 August 1977

Another bomb went off at a train station last night. No one was killed ... Alan fucked up James Lazell and called him spoofless (spineless). He kicked James in the balls and drew blood everywhere while James had to just stand there and take it like a man. Not like Alan who is a coward. I just do not understand that person. He is insane.

Tuesday, 9 August 1977

Last night was the worst night I have ever had at this school. I was woken up by Heron and taken to the washrooms. There I got fucked up and really balled at by the seniors for an absolutely incredibly unknown reason; for being spoofless and stroppy and not running for the phone, etc, etc! Dave (Fox) was also there. Evans was the worst. I really hate that cunt. They said I take advantage of Alan because he goes out with my sister and they said I just go to the rugby to watch Duncan play and not the school (even though I do not know why THAT is so wrong?). Because of what they said I got the impression that Alan was the cause (and this coming from a man who beats me every day – you can take your favouritism for all I care). Some form 4s were fucked up too and the next day some form 2s. It was really shit and they made me have a freezing shower which made me go into convulsions.

Later I saw Mandy. I so wish I could tell her.

Looking back, it is amazing that not once did a career officer ever sit me down and ask what I wanted. Not once did a social worker take me aside and inquire about who I was, what I needed, was I bullied? Sex, sexuality, issues at home? Bear in mind a war was raging and friends were being killed. Kids were in torment. Weekly evacuation drills on to the rugby fields created a state of intense fear. Children disappeared from our classroom after the holidays – killed in attacks on their homesteads. I went to three funerals in one day as a teenager, all of whom were either friends or fellow pupils killed in separate incidents – yet not one teacher took me aside and asked if I was okay.

Boarding school also produced an amorousness minus the eroticism. John Arton-Powell was one of the good guys. Naughty but good, if that makes any sense. He was the kind of chap who believed that if you did not have anything nice to say about a person, it's better to say nothing at all. When he did have an opinion, you sat up and listened. When Arton-Powell came on to my side of the room, I knew the tables might turn. Arton-Powell was a cheeky bugger and to get him onside was vital to my survival. He was also my greatest rival at cross-country. No other chap my age at school equalled me at long distance. He and I competed against each other year after year – some days I beat him and others he pipped me at the post. Mostly, though, he beat me.

This friendly rivalry grew to a crescendo in March 1977 when my fame dive-bombed at the inter-house cross-country. I was the star of Selous House. Arton-Powell was the star of Rhodes House. Parents had come from miles away. A feeling of anxiety and excitement rippled through the hostel. Colourful bunting had been hung up on poles along the fields. Groups of teachers and parents huddled and chatted amicably about how good their child was and how such-and-such was going to thrash your kid in the race. My parents behaved humbly by simply smiling; knowing that their son was in fact a sure winner. My performance all term had been nothing less than spectacular and I was expected to come first, so they had good reason. All morning people would approach me, a look of pride and reverence in their eyes. They would slap me on the back and give me a friendly squeeze around the shoulders or shake my hand in encouragement. I was the man that day. And this was the highlight of my athletic career.

This was it.

It was a Monday, and Mondays always meant malaria tablets. Absent-mindedly I took two of the quinine pills instead of one.

A disaster.

Initially, things went well, Arton-Powell and I pacing each other at the head of the pack. Nothing was going to beat us that day. We were invincible. The shouting from supporters, the roar of the crowd. The fame was going to my head. On the first lap I hurdled the gateposts with ease, flew across the water jump, sprinted through the flats and set the pace for the entire team. As the poison in the malaria tablets began to take effect, my legs got heavier, my breath shorter. Arton-Powell began to pull ahead. Other competitors passed me, some briefly glancing back in surprise. They had never beaten me before and now Wood was falling back in spectacular fashion. No amount of coaxing or cajoling would help. I eventually crossed the line in 20th place, and was greeted by an extremely angry team.

'Bad luck, old boy.'

'Don't worry – it couldn't be helped.'

'Oh well, you did your best.'

All I can say is that Arton-Powell also bombed that day and came in somewhere in the teens. And he had no quinine to blame it on. I was the shame of the hostel and no doubt my family, too. For Arton-Powell and me, our days of hero status in the cross-country team were over.

Yet this rivalry soon turned him into an object of my affection. Without warning I found that I was falling in love with my long-time opponent. A terribly confusing love-struck teenage crush with all its complexities and angst. Of course, I never told anyone, least of all him. That would have been the death of me. Even my diaries of this period were written in some stupid bloody code for fear of being found out.

3.4.2-4.6.21.3.8.16.6-3-15.17.18.5-8.22.4-3-16.18.23.6- 14.18.13.17-7.21.4.6.17-19.18.5.6.16.16 (translated: *It's terrible, I know, but I love Arton-Powell*). Page after page – hardly rocket science for Bletchley Park, but it took me forever to decode that wretched diary and the results were eye-wateringly pathetic. Poor Arton-Powell. I hope to god he never had an inkling and I apologise here and now. It would have killed him – not to mention me. Most kids face boyhood crushes, but mine were deeper and my frustration was extreme. I blush when translating some of the passages. Decoded, the messages are completely normal for a growing lad.

Monday, 26 March 1979

I have said nothing like this before, but I want to sleep with him. I absolutely love him. I know it's absurd.

I expect my love was much more hormonal than cerebral.

I love him because he has 'gripping' muscles, good looking, manly, 'big', good sense of humour, fit, etc ...

I do like the 'big' part – at least I had my priorities right. I believe I try to justify myself by saying that *I don't want to have (a complete) sexual relationship, but for someone to care for and love at night*, although I think those soppy lines was reserved for anyone who managed to get hold of my diary and decipher my code. My real feelings were somewhat more feral. Sadly, none of this was ever reciprocated. If anything, it was always going to end in tears.

Tuesday, 27 March 1979

When he is alone he says 'hullo' in a real nice way, but when others are around he is lousy.

My crushes were not directed only at Arton-Powell. There was a plethora of others, including teachers I absolutely ached to hold, to be held by, to be comforted by, but their names and faces have faded into the mists of time. Snatches of memory. I was once accosted in a car by an elderly professor from the University of Rhodesia. I had been hitch-hiking along Second Street Extension when this silver-haired, pink-skinned man picked me up. I watched mesmerised as his liver-spotted hand reached furtively across the gear stick and landed on my knee. 'Would you care to come back to the university with me young man?' he asked stroking my leg and glancing at me sideways with his watery eyes. A frisson of excitement rushed through me. No man (or woman come to think of it) had ever made a pass at me. Despite the age gap, I almost consented. But I had younger prey on my mind. I asked politely and slightly indignantly to be dropped off on the verge.

What did he see in me that instigated this incident. Had I given off a signal or was he simply a man who preyed upon young boys? I felt both anger and sadness. Is this it? Is this what becomes of homosexual people? It terrified me. Not so much the homo part but the age part. I was young, and like all young men, I was an ageist. Yet this incident puzzled me. I began to understand slowly that the person you imagine is nothing like the person you imagined him to be.

In abject desperation to hide my 'Greek' feelings, I felt compelled to find a girlfriend. I might have succeeded had I not been quite so ham-handed. I do feel sorry for some of those girls. God, the poor things had to put up with my fumbling hands and lack of knowledge. A hard squeeze of a breast was about as far as it went with eroticism. Eros would have blanched. Even the term 'get off with', or worse 'to clamp', was hardly inspiring. I 'got off with so-and-so' or 'I had a clamp with so-and-so' might induce a scramble around one's desk to hear all the gory details. My punk-rocker cousin Madeleine had a friend called Beverley. I adored Bev, and I don't think it was any misguided attempt to be straight. I truly adored her. Her style, her sexiness, her total lack of respect for school. Bev and Madeleine initiated me into that whole English music scene. It was delicious and extreme and irreverent and it went against the norm.

Through those two girls I learned about The Boomtown Rats and Bow Wow Wow. I struggled to understand The Jam and Joy Division and I fell on my sword over the The Sex Pistols and The Stranglers, two groups spoken of in hushed, if not disgusted tones, in a country still celebrating David Essex and Elaine Paige. Madeleine and Bev hung out with the Dragons, who frequented Spaniards T-Bone Disco. The Dragons were Rhodesia's answer to the Hells Angels and they rolled around the place like outlaws with their long hair, tortured hearts, wings, skulls, and leathers with spikes and chrome, and the ubiquitous tattoos and very loud bikes. It was hardly punk, but it was the next best thing. And there I was trying my best to blend in.

My determination to get Bev into bed and my sycophantic efforts to ingratiate myself with her biker friends eventually led to me designing their gang logo: a motorbike with fangs, wings, snake's tail and a forked tongue. Not my style, I might add, but certainly the highlight of my commercial art career, which began at 11 years old when I won the Air Rhodesia poster competition: *Flying Is Our Business. We Will Make It Your Pleasure.* I like to believe that there are men (and women) out there with my winged monster inked on their boobs. Try as I might, my heterosexual mating game was simply not up to par. Harleys and Yamahas won the day. Beverley attempted to fob me off on her other friends, but I consistently sprang back in a cloud of Guy Laroche, stove pipes and a paper-look jacket crackling with static electricity. Without a doubt, Bev knew me far better than I knew myself.

On Sundays, we had to be back at school for 6pm roll call (*Wood, see me after supper* ... groan). As soon as chapel was over and I had taken my daily thrashing, I would be up through the hole in the ceiling above the loos to join the smokers. This had been the smoking room for as far back as anyone could remember. Filthy and redolent of years and years of tobacco smoke, it was a wonder that the ceiling had never collapsed in on itself. The floor was thick with old empty packets, many going back to a time before sanctions – dusty cartons with names no longer available in the stores – layer upon layer, almost a foot deep. It was like an archaeological dig of fag-ends with each layer illustrating a different era. We loved the fact that here we were, puffing away only feet from the heads of those twatty prefects. There were always one or two reprobates sitting up in the gloom dragging on a B&H, undeterred by the fact that, should we be caught, we would be expelled. Occasionally, on beautiful evenings, we would lug a foam mattress up to the roof and lie out gazing at the Milky Way and the Southern Cross, quite oblivious to the fatal drop just inches away.

During those years at Prince Edward the amount of alcohol consumed was alarming. Even by today's binge-drinking standards, I am left in awe of our intrepid ways of bunking out, getting utterly smashed, and back at school the next day. It appears that no adults took control. Clearly those prefects were absolutely clueless. So, inevitably, my truancy, smoking (tobacco, I hasten to add), lack of concentration in ghastly subjects such as physics, chem and maths – not to mention the demise of my cross-country career – all led me down the grey gravel path to headmaster Raymond Suttle's office, where he sat me down and quietly, if not firmly, advised me that my days were over at Prince Edward School.

'Are you aware that there are 500 black kids out there clamouring to get into this school?'

'And did you not think another year at school is simply a waste of time for me, for the teachers and indeed for you?'

'And are you aware that doing A-level arts or English literature will not get you anywhere in life?'

He had a point.

'Let us be perfectly frank, Wood. Think long and hard about what I have just told you. You are no longer wanted here at Prince Edward School.'

I thought hard, but not long. I departed immediately.

It was February. I had successfully completed my matriculation the previous term and was into my first two weeks of the A-level year. To be honest, I was rather flattered that he even knew who I was. In the past five years I had not said one word to the man, never been into his office, never been congratulated for my excellent running. Hell, I'd never even been reprimanded by the man. His wife knew me better than he did – she was in charge of the costumes for *The Pirates of Penzance* and had many a conversation over the Singer sewing machine with my grandmother. And now here he was defining my life and paving the way to an uncertain future.

With the stroke of a pen, I was out.

Just 17 years old. No testimonial to prove my existence over the past few years. No turning back. That day, my friend Spike and I walked down to the recruitment office and immediately enrolled in the army. Spike, who had a future, who was actually bright and was clever enough to pass his A-levels was there, willing to join the army with me. To throw it all away. I had little to lose. He was a loyal friend, that boy.

I had no choice. My childhood ended that day. Okay, fuck it, my childhood probably ended way before that, but there was still a war raging and if academia did not need me, then maybe the military did. Wisely, Spike walked away, back to school.

I was in a state of shock. Anti-establishment I may have been, but I was, by any other standards, still a good kid. Well, I thought I was. My closely kept secret was, to my knowledge, still a secret.

From henceforth, it would all be about survival. I had been cut adrift. I was being weaned earlier than the rest of the pups. Like a runt suckling the hind teat, I was thrown to the lions. In the spirit of the times, I took it on the chin. I laughed. I rejoiced. I brazenly smoked a pack of Madison Toasted in front of the prefects. I had a Castle Lager with my mates. 'FUCK THEM!' I shouted from the stands. 'I'm joining the ARMY. I will show those pricks.'

I adored the limelight, momentarily. The sudden adoration of my peers as they saw me in a different light for the first time. Yet, beneath the surface, I was in a total fucking panic. The country may have been going through change, according to the suits in parliament, but the war was still full-on. The euphoria drained from me. I finally understood that I had made a momentous decision that could change my life forever.

All I could think was, 'At last ... my dad will understand.'

Despite my nerves, I felt stronger than I had ever felt in my life. I felt in control at last. My life was mine and mine alone. Those bullies at school who had made my life hell were already a distant memory. I was not doing this for them and they played no part in my future.

Prior to my dismissal from school on 27 February 1980, the first black boy in the history of Prince Edward became a boarder at Selous House. *Old Kingsley Mbeya has arrived at the hostel. I wonder what he's like?* my diary wonders. Kingsley Mbeya? What a great name I thought. The final entry ever in my diary reads: *That Kingsley bloke seems okay. He's not being ENTIRELY ignored, which is the main thing.*

With Kingsley came the relaxation of rules, Wart's retirement, the removal of initiation for youngsters ... and the end of an era.

As for Mbeya, he certainly seemed to have fared better than I.

5

Hunting, Shooting, Fishing

Back in the mid-1960s, much of sub-Saharan Africa was still in the last gasps of colonialism. Portugal was losing interest in its colonies. Beira, nestled in the curve of Mozambique on the Portuguese East African coast, was the height of sophistication to three little kids with mud between their toes. To the adults, it was exotic and terribly European.

Donning our rose-tinted specs, we would tiptoe around the sewer bubbling away merrily in the hotel lobby, reach across the slumbering receptionist and drop off our room keys. The hospitality industry was somewhat haphazard in Mozambique.

Communications were worse. Tarmac roads had such deep rough edges that they shredded your car tyres every time you tried to make way for an oncoming vehicle. The braver souls refused to get off the road for love or money and played a daring game of chicken, or *galinha*.

Hospitals were an absolute no-go area. People went there to die. And the idea of travel insurance was non-existent. But all of that meant nothing because the beaches were quite simply some of the best in Africa, if not the world, fringed with white coral sand that squeaked beneath your feet. And mile upon mile of great, roaring rollers tumbling in from the Indian Ocean.

There was also, of course, the food. The Mozambique prawns were world famous, the Vinho Verde and Mateus Rosé legendary. To farmers with straw growing out of their ears, this was heaven.

PETER WOOD

We usually drove the 350 miles to Beira. The train was an option, but this took three days. Driving meant that we could stock the car boot full of illegal goods, which we hoped to sell once in Mozambique. We stashed elephant tusks beneath the bedding, and under our feet a ton of gorgeous, colourful, semi-precious stone eggs, all the rage back then and something that would come back to haunt me later in life.

There were coolers full of fillet steaks and coils of *boerewors*[42] stacked up against spicy beef biltong wrapped in old copies of the *Rhodesia Herald*. Under our seats we shoved cartons of contraband cigarettes. Carton after carton of good old Rhodesian Virginia. Rarely did these efforts ever pay off. Rather than being short-changed by some clever grafter, we more often than not sheepishly smuggled the wretched stuff back into Rhodesia.

Sometimes smuggling did not stop at inanimate objects. A few times we even smuggled our poor nanny across the border. She didn't have a passport and as we neared the border post, nanny would be unceremoniously shoved down beneath our feet and covered in anything deemed suitable: blankets, fishing tackle, once even a jerry can of petrol. Poor dear nanny took it all in her stride. To be fair she absolutely loved these trips, often borrowing a bathing suit from one of the madams and going for a dip in the *makulu mvura*[43].

I have an abiding memory, as a six-year-old, of women sunbathing on the Beira beach, a glass of Mateus eternally clasped in hand. Each day was a different swimsuit with matching floral bathing cap. The men would lounge around drinking Laurentina lagers or smuggled stumpies[44] of Castle, keeping a casual eye on us kids

---

[42] South African sausage.

[43] Chilapalapa for 'big water'.

[44] Small stubby bottles.

getting dumped by huge waves that would send us careering towards an old, jagged and rusted shipwreck.

From a tender age I remember making sure those breakers would roll me up against the legs of the sexy Portuguese surfer boys. I was able to swim like an otter from the age of three, so my spluttering and blinking and blind reaching out for help was mostly a big act. The surfers would gladly gather me up against their lithe, oiled and bronzed bodies and carry me to the shallows.

Their body-hugging Speedos excited me. It was confusing to say the least. There was no way of knowing why I felt this way. No person to speak to about it. No literature to help as guidance. The desire to make a fool of myself in front of the surfers was far stronger than the need to repress it. I knew it was 'wrong', but I was too young to be able to do anything about it.

As determined as I was to get a cop of the hairy, oiled legs of the surfers, I was equally determined to hide these strange, queer feelings, particularly as I grew up and became more aware. This would be the first step on a long journey towards becoming tougher, rowdier and more obnoxious than anyone else on the block. I constructed a smokescreen that would dog me most of my young days. Frankly, I was the most vocal of all my gang and my diaries are pretty clear about this.

By the time I was in my teens, I had become expert at deception. My walls covered in James Dean and *Grease* posters had nothing to do with rebellion or Olivia and everything to do with John and James. I would listen over tea as wives nonchalantly waved their hands and spoke about having nothing against queers.

'I just worry that they will grow up lonely,' they would say.

My smokescreens of asexual and androgynous pop and film

stars, my swearing, my deliberate anti-fashion sensibilities and my pretence at being an alpha male led me spiralling down a dark tunnel. In short, I developed extreme, internalised issues around my sexuality leading me horribly close to becoming a nasty little homophobic racist, just for the sake of smoke and mirrors. And deep down, even back then, I hated it and hated myself for it.

The music never stopped in Beira, though, and having a nanny meant that the old folks could now go out and party. By all accounts, Beira was the Paris of Africa. By day the beaches were a constant parade of scantily-clad sun-worshippers, but by night the city came alive. Big, bouffant hairdos, false eyelashes, glittering sequinned gowns in midnight blue and silver. The men in smart shirts and sharp slacks and Brylcreemed hair, mingling unsuspectingly with the pimps and mulatto rent boys outside the nightclubs.

First a meal at Johnny the Greek for his famous garlic prawns swimming in butter and lemon and a few bottles of Vinho Verde to wash it down, then a short stagger down the street to the Moulin Rouge. Seedy by day, seedier by night, this was a favourite club where you could mix with the glamorous and the gorgeous, the whores, the thieves and the shit-kickers.

One evening, the group piled into their cars and drove off to the club, its neon windmill flickering in the oily puddles on the side street. Dark-skinned women with large afros and tight frocks stretched over their ample breasts beckoned to the men in a suggestive manner.

'Vem cá, bonitão. Anda comigo, meu querido.'

'Come here. Come with me, my darling.'

'És mesmo giro! Queres beber um copo comigo?'

'Ooh, so handsome! Would you have a drink with me?'

When they received little response, the language became slightly more colourful.

'Foda, foda! Fuck, fuck!' they would jerk their hips in a suggestive, humping motion.

'Ah! Estou a pérdere o méu témpo. Foda-se!'

'I am wasting my time. Fuck you!'

The wives would laugh, hugging their husbands in a proprietorial manner, having understood absolutely none of the dialogue.

'Come on, sweetheart. Let's get inside. I'm dying for a drink.'

By now, the place was at full throttle. Throngs of Portuguese, South African and Rhodesian men, uncomfortable in jackets and ties, foreheads shining with sweat in the fuggy atmosphere, would loosen their collars and roll up their sleeves. Mulatto waitresses, bosoms spilling out of their décolletages, carried trays of cocktails and champagne above the heads of the couples slow-dancing on the floor.

The noise from the side rooms where the illegal gaming took place reached a crescendo each time someone won a bet. 'Olé, olé, olé!' The clack of the roulette, the laughter, the fado and the jazz bands barely visible across the room through the fog of cigarette smoke. In darker corners, hungry eyes devoured the sexy Latino arses of the women, and the men. Overhead, red-shaded chandeliers cast an ethereal hue on the faces of the beautiful and the horny.

Des Bentley, a family friend and true gentleman in every sense of the word (actual name: Desmond Ponsonby Muloch Bentley, if you please, but nicknamed Mule Cock, for obvious reasons), was left faffing about in the car, locking doors and closing windows while the rest of the gang trooped into the nightclub.

If anyone in the Umvukwes district epitomised Englishness and charm, it was old Mule Cock. Educated at Hilton College, arguably South Africa's premier boarding school, Des embodied all that was elegant and sophisticated in a man. An accomplished cricketer and horseman, Cary Grant good looks and a successful farmer, he was quite a man.

Dressed to the nines, looking utterly charming and undeniably handsome, he checked the back seat for any left items, took a backwards step, and plunged straight into an open manhole, sinking up to his neck in shit.

'And bloody Portuguese shit!' he liked to remind us later.

It was a dilemma few people would have handled with such style and aplomb. His wife Myrtle had the hotel keys and all the money. Des had little choice. Pulling himself out of the sewer, he glared at the two tarts who two minutes earlier had been harassing him, and chin held high as if nothing in the world was amiss, he walked up the steps and into the club. Pausing briefly to take in the crowd and locate his wife, he straightened his shoulders and strode across the room to Myrtle.

'Meems, darling. Please may I have the keys?'

He held out a soiled hand.

'What the hell are you looking at?' he said to a waiter.

The man's tray quivered in his hand, rattling the empty glasses.

'Now, please, darling. If you don't mind.'

Myrtle gingerly dropped the keys into his hand. With that, he about-turned and walked proudly back out on to the street and, oblivious to the stares of revellers along the way, down to the beach, where he quietly dug a hole, removed all his clothes and buried them in the sand. After a dip in the sea to wash off the shit, he walked along the beach, stark naked, through a stunned hotel lobby and back up to his room. I expect the concierge would have copped an eyeful of dear Mule Cock had he not been asleep at his desk.

One hour later, Des was back at the nightclub ordering a well-earned drink, much to the admiration and cheers of all around him.

Every evening when the adults were out, their children were left to fend for themselves. Looking back, it seems extraordinary that a bunch of farm kids should be left to their own devices running riot through a foreign hotel. Then again, we spent so much time away from our folks they probably didn't even notice.

Back then, the hotel of choice for most farmers was the Estoril, a rather shabby family-style cinder block on the main promenade. Next door was the posher Dom Carlos. Mandy, Duncan and I, together with Peggy and Jenny Strong and the Hammond kids, were given the freedom of the place, annoying other guests by constantly going up and down in the lifts. This was endless fun. Hell, we had never been in a lift before. We would run down the corridors singing the latest Petula Clark song, appropriately called *Downtown*, or our favourite Skeeter Davis song *Sunglasses*, tuneless and repetitive until one or more guest would poke their heads out the door and scream at us to 'bugger orf'.

The parents had told us that we could go to the Dom Carlos as a treat and eat seafood. Just put it on the hotel account, darlings. And so we did, making the most of it. Well, at least I did. I always have had expensive tastes. Seated in the plush, velvety banquet staring down at the confusion of cutlery: a butter knife, soup spoon, fish knife and meat knife, a white napkin starched into a nun's cornette, and then there was the menu. Encased in burgundy leather with gold embossed text and a green tassel, pages of delicacies seemed to fight for space on each sheet of heavy` bonded, cream vellum paper. A plethora of exotic foods, all magnificently scripted in Portuguese curlicues and flourishes: *ostras, camarões, lagostim, peixe, cereja amêijoas pedra*. Oysters, shrimp, crayfish, king fish, cherry stone clams, the complete *frutos do mar*.

'Peggy, take control,' my sister whispered.

Peggy stared at us as if we had asked her to abseil off the top of a granite *kopje*.

'Okay. Well, who knows Portuguese?' cut in Duncan.

I knew one word. Thermidor.

'Lagosta thermidor por favor, waiter,' I said with as much conviction as I could muster.

'Are you mad?' my brother said. 'Waiter, I will have the spaghetti. So will my sister.'

'So will we,' chorused Peggy and Jenny.

The waiter retreated through the swing doors, returning 15 minutes later with a large tray held above his shoulder. Delicious aromas of cognac and gruyere escaped from the bubbling shellfish as the waiter lifted the silver cloche in a blood-and-thunder swipe, his pinky extended to show off his long, hooked nail, and like a matador proudly performing his final *pase de pecho* before plunging his sword between the shoulders of the raging bull, he triumphantly exclaimed, 'Surprisa!' On the plate, beneath a rather small lump of bubbling cheese, sat my *lagosta*. What a disappointment.

Unfortunately, when it came time to pay the bill, the maître d', by now quite fed up with these awful precocious children, refused to accept credit. Flapping his hands in a fabulously camp way, and with strangulated vowels, quite possibly from the painfully tight trousers he was wearing, he croaked at us all, 'You children will be doing zee deeshes tonight!'

Crikey, we thought, washing dishes was as good as a stint in jail. And a Beira jail at that! Worse, we had never been made to wash-up before. Back home, we had staff to do that kind of thing. In a panic, we rushed back to the Estoril, running up and down the corridors knocking on the doors of sleepy and extremely irritated guests explaining our situation and asking for money. With a tatty piece of paper, Peggy (being the sanest and most administrative-minded) wrote down each name, room number and amount:

» *Rm 412:* Mr Edward Jenkins, Crossroads Farm – 4 escudos
» *Rm 301:* Mrs Jane Kemp, Bulawayo – 8 escudos
» *Rm 323:* Mr & Mrs (scribble – can't remember) – 10 escudos

And so on, until finally we reached the right amount. Sheepishly walking back to the Dom Carlos, hangdog looks and pockets jingling with coins, we paid the bill, much to the sniggering of some diners and, I believe, to the admiration of the manager. I doubt if he expected us to return. Good, honest Rhodesian kids.

Beira was amazing, but without a doubt the best holidays were always the trips we made down to the Zambezi Valley, or 'The Vellie' as my dad's great pal Ben Norton called it in his broad South African accent. We were often invited to join our fathers at their annual hunting camps along the river.

Most of the white school kids went to South Africa and Mozambique, and the lucky few to London, returning laden with goodies never seen in Rhodesia such as Quality Street and Black Magic chocolates and Wrangler jeans. But we never really felt jealous. We knew that what we had was unique. In fact, now that it has all gone, those wondrous weeks spent on those camping trips are even more precious.

The hunting camps were allocated by auction and you might get anything from A, B or C camp (which was upriver of a small town called Chirundu), or D camp down to K camp right at the bottom of the valley. All camps were on the river, situated under the shade of the huge, leafy sausage trees[45] whose massive phallic pods could kill a grown man should they fall on his head.

The Zambezi is a quick route from the centre of the continent down to the Indian Ocean. Tamarind trees[46] also grew in abundance along the river. Indigenous to tropical Africa (not India as the Latin name suggests) it was believed they had been brought down from Central Africa by Arab slave traders. The fruit is used to add a sour note to Sri Lankan fish curries, but in Rhodesia the closest we ever got to a curry was powder from a packet, sprinkled with desiccated coconut and raisins. Without these riverine trees, few people could have withstood the constant onslaught of the unrelenting Zambezi sun.

All camps were stocked with plenty of grog and an overabundance of food, but still it was extremely rough and ready. They were definitely not the romantic *Out of Africa* posh safari-style camps of the Kenyan set. Don't get me wrong, we always travelled with a circus of servants and nannies and truck-loads of fabulous produce. But no one had tents, or smart khaki safari outfits run

---

[45] *Kigelia africana.*

[46] *Tamarindus indica.*

up by an Indian tailor in downtown Nairobi. At these camps we just slept under the African stars with, if you were lucky, a flimsy mozzie net to protect you against wild animals. In their own way, these camps were spectacular for the very fact that they were pared back and raw.

As many as 15 or 20 people might turn up, and as many servants, plus scores of kids and hangers-on. Often, there was only one long drop as a toilet and one zinc tub to bathe in. Generally the camp only had two official hunters, always with a 'bag' of big game. The National Parks had an auction each year by allocating each camp along the river with a 'bag of animals'. Some camps might have a bag with big game and antelope while others might simply have a bag of fowl and fish. Hunters would bid for the camps depending on what they were prepared to pay. Back then, the bags were not only exotic but also rather large, what with game such as elephant, buffalo, rhino, hippo, and antelope of all varieties, and for the pot, as many guinea fowl and partridges as one could shoot.

With all the hunting, untidy piles of tusks would be heaped under a tree, the odd hippo skull or rows of buffalo trophies drying in the sun, their skins pegged out nearby and salted. It must seem strange, in fact it must disgust many people now, as indeed it does me. But in the 1960s no one thought much about shooting an elephant or a rhino. Game roamed all over the Zambezi Valley and was plentiful. Rangers ensured that the hunters stuck to what was in their bag. If you wounded an animal and could not track it down, you were not allowed to shoot another. It was, and still is to a degree, strictly controlled. Morality aside, it is believed that more elephant roamed the Zambezi Valley in the 1960s than at the turn of the century.

Getting to the hunting camps was as much of an adventure as being there. As you wind around the Makuti hills, you are met with a sight that is difficult to forget, the Zambezi escarpment.

Rounding one of the many hairpin bends, trying to ignore the treacherous drop of a few hundred feet below, you are greeted first by the unusual aroma of the potato tree, the scent delicious as a roasting potato, and then visually by the massive, flat expanse of the middle Zambezi Valley, stretching from the Kariba gorge in the far eastern side all the way to the Cabora Basa basin in Mozambique.

In the 1960s these camps were quite untamed, the kids all kipping down in a row at the far end of the camp, falling asleep snug in our sleeping bags while listening to the hysterical laughter of hyenas or the low grunt of a male lion, and dreamily watching shooting stars skitter past the Southern Cross. It was magical. Out of earshot, the parents would carouse and tell hunting stories around a roaring camp fire as they were served canapés of goujons of bream or kudu sweetbreads on melba toast. The grog would flow and one wonders what they could have done to protect us kids should a wild animal have come into camp, as often the wild animals did.

The Zambezi camps attracted many night predators. When an animal such as a buffalo had been shot, it was hauled back to camp on a Land Rover, hung up with a block and tackle, and gutted and skinned. As kids, we loved watching this, squeezing our noses when the intestinal sack was pierced and the green shit spilled out on the ground. It was a busy day for dung beetles, scuttling busily across the dirt. Measuring the trophies, weighing the tusks, admiring the beautiful subtle colours of a reedbuck skin or the coarse, prickly hair of a waterbuck. There is a photo of me standing inside the hollowed-out foot of an elephant surrounded by hunting trophies. I am bawling my eyes out.

These elephant feet were used as coffee tables or litter bins. Meat from antelope and buffalo was cut into strips for biltong and placed in zinc tubs of brine for a day, then spiced with herbs and ground coriander and hung up to dry in long lines. Biltong was the Rhodesian's favourite snack, always eaten with a beer.

All the blood and guts made these camps a magnet for scavengers. A 'boneyard' was always established a few hundred yards out of camp where the hyenas and jackals would squabble and fight over the carrion all night long, cackling and whooping like mad fishwives. Over the years, the boneyards would become littered with the eerily white skulls of elephant, buffalo and impala, trophies too small or considered unworthy of taking home. But it was the rib cages and massive femurs that stick in my mind, like a battlefield in a Tolkien epic. Which I suppose it was, really. Man versus beast. At night, the skulls and hip bones and ribs would glow in the moonlight like unearthly faerie kingdoms.

During the hunting season the fresh offal also attracted lions and leopards. It was not unusual for lion or leopard spoor[47] to be seen in the sand between our camp beds in the mornings as they sniffed out the rows of biltong, rarely bothering us but still a bit too close for comfort. One intrepid leopard managed to reach the drying meat and spent the night quietly eating the strips, spitting out the metal clips used to hang it up. In the morning, we were staggered to see these small, neat piles of clips below the now-empty line of meat. Never ones to waste, we picked them up and used them again for the next batch of biltong.

One particular year, the boneyard had been situated a little too close to the camp and the hyenas became a menace, skulking on the periphery of the camp at night. Long before the days of *National Geographic* or Attenborough, we had little idea that these beasts were as predatory and dangerous as lions. One night, while sitting around the fire, someone pointed to the row of sleeping kids at the edge of the camp.

---

[47] From the Afrikaans *spoor* and Old English *spor* meaning 'footprint', 'track' or 'trace'.

'My god, Libby. Look! A hyena. I think it is sniffing Pete's head.'

Sure enough, a massive hyena, with jaws that could crush a skull like an egg, was inches from my slumbering head.

'Go away! Voetsak! Shoo!' the adults gesticulated.

The hyena shrank guiltily back into the shadows like Shylock seeking out his pound of flesh. The old folks casually went back to their drinks, laughing at the incident. That particular year was the worst I can remember for hyenas. They were everywhere around that camp, their hunched, sinister shadows flitting between thorn bush and *mopane*[48] trees casting long, ghost-like shadows in the moonlight.

One night, my sister Mandy and I wanted to have a pee. Loos were basic long drops with a flimsy hessian fence around for privacy rather than safety. The other kids had gone to sleep, so Mandy and I tiptoed the 100 yards or so along the dark path in the pitch-black to the long drop. While Mandy was sitting on the can, we heard a movement outside. A scuffling. A snuffling. A large dark shadow. Then the inevitable terrifying high, pitched giggle.

The sloped form of a huge hyena appeared, slinking along like a large, slavering dog, the nape of its neck a shag of spiky hair, its slobbering face inches from the two of us, peering through the gaps in the hessian fence. It looked very hungry. Around and around it walked, trying to find a way in. We were perfect morsels for this animal. Absolutely petrified, we sat rigid on the lavatory not daring to move. I was only five and Mandy was seven years old. Incredibly, we never screamed out. That was simply not done in those days. The adults would think us sissy.

---

[48] *Colophospermum mopane* are common to hot low-lying areas in southern Africa.

And honestly, who would have heard us? Finally, after what seemed like an eternity, the hyena gave up and went searching for easier prey. The two of us made a dash for it through the bush and into our sleeping bags and the safety of the distant murmur of a couple of diehard adults still drinking Bols brandies around the glowing embers of the fire.

Back at school during the 'show-and-tell', when other kids talked or wrote about their experiences at the beach or trout fishing in the Eastern Highlands, I was sent into the corner for telling fibs about such an idiotic thing called a 'boneyard'.

'That child lives in some dream world,' Miss McCarthy remarked.

Not all hyenas were quite so benign. As an adult, my brother Duncan once woke up in the dead of night with a heavy animal on top of him. Still half asleep, he put his hands on the rough, wiry head and patted it.

'Get off me Sammy, you stupid dog,' he groaned sleepily.

A fetid, warm breath enveloped him and immediately he was awake and alert. There, looking down at him in the moonlight, was a huge hyena, its watery yellow eyes sizing him up, its mouth slobbery with spittle. The animal already had his sleeping bag in its mouth and began to drag him away into the bush.

'Jesus Christ! Get the fuck off me,' he shouted, beating the beast on the head with his fists once he had managed to extricate his arms from the tight sleeping sack.

Alarmed by his noise and beating fists, the animal dropped him and sloped off, giggling and whooping. Picking himself up, Duncan grabbed his torn sleeping bag and staggered back to his camp bed. Looking over in amazement at his still, sleeping hunting companion Angus Black, he shrugged and went back to sleep. Unsurprisingly, Angus didn't believe Duncan when he related the tale over breakfast.

It was easy to forget that the bush was teeming with dangerous wildlife, and it beggars belief that more people weren't killed. I do remember, with morbid fascination, when one of the more infamous, albeit eccentric couples, Nigel and Corona Thornycroft, both of whom were avid hunters and conservationists and fearless to the point of lunacy, came staggering back into camp covered in blood, their clothes tattered and torn. Corona was shoeless but wearing socks, now matted in burs and blackjacks and mud.

I'll let my father tell this one.

As published in *The Hunter* magazine in the late 1980s:

Buffalo & Birdshot

It was the second last day of a successful two-week hunt in the Zambezi Valley. The last of 16 buffalo, four elephant, numerous impala, kudu and two zebra and warthog had been felled without wounding, so Gerry von Memerty, Norman Travers and myself bundled up all the camp's visitors and kids and set off for a good bream pool to supplement the camp's pot with some fish.

On the way, we put up a huge flock of guinea fowl. This was too much for Nigel, one of our visitors, who was by far the best 12-bore shot I have known. As he set off with his Purdy, he stopped, and with difficulty persuaded his wife, Corona, to tag along – fortunately, as it happened, with her gun.

After about an hour of fishing, we heard, apart from the odd shot, suddenly a barrage of shots – bang, bang, bang, bang! We didn't think too much about it as guinea fowl in those days were unlimited. However, at sundown, we set off in the direction from where we had heard the last shots.

We had travelled about one kilometre when we came upon our friends in a pretty bad shape; cut and bruised. On enquiring what had happened, Nigel, in his very English accent, said: 'We have just been attacked by a jolly old wounded buffalo.' Upon arriving at the scene, sure enough, there lay a dead bull.

They told us the story of what happened. Walking through the grass and bush about 20 yards apart, bagging birds as they flew up, Corona spotted the buffalo bull at quite close range and yelled a warning to Nigel whereupon it charged straight at her spouse, hitting him at full speed, sending his gun flying and broken in two pieces. The bull then proceeded to shake and gore Nigel like a terrier with a rat. He managed to pull his torso close against the beast's face to avoid the points of the horns with his legs hugging round its neck. Amongst much shouted instructions like 'Shoot it in the eyes darling,' Corona, with her gun, and with courage, came round to the left side and proceeded to pump double shots of No. 6 into the bull's shoulder at point-blank range. Ten shots did the trick.

On examining the carcass, we found an old gunshot wound in the back leg, which had given him a mean attitude to life, but was no handicap to attack. The lesson in this account is never to hunt alone, even after guinea fowl. Had Corona gone fishing with the rest of us, the ending would have been a lot more tragic. As it happened, Nigel suffered three broken ribs and collarbone, not to mention a face that looked as though it had gone 10 rounds with Mike Tyson, but being a tough old bird of 53, he soon recovered.

If there is another hunter, male or female, who has killed a bull buffalo with birdshot, I would like to hear it!

John Wood, M'sitwe Farm, Mvurwi (Umvukwes)

One can just hear Nigel shouting in that wonderful English accent, 'Bloody hurry up darling. I can hardly hold the damn thing orf me much longer!'

'Good heavens,' groaned Nigel as he eased himself out from under the dead animal. 'We don't have a buffalo in our bag. How on earth are we going to explain this to National Parks?'

When Nigel finally staggered back into camp, his appearance hardly raised an eyebrow. Looking up from their deck chairs on seeing the bedraggled pair, one of the hunters simply remarked, 'I suppose this means we won't have any fowl for supper tonight?'

Nigel and Corona were brave, but they were also lucky. And no matter how experienced you were as a hunter, tragedy did occasionally strike, sometimes quite out of the blue. The hunters were always on foot and often traipsing many miles from camp in what is known as jesse-bush – a thick, virtually impenetrable thorn scrub common to the Zambezi Valley. So thick is the vegetation that visibility is reduced to only a few yards at best – ideal country for the Cape buffalo.

Woody's old pal, Gerry von Memerty, was an avid hunter, with a particular penchant for elephants. He loved the challenge and had made quite a name for himself as one of the country's premier big game hunters. In the early days, Gerry would often accompany my dad on these hunting trips.

Later in life, as world opinion swung away from the slaughter of elephants, as wildlife stocks in Africa began to diminish and in some cases were driven to extinction, Gerry became an elephant conservationist. Always armed with his .458 Winchester Magnum, he would take tourists, movie stars and National Parks officials deep into the African bush, showing them and teaching them about wildlife.

They say an elephant never forgets, and in a tragic stroke of bitter irony, on one excursion in the jesse-bush, Gerry was charged and killed by an enraged female elephant, which pierced his heart with its tusk. Gerry died instantly. He had no time to react nor any chance of survival. However, what happened next made this story a thing of legend. His party of guests and the National Parks guide watched as the herd of elephants surrounded Gerry's limp body, and throughout the night would let neither man nor beast anywhere near him. Trumpeting and flailing their trunks, they would drive off predators attracted by the smell of blood. The National Parks guide said that he had never seen anything like it in his years patrolling the bush.

'It was like they were trying to protect him. Not once, as is often the case, did they kneel down and gore his body. With our tour group only 50 yards away, a herd of elephants will usually disperse into the bush. Not so this time,' he said.

'Honestly, I think that the matriarch elephant that killed Gerry not only knew who he was, but in some strange, weird way, felt that it needed to protect this man who had spent so many years in the bush hunting them down,' the guide added.

'Surely then, the elephant would have hated Gerry?' one tourist remarked.

'Hate? Respect? Who knows?' the guide replied, 'but you can bet your bottom dollar that at some stage the scent of Gerry triggered something in the elephant's brain. Had Gerry tried to shoot it once upon a time?' he shrugged in that lovely African way, 'maybe, hey? We will just never know.'

By daybreak, the herd finally and silently disappeared into the scrub and the guide was able to retrieve Gerry's body. At the funeral, Robert Louis Stevenson's haunting *Requiem* was read to the packed congregation, ending with the line, so apt for Gerry:

Home is the sailor, home from the sea
And the hunter home from the hill

In 1972, my father and his friend Bill Francis decided to go on what back then must have been a very hazardous boat trip down the Zambezi River from the small, dusty border town of Chirundu all the way to one of the camps on the far eastern end of the river near Mozambique, a trip of some 75 miles.

They decided that a trip such as this would build character, so they invited me along. I was ten years old. The Rhodesian Bush War was just kicking in and every night insurgents were streaming across the Zambezi River from Zambia to attack farmsteads. The Zambezi had become what was known as 'the sharp end'. Hunting camps and holidaying along the river had been forbidden because of the fighting, and in many ways the entire valley had become a no-man's land. This was no place to be caught out. It probably was not the place for a kid, either.

What made this little adventure so exciting, or foolish, was the fact that we chose to do the whole trip in one day in a small, unsheltered outboard boat through totally uncharted territory. The deep, navigable channels in the river were constantly shifting and the police gave us permission in the hope that we might be able to map out the river for future operations.

Early one morning, before sunrise, we set off under the majestic 382-metre steel-framed Otto Beit Bridge. The wide, fast-flowing river took the small boat downstream past tiny African hamlets, bathing women, kids splashing in the shallows oblivious to the danger of crocodiles. It was a scene reminiscent of the Thomas Baines[49] landscapes that adorned the walls of the Meikles Hotel in Salisbury.

---

[49](John) Thomas Baines (27 November 1820-8 May 1875) was an English artist and explorer of southern Africa and Australia.

A few miles downstream, the bush on the Rhodesian side became wilder, teeming with buffalo and elephant, waterbuck and kudu. Huge crocs slid off the sand banks and into the water as we approached and pods of 20 to 30 hippo wallowed in the shallows. The green river was difficult to navigate and submerged sandbanks meant that we had to jump into the water, often up to our waists, to push the boat off.

Around mid-morning we saw a small herd of elephants frolicking in a narrow channel off the main river, spraying themselves with water and mud, the young males sparring with one another. Slowly, we drifted over until we were almost within touching distance, watching silently as the largest land mammals in the world played like children in the water.

All of a sudden, there was a hell of a commotion. We had managed to spook a large, angry male hippo that had been grazing the grass on the shoreline. The rule is never get between a hippo and deep water. And that is exactly where we were. I remember the noise as this massive beast crashed through the undergrowth almost right on top of us. He was clearly wounded and bore scars all over his back from territorial fights with other males. There was no time to react and within seconds the huge bull was on to us, thundering into the water on the attack, his shiny pink mouth big enough to swallow a kid my size, his teeth certainly big enough to rip the small boat in half, his murderous, rheumy eyes mad with pain.

As luck would have it the channel we were in was deep, and as the hippo hit the water only yards from us, sending a massive tidal wave up and over the tiny boat almost capsizing us, he immediately sank from view, unable to reach our boat. With lightning speed, upturning beer bottles, fishing tackle and worms, Bill started the engine and managed to make a break for it before the hippo's huge head emerged from the water a few feet away. For once, our usually useless outboard motor saved the day. It was a close shave and one we would laugh about later around the camp fire.

The rest of the journey was not to get any easier. Constantly hitting submerged tree stumps and sandbanks, we were losing the daylight and the camp we were headed to was still many miles downriver. Our situation was beginning to look grim and about to get a whole lot worse. The nights in Africa can be dense, and without a spotlight and no moon we soon got lost between islands and channels and reed beds. When we hit a particularly troublesome spit of sand, Bill got out to push and in the darkness gashed his leg badly on the prop. We tried to bind his wound as best we could, given the lack of visibility or a first aid kit, but as the hours passed he began to fade.

I had never witnessed a man dying before and Bill was losing so much blood that he was, without doubt going to die unless we could get help fast. In the pitch-black, we had no way of telling where the camp was. Dark shapes would loom up in the night, floating islands and reed beds, fallen trees and submerged rocks. Every time we shifted, we would slide across the floor in Bill's blood, sticky with the strong metallic smell of iron.

Then, away in the distance on the Rhodesian side, we saw the pinprick of a fire. As we drew nearer, we noticed that the fire was being used as a signal, fanned by silhouettes of people, like Cornish wreckers or moon-cursers, only this time trying to lure us to safety rather than death. Our host at the camp, the usually indomitable Des Bentley, had understandably grown concerned about our whereabouts and had built the fire to draw us in. Carrying Bill's limp frame from the boat, the hunters saw what a desperate situation he was in and someone managed to drive to the nearest South African Police camp. They were on exercise about 20 miles away. Their medic took one look at Bill and ordered a military helicopter to 'casevac' him to safety, saving his life.

For me, perhaps the most memorable and fun of all the camps were those spent at B camp, upriver from Chirundu. My father and his pal, Ben Norton, would invite 'us mob', as he liked to call Duncan, Mandy, me and his son, Larry, down for a week or so, driving over interminably rough roads, laden to the hilt with fruit, veg, crates of beer and soft drinks, sleeping gear, fishing tackle and, perched on the top, a servant or two. B camp was one of the most beautiful on that stretch of river and was always sought after by the hunters and campers for the cool shade cast from the huge riverine trees.

For the children, it meant untold adventures from dawn until dusk, followed by hot steaming baths in a tin tub, scrubbed clean of the dust and mud, then into pyjamas to sit around the camp fire listening to John or Ben or Bill or any of their mates telling fabulous hunting stories.

During the day, when the men went out, we would be taken by boat downriver to swim in shallow pools, go fishing for tiger fish or bream, and have delicious picnics under the leafy African mahogany trees while herds of impala grazed the new grass on the floodplain. The red, eroded cliffs along the river, were pitted from the nests of hundreds of brightly coloured, carmine bee-eaters[50], their rich crimson and turquoise feathers flashing in the afternoon sun.

We Woods never professed to be great fishermen. Indeed, many a joke was made about our appalling tackle, useless technique, and rampant theft from other folks' fishing boxes. When the Woods were in the vicinity, everything needed to be clearly labelled with your name, or locked away or tied down, preferably to your ankle. Otherwise it simply went missing.

We were not kleptomaniacs. We simply took advantage of

---

[50] *Merops nubicoides.*

any given situation. To this day I have no idea why I ended up with that wonderful Mitchell reel in my box, nor that fabulous imported float so ideal for catching bream, but somehow my tackle box never needed replenishing.

Fishermen are strangely, superstitious creatures. You can only have your first beer after you have caught your first fish. You must sit in the sun all day without any sun lotion in case the fish can smell the Coppertone. Don't eat oranges. Bream hate the smell, apparently. And never, ever lend anything from your tackle box. Selfish bastards.

On one occasion, we went fishing at the rather ominously named Crocodile Pools. The place lived up to its name with sandbanks covered in the sluggish, black, basking crocs, the deeper channels dotted with the comical heads of inquisitive hippos. A Goliath heron stood on one leg gazing into its own reflection and hundreds of feet above, the black-and-white dot of a fish eagle soared in the thermals. The men had taken a day off from hunting and were fishing from a large tree trunk that had fallen into the river during the previous rainy season. It was one of those airless, insanely hot days, and Larry and I kept whinging about the heat and wanted to go swimming.

His dad, Ben, wiped his forehead and looked warily across at the reptiles, their mouths open in grotesque postures as they soaked up the sun. The river there was relatively shallow with a sandy bottom.

'Geez, you kids are annoying,' he groaned.

'But okay, if you want to damn well swim, go and swim over there in that sandy bit. And look out for crocs! You should be able to see them against the sandy bottom. Mark my word, Larry – they swim a lot faster than you my boy.'

Delighted, we ran splashing into the warm, crystal-clear water of Crocodile Pools, oblivious to the now wide awake crocs and hippos snorting only 50 yards away.

'And don't do anything stupid!' Ben shouted at us as an afterthought.

We had been keeping a wary eye out for the reptiles, which had now silently slipped into the water. But one thing escaped our attention. Not far away, on a sandbank, a large, black log covered in dead leaves, reeds and branches seemed to have been washed up, possibly during the floods. Without warning and to our horror, the entire pile stood up and slowly slid into the water. It was the biggest croc any of us had ever seen, and it was only yards from where we were swimming. Squealing and laughing, we ran tumbling over each other to get out of the water. It was a close shave and sadly spelled the end of any swimming that day.

I do not recall a time when we weren't drifting around hippos, avoiding crocs, getting out of the way of elephants or trying not to be charged by buffalo. It seemed that we did not have a care in the world. The truth is that we were actually very well educated in bush lore and were far more aware of our surroundings than most kids our age.

Still, hippos were a nuisance, and constantly gave me a headache when fishing.

Sometimes it was just down to good old-fashioned luck. When I was a little older, we were on a trip upriver from Chirundu. My pal George Moorcroft, his two young daughters, Carey-Ann and Tara, his wife Calla, my cousin Kerry Grier and I took the small outboard upstream to catch some bream.

'George,' I shouted over the roar of the engine, 'are you sure we should be going so far? Don't forget this is Yellow Boat and it has a bloody mind of its own.'

'Shit, man, Pete,' laughed George, 'I'm a mechanic...'

The rest of his reply was whipped away by the wind and drifted downstream. Yellow Boat belonged to my father and the Wood family were notoriously bad with engines. I had very little faith in this outboard. As if on cue, about ten miles upriver, our engine conked out. Even George's magic was not going to help here. This time, we had no fuel.

Kerry was a lawyer and in her unflappable manner summarised the situation.

'Well, you can't blame it on your boat this time. We will just have to drift downriver until we get back to Chirundu.' Kerry spoke with a precise, clipped voice more suitable for a courtroom.

It was a sound idea, except for one thing. We had one small, rather useless oar on a swiftly flowing river with many submerged sandbanks, crocodiles and, of course, massive pods of hippos to navigate around. What could be more simple? It all went well for the first hour, notwithstanding the sandbanks. George kept up spirits by singing Shona songs beneath the searing sun. Occasionally, in awe, we would watch a herd of elephants crossing the river in a line, one trunk holding the tail of the other like a circus act. Or stop singing to gaze at the massive curled antlers of a kudu antelope on the bank. It all seemed so idyllic. At times we would drift almost to a stop and at others would get caught midstream and pick up the knots. And therein lay the problem.

With no steering mechanism, we were at the mercy of Mother Nature and soon found ourselves drifting at some considerable speed straight towards a pod of about 80 hippos, with calves.

The hippos by now were thrashing and leaping in the water baring their massive jaws and tusks. Helpless, we careered towards them. Closer and closer.

Finally, George felt that this was the time to try to explain to the children the imminent danger and I clearly remember this terrified father telling his two brave daughters, 'Now listen to me Carey-Ann and Tara, this is important ... we are going to hit these hippos full on. The boat won't stand a chance. Some of us might get killed. So when I tell you to jump, I want you two to swim like hell towards that island over there. Don't worry, I will be right behind you. Do not look back – just swim. Do you understand?' Both girls nodded in unison.

Incredibly, when so much danger was at hand, there was little to panic about. No histrionics. No crying or screaming. Just absolute silence as all on board realised that this was it. Quietly, we looked to one another for courage and assurance, none of which was forthcoming.

Then from the silence, we once again heard Kerry's steady, cool voice.

'Why don't us adults just jump out and try and pull the boat by swimming? We have nothing to lose.'

It seemed obvious. No one at that moment particularly cared about crocs.

'Christ, a croc can only take one person. These hippos could kill the lot of us. We need to save the children.'

That was our primary concern. Judging by the speed of the current, we would reach the hippos within 20 seconds. The noise they were making was terrifying. Looking towards the heaving mass of shiny, brown bodies, we took our cue and jumped.

And hit the river bed.

The water was only a few feet deep. Laughing with hysteria and terror, we grabbed the boat and dragged it upriver, against the current and out of harm's way, finally collapsing in a heap of ragged nerves on the nearest island. Once we had gathered our senses we set off again, this time finding a less dangerous current, finally drifting into Chirundu bedraggled and deliriously happy. Just another day's fishing.

Sadly these wonderful trips to the valley were stopped in the mid-1970s after the war escalated and the valley became a no-go area for non-military. It would be another eight years before we would see our beloved Zambezi Valley again.

But by then it was another country.

6

Behind Every Great Man

The Rhodesian bush War crept up on us. It seemed that one moment we were living in a kind of utopia and the next we were at war. At least for those of us on farms. For many city dwellers it hardly seemed to have started at all. At times, they went about their daily lives unaware of the stress that was being heaped upon us out in the countryside. There were times when I felt that even my gran was quite oblivious to it all. It drove my mum crazy.

On 21 December 1972, a group of ten ZANLA guerrillas attacked the farmstead of the De Borgrave family in Centenary. Adrian De Borgrave was my age and had boarded at Umvukwes Junior School with me. Naturally we were all shocked to hear that the gang had shot up the farm with AK-47s and thrown grenades through the windows. Fortunately, nobody had been killed. For us farming folks, the war had officially begun.

The advent of war intruded into a rural community that was two or three generations old. Many of these folk had ancestors stretching back to the time when Lobengula ruled the Matabele. Exiles or adventurers of empire, they had arrived after circuitous and colourful family histories, and now felt as entitled as anyone to live there, and were prepared to fight for what they saw as their homeland under attack. And in this, as in previous generations, women were to the fore.

The majority of farm labourers were also immigrants from Malawi, Mozambique and beyond. They too would find themselves caught up in the politics of war.

African stores are always a hive of activity, music and gossip. The Kelston Ranch store on the Haringtons' farm next door to us was no different. Everything was hanging from the roof or bulging off the shelves. The single-roomed building was redolent of the sweet, musty smell of green soap, fresh bread and boiled sweets and always the pungent stench of rat droppings.

The storekeeper, often a highly respected person in the neighbourhood who doubled as the school teacher for the local farm kids, could often be seen chatting amiably and wrapping the purchases in brown paper. Sacks of mealie-meal, Vick's VapoRub, Nivea, Surf, Lion matches, long bars of carbolic soap, Coke, Fanta, Sparletta grape drink, batteries, candles, ink, cooking oil, even the odd bicycle suspended from the rafters. And the tailor in the corner constantly clacking and whirring away on his manual Singer with his swatches of brightly coloured textiles, from eye-popping printed polyesters and crimplenes, to navy blue wools and cool white cottons. 555s and Madison and Kingsgate cigarettes, sold either by the box or singly. Jars full of suckers, Gobstoppers and lollipops adorned the counter top. Noisy loiterers sat about the veranda chatting and smoking, occasionally shooing away chickens and the odd goat.

Outside the store grew an old mango tree, depleted of fruit but always offering its shade to several people whiling away the time. This was the ideal place for talk – and talk they did. The Africans from the Victory Block probably knew more about what was happening in the distant corners of the land than any of us whites ever did. Bush telegraph – call it what you will – chatter in the compound and at the stores was the lifeline for these folk.

The morning of 22 December 1972 would have been no different to any other were it not for the constant comings and goings of men and women in the Kelston store discussing the attack from the night before. News travelled fast. How they knew was anyone's guess. Pictures of Adrian's bullet-riddled bedroom were plastered in the *Rhodesia Herald*, but that would not be delivered until the next day. The headline photo showed bullet holes running in an arc across Adrian's whitewashed walls.

The rural population had good reason to be alarmed. No good ever came of this sort of thing – particularly for the peasant farmers. The atrocities by the Kenyan Mau Mau were still etched in the minds of the white folk, too. Farmhouses were barely protected, with many homes built to withstand hot weather rather than grenade attacks. Our own house was one such dwelling, with every room opening up on to a wide veranda. I expect our farm workers were even more worried than us, and would have felt even less protected. Farms were remote and communications awful back then. The best we could do for security was a couple of dogs that would sooner drown the intruder with slobber and drool than attack them.

All adult white men had to do call-up duty or police reserve. This was later known as PATU – the Police Anti-Terrorist Unit. It was essentially a 'Dad's Army', largely made up of farmers who knew how to wield a weapon. Initially, PATU took the men away from their work only a few days a year, but as the war escalated they were gone for weeks at a time, patrolling in dense bush and often making contact with guerrillas far fitter and better armed than they, although arguably with less training or discipline. Well, that's what we were led to believe. It was tough on the men and tougher on the women who were left to defend their homes and children alone. Yet many women believed it did wonders for their marriages.

'Honestly Libby, I love having the old bugger out of the house,' some housewife would say. One wonders what they got up to when the cats were away.

For many women, the war was a rallying cry. Their ancestors had lived through the Matabele rebellion of 1893 and the Mashona rebellion of 1896, and it was the women, including my great-grandmother Bella-Kay Burnet (nee Stuart), who kept the home fires burning. Known as the First Chimurenga, or revolutionary struggle in Shona, King Lobengula's 80,000 spearmen and 20,000 riflemen began attacking settlers and farmers. The pioneering women were often left alone and formed protective groups to defend themselves against marauding Matabele and Mashona.

My great-grandfather Tom Burnet was, like many pioneers, the third son of a wealthy landed family in Scotland. Hailing from Crathes Castle[51] near Dundee, the third in line was sent out into the world to earn his living. The empire was at its height and he was spoiled for choice. I don't suppose this was particularly unusual, as most third sons became preachers, missionaries or pioneers. Cecil John Rhodes and the BSAC (British South Africa Company) sought eager applicants from wealthy families. Children from rich families were more likely to get help from the British government in case of attack from 'savages'.

For the 180 young men who joined up, including Tom, it was a journey into the unknown, but it accomplished its mission and they hoisted the Union Jack on the site of present-day Harare on 13 September 1890. Tom married Bella-Kay Stuart, a successful opera singer from Dundee and distant relation of Mary Queen of Scots, so we are led to believe. I suppose all Stuarts are really, but I think this time it was true. Leaving his young bride in Scotland, Tom ventured forth with Rhodes and his pioneers to help open up the Southern African hinterland that would later become Southern Rhodesia.

---

[51] Crathes Castle is a 16th-century fortress near Banchory in Aberdeenshire, Scotland. The castle was built by the Burnetts (or Burnet) of Leys and was held in that family for almost 400 years.

Bella-Kay joined him, possibly towards the beginning of the 1890s. Alighting from the boat in Cape Town and straight on to a dusty, hot train up to Kimberley, Bella-Kay then trekked north behind a mule to join her husband. They lived in a pole-and-mud hut in Fort Bulawayo. One can hardly imagine the complete change of lifestyle for a woman of Bella-Kay's standing who was a protégé of the famous Australian soprano, Dame Nellie Melba[52].

She never really did settle down, this one. Like a White Russian in exile, not exactly surrounded by her tasteful paintings, tapestries and libraries from home (these would come many months later, moth-eaten and ruined beyond repair) but at least she had her beloved pianos, her scores and her music, and several crates of gowns by Worth in Paris. Together with all her fur coats and stoles, feathered Victorian hats and buttoned kid gloves, scattered with the droppings of mice and the odd black mamba, these pioneer wives must have cut rather ridiculous figures to the near-naked Bantus and Matabele.

King Lobengula's *kraal*[53] was but spitting distance from their home. It was a far cry from the footlights of Covent Garden, or her school in Edinburgh which had demanded the highest of standards, deportment and discipline.

But they were brave and resilient, these extraordinary women, arranging roses in a wattle-and-daub hut one moment and helping defend their homesteads against attack the next.

Bella-Kay always maintained it was Rhodes' funeral that finally

---

[52] Dame Nellie Melba GBE (19 May 1861-23 February 1931) was an Australian operatic soprano. She became one of the most famous singers of the late Victorian era and early 20th century. It is believed that given the opportunity, Bella-Kay would have been the next Nellie.

[53] A traditional African hut village typically enclosed by a fence.

killed her husband. Tom was a pall-bearer and had to traipse up the Matopos hills carrying Rhodes' coffin. No mean feat considering Rhodes' coffin was massive, consisting as it did of three separate coffins. There was an outer shell of Matabele teak, which enclosed two inner coffins, each made of metal. Attached to the sides of the outer coffin were eight huge handles of beaten brass bearing Rhodes' monogram. These were cast, beaten, finished and delivered for fixing within four days of the order being given, a team of artisans having worked night and day to complete the job.

The coffin was then transported by ox-drawn wagon to Rhodes' final resting place at Malindidzimu in the Matopos hills, a special road of more than 15 miles having been carved through the rocky terrain over the preceding days by a thousand-strong team of Matabele. Bella-Kay watched as the Matabele nation saluted Rhodes' coffin. 'BAYETE!' The royal salute given by an *impi*[54] of Matabele warriors as he was finally lowered into his granite grave. It was the first and only time this tribal blessing was given to a white man.

Having survived two rebellions, Bella-Kay lived to the ripe old age of 91. Known affectionately as 'The Rhodesian Nightingale', she openly loathed her adopted country to the day she died. Only once did she go back to her beloved Dundee, where the mayor hung bunting across the street with the words 'Welcome back Bella-Kay Stuart'.

Perhaps I paint a rather rose-tinted picture of dear Bella-Kay. Despite the 'done thing', I am reliably informed that she was a frightful bitch and one day just decided to leave her poor husband in a nursing home in Bulawayo and head for the hills of Mashonaland, but not before having had a rather public affair

---

[54]Zulu term meaning 'an armed body of men'. In English it is often used to refer specifically to a Zulu regiment.

with Jock, the father of the future Rhodesian prime minister Ian Douglas Smith[55].

Old man Smith would often go up to Bulawayo to listen to Bella-Kay's singing, although most people in the know believed it certainly wasn't the voice he was after. Tom Burnet's health deteriorated quickly after that, not helped by lugging that coffin up the Malindidzimu hill, and when he was finally laid to rest they took the original pioneer flag out of the Bulawayo Museum to drape across the coffin, 'Quickly returning it afterwards, of course,' Bella-Kay was quick to tell people.

And so Bella-Kay packed up her gowns, hats and gloves, loaded her two Steinway pianos on to a wagon with a team of 16 oxen, and together with her three children, my grandfather Gordon and his two sisters Isobel and Jane, set off on the long 400 mile trek to Fort Salisbury on the Mashonaland Plateau.

Day after day, the span of oxen drew her convoy away from the lowveld[56] and heat and tsetse fly. The three young children would have taken note of the change of flora and fauna. The flat, dry plains of Matabeleland, the thorn scrub, giant, leafless baobab trees and delicate lime-green *mopane* slowly making way for vibrant and colourful *msasa*, *mnondu*, *mobola* plum, bloodwood and monkey bread. This was spring, the rains had come early that year. The *msasa* trees were displaying a riot of colour, almost lurid after the greyness of the lowveld; carmine, fuchsia, magenta and darker chestnuts. Even the granite *kopjes* seemed more vivid with streaks of rust and red lichens. The

---

[55] Ian Douglas Smith, GCLM, ID (8 April 1919-20 November 2007) was a politician, farmer and fighter pilot who served as prime minister of Rhodesia (or Southern Rhodesia) from 1964-1979. His country's first native-born premier, he led the mostly white minority government that unilaterally declared independence from the United Kingdom in 1965.

[56] A region of land situated at a low altitude, especially in the low-lying region of southern Africa.

wide, shallow crocodile-infested rivers gradually gave way to the balancing rocks of the Midlands and the downy hills of the Great Dyke. The huts on the side of the track were less robust than those of the Matabele and made of mud and elephant grass, sometimes with rust-coloured patterns, totems and animals painted crudely on the walls.

I have a framed black-and-white photo on my wall of some of these tough colonial Victorians at a picnic in the bush. The women are lying about on a blanket under the *msasa* trees like Manet's *Le Déjeuner sur l'herbe*, only with clothes on, broken bread, hard-boiled eggs and jars of pickles and a bottle of what looks like port strategically placed around them. What I love most about this photo is that, clearly, neither the photographer nor the subjects noticed a man a few yards behind them, out cold on a rock, a half-empty bottle of bourbon nearby.

Here in the Midlands, rivers were stronger, deeper and more violent. The massive cumulus thunder clouds overhead were testament to the heavy rains this part of the world endured. After several weeks of bellowing cattle, cracking *sjambok*[57], dust and mud, her trek drew up to the banks of the great Hunyani River, Bella-Kay's last major hurdle before reaching civilisation.

The drift normally used by the oxen was now a quagmire of mud and raging, frothy reddish-brown water. Branches and the occasional tree were swept past by the deluge. Teams of men drew the oxen and wagons slowly into the maelstrom, the 16 beasts bellowing in terror. Helpless, Bella-Kay watched as her 990-pound Steinway was swept off the wagon by the current, floating majestically down the river and around the bend, never to be seen again; the ivory and ebony returned to the African bush from whence they came.

---

[57](In South Africa) a long, stiff whip, originally made of rhinoceros hide.

'I felt quite desolate and perfectly helpless,' she told people later.

'That beautiful thing dashed upon the rapids downstream. It was inlaid with walnut you know? And gold leaf lettering beneath the lid. It was meant for life without dust and dry air. A life in some large cool, clean Scottish home cut from the granite of Aberdeen. I never forgave the country after that.'

Bella-Kay kept singing most of her life, giving lessons on her surviving piano to budding sopranos and mezzo-sopranos in the high notes of *Una voce poco fa* in Salisbury and often performing to stunned audiences or visiting dignitaries at the theatre or embassies, or the newly built Meikles Hotel.

She was still alive when I was a toddler and I have a distant memory of an imposing woman – rather like Queen Mary, with a fur stole, large bosom draped in strings of pearls. Perhaps that was just my theatrical side coming out. Of course, not everyone was enamoured with Bella-Kay. After all she was rather a harridan.

My mother's cousin, Mick Grier, once famously said, 'The only reason I went to her funeral was to make sure the woman was dead.' Rest in peace Bella-Kay.

Those tough colonial women who defended their homes and supported their husbands through the hardships of the rebellions left behind a legacy that would alarm their great-granddaughters. History seemed to be repeating itself. Once again the women were forced to fend for themselves while the men went to war. Like their great-grandmothers, the farm women suddenly found themselves learning new skills. Many, such as my mother, did not even know where the tobacco seed beds were. Many would never have dreamed that they might have to run a farm. Other more urgent skills such as first-aid (A for Airways, B for Bleeding, C for Chest and/or Casevac. 'And ladies, always keep tampons handy, they are the best dressing for gunshot wounds'), radio work (Alpha, Bravo, Charlie Ov-ah), how to load or dismantle a rifle and, of course, how to shoot, became fundamental to their survival.

Target practice was one of the highlights of the month and allowed the women to get together and gossip.

'I much prefer the Uzi,' remarked my mother to a friend. 'At least it doesn't leave ghastly bruises on your shoulder like the automatic shotgun. I mean honestly, try wearing a halter-neck with those awful dark marks!'

Target practice was held at a range specially built on the Girdlestones' farm, Prangmere. Women from all over the Victory Block would congregate with the kids and nannies. My mum was on her knees looking at a canvass sheet covered in an assortment of strange looking steel components from a disassembled FN rifle.

'I know, Libby, I couldn't agree more. And as for this FN, I break a bloody nail every time I try to fill the magazine.'

Several woman nodded assent. 'Too true, Roseanne, but the one I hate is the Browning pistol. That hair trigger gives me the heebie-jeebies. God, now how on earth do we reassemble this flipping weapon? Do we really need to understand this?'

'Keep those kids OUT of the firing range,' Andy Laing, the rather dashing police chief would bark.

'This is not a bloody playground. Right. Assemble your weapons please, ladies. Concentrate please.'

This was followed by a jangle of silver and ivory bracelets as the wives began to put the rifles back together.

Target practice day was like a fete. This was the 1970s and these were no ordinary farm women. Hair was teased up and sprayed, eyeliner applied, fetching A-line frocks and flared paisley slacks were donned, and yes, Uzi's were slung over the shoulder like an accessory. I have a lasting memory of a line of women, all dressed to kill (quite literally) standing in a row, loading magazines with rounds, and letting loose into a bank of targets shaped like soldiers.

The weapon the women loathed above all was a Belgian-made semi-automatic called the FN, or Fabrique Nationale. Heavy, cumbersome and utterly deadly, it fired 7.62mm rounds and could tear a man to pieces. It was the weapon of choice in the army, but for a housewife it had a kick like a mule. Whereas the Uzi – or the locally made 'Rhuzi' – could be fired from the hip like Bonnie and Clyde. After practice, the women would gather up the bairns and jump into their cars and head back to the Girdlestones for tea and scones and lashings of gossip.

Being brought up with guns did not mean you were safe from them. Accidents happened all the time: ADs as they were known, or the rather unfortunate 'accidental discharge', which sounds more like a wet dream. When I was home on R&R from the army, my FN went everywhere with me, it never left my side. One afternoon I was chatting to my mum in her room. She was titivating at her dressing table, gossiping about this or that. I had removed the magazine from the rifle and was cradling the weapon in my arms. Then I made the rookie mistake that might have changed my life. I pulled the trigger.

Stupid.

Idiot.

Fuckwit.

All that training for nothing. At first there was a sound, so close, so loud that it did not register. Then within a millisecond the crash resounded all around us, reverberating off the walls of the bedroom. Staring at me, silent, unmoving, lipstick poised, was my mother with a neat round crater in the wall two inches from her head. My body froze. Then my father was shouting from the veranda 'IS EVERYONE OKAY?' We both shouted back that we were fine.

My father knew better than to come in and give me 40,000 words. Everyone was fine. That's all he needed to hear. 'Christ,' whispered my mum, and then she turned and went back to her titivating, her hand slightly shaking from the shock as she teased her hair with a comb. The incident was never mentioned again. That deadly round lay embedded in the wall as if a reminder that once, just once, I nearly killed my mother.

During 1978 and 1979 the war escalated. Soon, most farm wives were riding shotgun whenever they went out. The fighting was never going to stop the party, but having an Uzi tucked under the front seat was extremely comforting. At the club, guns had to be left at the door, a strange sight for most urbanites seeing a group of smartly dressed women rack up their weapons before going into the bar to order a Cinzano and soda.

Most farm wives also had to do a three-day stint each month, manning the radios at the police station at Sipolilo. I suspect many of them loved this. Granted, they had to wear dreary grey police uniforms, but they also had carte blanche to flirt outrageously with the cops, including the handsome OC.

Often the reality of war would shatter the monotony of the radio room. One time, a neighbour, Roseanne Henderson, was manning the radio. Her husband was named John, as was my father. As was a young Englishman called John Foster, a bachelor who had recently come out from the UK to live in Rhodesia.

We called him John the Pom. The three Johns were all out on patrol together when their armoured vehicle was hit by an RPG. In a totally fluke shot, the rocket penetrated the cabin, causing mayhem and carnage.

Manning the radio back at base, Roseanne heard that 'John had been killed'. Not knowing which John it was, she sat in abject terror, waiting for that radio to buzz. It takes a very special kind of person to keep control in a situation like that. Roseanne also was expected to feed the rest of the farming community information and news through the agric-alert, a radio system connecting all the farmers in the district. This was powered by a car battery in case the terrorists had cut the electricity lines. Each farm had a call sign. Ours was Tango-Whisky Two-Three. It allowed farmers to speak to other farmers when their homes were being attacked, at any time of day or night.

That day the Victory Block community held its breath and waited. And waited. Hearing the brave voice of Roseanne telling everyone that a man was down, and that his name was John must have been horrific for her, for my mother and for the community. Finally, when she got word that it was John the Pom, she rather guiltily breathed a long sigh of relief. John the Pom had no wife or children. I suspect my own mother was also terribly relieved to find out that her own John was also safe.

Incredibly, my own father had changed seats with John the Pom only minutes before the ambush. If you had to believe in fate perhaps that was the time. My father believed it was fate that John the Pom should swap seats at the last minute, and in doing so saved the lives of men who had children and wives to support. John was loved in the district and his loss was a terrible shock and a terrifying jolt for the community.

I was home for the holidays with my pals Spike and Horts and I remember my father arriving back at the house that evening still covered in blood. It was late and they had wrapped the dead body up in a tarp and stashed it under an avocado tree at the Henderson's house.

'We didn't know what to do with it,' my dad said. He was exhausted and threw himself on the sofa, poured himself a cold Castle Lager and stared at *Dallas*, which was playing on TV.

An extract from my diary dated Tuesday, 10 July 1979 reads:

Exeat[58] weekend:

John was called out on duty and about 6.15pm. Their unit were driving in a Crocodile[59] *when they were ambushed by terrorists. By sheer fluke an RPG rocket managed to hit their vehicle at the exact right angle, the missile entering the* crocodile *and killing John Foster, known as John the Pom, and a guard-force man. Local farmer Tim Strong was also injured. It was absolutely gruesome. Poor John the Pom. Our own John had his blood all over him. This war is really beyond a joke now. John the Pom was just such a nice bloke. What an end to an already horrible weekend.*

Mum was called out to do her medics course for three days.

Early Tuesday morning John drove us kids back to town. The car broke down and we needed to be pushed. John yelled at us. Shit we can never do anything right. I hate him you know. It's terrible because he is my father but I've never liked him. Oh shit it's terrible and I am so depressed. We managed to change the battery in Umvukwes village and drove on into town – the atmosphere was awful. Spike and Horts never came to school so

---

[58] Permission for a temporary absence granted by a college, boarding school or other institution.

[59] A 'crocodile' was a bullet-resistant armoured vehicle.

I tried to sleep in the afternoon. But it did no good. I really feel down in the dumps. You know it's incredible how hard war makes one because when we told Dunc about John the Pom he hardly reacted. He just seemed so casual. Like it was an everyday thing. Of course, that does not mean he has no feelings.

For a father, the pressures of war, of losing a friend in front of you, of trying to defend your country, not to mention your family, must have seemed insurmountable for Woody. Little wonder that he was so uptight and cranky with his wayward child. Having other people's kids to look after was just an added pressure. But from my teenage eyes he was just a twat. He never seemed to let up on my sister or on me. He was doing his best, but at the time growing up in this environment was not easy.

Domestic life had to change to fit into war. Windows of homes had grenade screens installed, often just some chicken wire across the window. Security fences were erected around gardens, often disguised with creepers and shrubs, or better still, sharp pointy sisals. No grenade screen or security fence could ever stop an RPG or a round from an AK-47 but one went to bed slightly less worried.

Women lived in constant fear but the *laagers*[60] they formed, much like their ancestors, often had a party atmosphere, swapping recipes, knitting patterns and certainly getting quite sloshed along the way. Our friends the Moorcrofts were with us one night. The men were once again all out on PATU. George Moorcroft, who is my age, was sleeping with his brother in the cottage across the lawn from the main house. This was before we had the security fence erected. When George was in bed that night, he saw a black face appear at the window. It chilled him to the bone and he rushed across the lawn to tell us.

---

[60] From the Dutch meaning an entrenched position or viewpoint which can be defended against attack.

'Now are you sure, George?' Mona, his mum, asked. 'Was it a face you saw?'

'I swear, mum. Jeez, come on. I know what I saw,' George said.

'Well, all the staff have gone home. It couldn't have been Fred or Konda,' my mother said. 'It's late – who do you think it was?'

We immediately got on to the agric-alert, although there was really little anyone could do. Ultimately, we knew we were on our own. Dirt roads were occasionally mined and no one could travel on them until they had been given the all clear. The distant, crackly voice of the woman on police reserve duty over 50 miles away did little to allay our fears.

'And where are those bloody useless dogs of ours?' my mum asked. 'Great guard dogs they make!'

It was then that we noticed that the dogs were gone. They would have barked had someone been prowling around. It was a mystery, but not unknown for the dogs to all go off hunting at night. Still, it was several days before they mysteriously re-appeared and only after the war ended and stories emerged did we find out that our home was due to be attacked that night.

My childhood friend, Alec, had allegedly been complicit in this attempt on our lives.

Alec, my one-time best friend before I went to school. Alec, whom I had played with in the sand down at the river, climbed *kopjes* and splashed in the zinc tub down at the compound. While I went off to high school, Alec went to war. Alec, now a teenage lad, had become a *mujiba*, those essential links between the terrorists and the local community.

Incredibly this group of some 15 guerrillas had been camping only a few hundred yards from our home for a fortnight, the bush so dense it was impossible to know. The Special Branch informed us that they had watched my mother go riding each morning as they made plans to attack our home.

We will never really know what made them change their minds and scrap the attack. Perhaps they felt safe on the farm and it was common knowledge that M'sitwe was used by them for R&R. An attack would compromise their position. Another unlikely scenario was that they wanted to kill my father, not the women and kids. These men were not exactly known for their chivalry. Whatever the reason, the one thing we do know is that the war came very close to us that night, even if we didn't have a clue at the time.

For many, it came too close. Way too close. In 1978, my wonderfully kind uncle David Ward was ambushed in Mazoe in broad daylight on his way home. Mazoe was not considered a hot area and it came as a shock to all of us when we heard that he had been killed. David's wife, my aunt Maggie, and her four children were only a few miles away at home on Kincardine, waiting for him to return from another uneventful day at work. It broke all of our hearts, and for those of us who knew David, the damage was irreversible. That same year my classmate Colin Tilley was killed by terrorists at the gate of his home. Murdered in daylight trying to get into his house. He was only 15. Another ghastly tragedy.

My diary speaks for itself.

Wednesday, 13 December 1978

Three farms were attacked this evening. John is meant to be helping because he is in charge. Of course, we get little sleep because of the agric-alert. The thing is constantly going off. Many compounds in the district have been burned to the ground, and there is no thatching grass at this time of year. The Beresford farm has been attacked – it is their third time.

Friday, 15 December 1978

Sid Moorcroft's dad was killed by terrorists. That poor family have had it so bad.

Sunday, 17 December 1978

We went to Sheena (Philp's) wedding last night, but had to leave Salisbury at about 6am to get home because John was called out on duty. There has been a lot of trouble in Mutorashanga. Mum and I went to a panto (Snow White) at the Horseshoe Club, which was excellent because everyone forgot their lines. It was spooky driving home that night. We should not have been on the road.

Tuesday, 19 December 1978

Went to the Girdlestones for shooting practice. I got 10/10 which I thought was damn good (although John said I should get top marks anyway). Mum only got 3/10!

Wednesday, 20 December 1978

There has been a lot of activity on Chiwi Estates. The agric-alert has been going crazy. The estates have been attacked and I think someone has been killed. I will tell you just now – yes, a bloke called Joubert has been killed. It just never ends does it? John has been called out again.

Thursday, 21 December 1978

Both mum and John have been called out – mum to do radio duty. I can't stay at home alone, so I am going to the Philps who are having a party tonight. I will sleep there.

Sunday, 24 December 1978 (Christmas eve)

The Haringtons had a carol service where I read one of the lessons. Halfway through all the men were called out because the Muir of Ord store had been attacked leaving only the women, kids and Father French singing carols. All our men had a contact with the terrorists. There was a Lima Mike[61] down the road. Everyone is very fraught.

Monday, 25 December 1978 (Christmas day)

John is still out on duty. A whole family from Shamva and all their relations out for Christmas were killed today. One of them was a Bennett and I think he went to Umvukwes School – he has been abducted and it is just so awful – all of the others dead.

That Boxing Day we had more than 50 people turn up for a lunch garden party. Mostly women or elderly, or the very young. All the men were out on patrol. Life went on. My mother, of course, would never have considered cancelling, perish the thought. Anyway, back then the idea of trying to get hold of everyone on a party-line phone was fanciful. Imagine the cacophony of ringing and trings and tringing, my mother would say.

'I suppose you could use the agric-alert, mum,' I suggested rather feebly.

'God, no!' said mum. 'That's highly illegal – and anyway not everyone on the other end has been invited. I would be mortified if they knew I was throwing a do.'

So, 'Lima Mikes' aside, the entire district donned their frocks and drove the 20-odd miles to our farm for a fabulous day of revelry and way too much punch.

---

[61] Military alphabet short form for a 'landmine'.

The war just never seemed to end that year and my father often slept down at the barns to protect the crop from being torched. Many people were not quite so lucky. Our neighbour Heath Laurent had 70 bales of tobacco burned at a cost of US$4,000. A considerable amount of money back then. Some people lost their entire crops. Day to day, we waited. Holding our breath.

Thursday, 25 January 1979

Terrs[62] have been spotted near Matimba on our farm. Vaughn Davis house was burned down. Mum got a mysterious phone call. John was called out because shots were heard on Muir of Ord. Dave Dolphin was nearly killed because one PATU stick wasn't told that he was down at the store checking up on the shots that had been heard. Of course all they saw was this figure and so opened fire. Luckily, they missed him.

Tuesday, 15 May 1979

It has been a terrible week. First the Vassards hitting a LM (landmine). Then Doug Muir getting killed, then Bill Meaker being attacked. Then the Ervines attacked, and now Mike Chance getting killed. This war is getting beyond a joke now. Dear God, please protect Duncan. Poor Mike only had a month and a half to go in the army. John's PATU stick was called out and they killed 2 terrs. No one in the stick seems to know who shot the killing bullets. Loads of contacts are going on in the district.

Played squash with the Halls.

By now the men were being called out nightly on PATU duty. Night after night the agric-alerts would burst into static as farm after farm was attacked. With farmers out on patrol all the time, the farm management was left up to the wives and children.

---

[62] Common short form for a 'terrorist'.

Thursday, 17 May 1979

I am on my own today and I can hear a contact going on right at the moment. Still I had to dip the cattle. I wanted to go to the club but have been told to stay put as it is too dangerous to travel. Someone was killed by a landmine nearby in Mutorashanga.

Monday, 21 May 1979

Woke up early and went to town. It was like going to your doom. We collected Mandy and went to Mike Chance's funeral. It was absolutely terrible. Just terrible and very moving. It was a military funeral – the bugle, the Last Post, the flag over the coffin, the final gun salute. The family naturally just broke down then, especially when the troops saluted the coffin. God what a waste of a wonderful man. Lou-Anne had to be carried out sobbing. Later there was a wake and drinks in the Stuart Room at The Meikles Hotel. Funnily enough the Chance family were incredible – so strong.

That day there were three funerals. All friends of mine.

And the war on the farms continued.

Friday, 25 May 1979

Sid Moorcroft's farm was attacked again last night. Bugs was there alone and a reaction stick made up of farmers from Raffingora were hit by a 'zulu' injuring nearly everyone in the vehicle. Most have been sent to hospital. Some may die. It's pretty terrible. Shit, I really love my family. I was just thinking that if any of them are killed my whole life would change. And it could happen at any time. I just want to cry thinking about it.

These buggers who were blown up at Sid's farm are in a terrible way. Mike Graham has lost an eye and may lose the other (he did). *Another chap was shot in the neck. Mum is on radio duty at the moment listening to it all.*

The Rhodesia Broadcasting Corporation anchors would issue a communiqué every night at 8pm beginning with 'the security forces regret to announce the death in action of...' If the person or people killed were not known to us we would all breathe a sigh of relief and go back to our supper. White people were always announced first, despite the Rhodesian army being 60 per cent black. We knew few black soldiers, so if the communiqué began with an indigenous name my mum would tell us to get back to the table before the scoff got cold. Still, it was hard to understand the anxiety we were all faced with. Day in, and day out.

My aunt Sue and cousins Madeleine and Mark seemed desensitised by it all. The kids had grown up in the UK, so we accepted that they might be more liberal. Indeed we rather enjoyed their liberal attitude. It was not exactly difficult to appear liberal in a country like Rhodesia. Their father, Andrew, was a 'raging liberal', to quote my dad.

My father aside, the rest of us pretty much understood that everyone has a right to their own political leanings. But it hurt us all the same when they taped a 'Zimbabwe' poster on to their wall illustrating two freedom fighters. It seemed remarkably insensitive. Naturally this culminated in a massive row, with my brother storming into their flat and tearing it down. My maternal cousins were provocative to say the least, egged on as always by my uncle Andrew, whose left-wing views were always at the back of their minds. As much as I adored my cousins, I was also terribly mystified by their overt pro-ZANU stance.

Monday, 28 May 1979

I swear if anything happens to Duncan in this war I'd kill Sue, Mark & Madeleine for daring to put up such a poster of that

*hideous Zimbabwe guerrilla. What on earth were they thinking.
I had a terrible dream that Dunc was killed and Ganty (my gran)
thinks it is an omen that Duncan left last night without saying
goodbye. God please look after him.*

Tuesday, 29 May 1979

We became Zimbabwe-Rhodesia today.

*Big dramas today. It's terrible to see our family torn apart because
of this war. Relationships have broken down. Duncan had an
enormous row with Sue and Madeleine over that poster. He tore
it up and Madeleine threw herself at him and there was shouting
and bellowing. Duncan nearly hit Madeleine! I believe it was
really bad. Already the filial bond has been broken. There is no
way to repair it but the terrible thing is that I love Madeleine and
at the same time I couldn't bear to defy my family and country.
So therefore the only thing I have to do is try and play cool with
Madeleine and be on Duncan's side.*

Shit it's a lousy war.

Our lives are in turmoil – but that's war!

Played rugby.

Of course, blood is thicker than water and certainly stronger
than government. I called Madeleine the next day and we
made up.

Thursday, 31 May 1979

*Mum called. John had been called out on duty. His stick killed 6
to 8 terrorists.*

That same month some guerrillas had been captured and

interrogated. Special Branch called to tell my father that he was now a marked man. Our lives seemed to have been turned upside down. The family was at loggerheads with each other. Our house was quite possibly being watched at night. We were allowed only one light on after dark. I have no idea how that would have helped. We were hardly being aerial bombed and any guerrilla worth his mettle would know exactly where to find our house, even in the dark.

Even Paul, our wonderful black farm manager, was caught up in it and arrested for collaboration. I suspect Paul had little choice, seeing as he had the barrel of an AK-47 pointed at his head.

Thursday, 7 June 1979

Paul our manager has been given 5 years in jail because he collaborated with the terrs. It's terrible but has to be done. I feel so sorry for him but on the other hand it is because of him that my family may be killed. The trouble with a clever black guy like him is that when he comes out of prison he will most certainly be a terr-lover and a white-hater. It seems little will be achieved but surely he must know he did wrong? After all, he is now fighting against his own country: Zimbabwe.

Paul was released from prison the next month having only spent a few weeks in jail. I was relieved, and although he did come back to the farm to ask for his job back, it was simply untenable. I have no idea where he is or what he is doing. Nor do I know where his convictions lie. But I do hope that he is doing well for himself.

Of course, life was not without its funny side.

One day, just before lunch, an almighty racket suddenly descended upon the house. It sounded like a spaceship was about to land on us. Running outside, we were delighted to see about eight or nine French-made Alouette helicopters hovering just feet above the lawn in perfect V formation, the air around the house looked like a soup of swirling, twisting nasturtiums and marigolds, the odd canna lily whipping across our paths like a rag doll. A hurricane of leaves and plants flying through the air, the dogs tearing about in a frenzy, a terrified garden boy ducking for cover beneath a now-flattened bougainvillea. It looked and sounded like a scene from a Vietnam war movie.

And there, sitting in the seat of the lead chopper, was my mum's cousin, Air Commodore Mick Grier, a wicked smile splitting his face from side to side. Then they dipped across the lawn as one to position themselves above the swimming pool, and with a flick of his thumb, Mick ordered his boys to jump. The three of us kids watched in astonishment as one after another, fully loaded, the men leapt into our pool, emerging laughing and spluttering and ready for a well-earned beer. The choppers turned and flew down to the stables, where they landed on the nearest available flat piece of land, scattering the horses who were skittish at the best of times. It was without doubt the most dramatic entrance I had ever witnessed, not to mention highly irregular.

'Sorry, Libby,' Mick said, giving her a big hug. 'I just couldn't resist – I saw your call sign TW23 laid out in white bricks as we flew over and thought, bugger it, I haven't seen my cousin for yonks. And anyway, it's almost time for a G&T! We've just returned from a contact near the escarpment. Quite a firefight, I can tell you.'

Later, after a rowdy lunch, and half-hearted ticking off from my mum for buggering up her garden, Mick attached my father to a winch and flew him over the farm, dangling from a rope. Had he lifted his arms he would have simply slipped to his death. My father is, to my knowledge, the only man ever to set foot on the pinnacle of Matimba, the tallest and most inaccessible tower of granite in the district. We were green with envy, but still so happy to see Mick turn up unannounced in such a wonderfully eccentric manner. I think the horses are still running.

Never a dull moment was to be had on a Rhodesian farm.

By the end of the war, some 30,000 people had been killed on both sides, many of whom were civilians. For those women at the sharp end, often lonely and remote with husbands away on active duty, their bravery, stoicism and unwavering spirit helped make those turbulent years for a kid such as me seem almost like an adventure.

Almost.

7

The Seychelles and the Submariner

One evening, during the height of the civil war, we were driving like the clappers back to the farm. It was late and there was a curfew. My beloved uncle David Ward had been killed in an ambush a year earlier on this very stretch of road. But in the usual indomitable, Rhodesian way, we all felt life must go on. Besides, we had a Mercedes S-Class and, god willing, the car that the adverts claimed was 'the best or nothing' would pull us through.

That night my friend James Hughes was in the car with us. My dad was driving and my mum in the passenger seat relaxing. Cruising well over 80 mph along the curving roads near Mazoe, I turned to James and pulled out a small glass vial, a free sample of the latest fragrance by Fabergé called Babe. All the cosmetic companies ignored the UN sanctions on Rhodesia.

'What do you think of this?' I asked James, cracking open the vial and passing it to him to smell. The heady scent of ambergris and roasted citrus filled the cabin. James had been with me earlier that day when we had been seduced by the QV Pharmacy girl into taking a sample home with us. Country bumpkins such as us were always reeled in by those blue-eye-shadowed, big-haired dames.

Without warning, my father slammed on the brakes, the car screeching across the tarmac, wheels burning rubber, all 3,373 pounds of steel grinding under his control. What the hell was happening? Both James and I were thrown forwards and then back against the seat. My mother let out a short scream. Was it an ambush? God no, not here, not on this stretch of road. The terror of the moment gripped us. Within seconds the car had come to a silent, hissing stop.

Absolute silence.

Darkness.

No one dared move. Then out of the gloom, my father reached across the back of the seat, grabbed the perfume and hurled it out the window. The stunned silence seemed to last a decade.

'What the bloody hell is wrong with you?' boomed his voice. 'Why don't you smell like a MAN? Why don't you smell like LIFEBUOY?'

More stunned silence. Lifebuoy was the red, army-issue soap from the second world war, for god's sake. I shrank back into my seat. I knew what was about to happen.

'... AND another thing – WHAT THE FUCK DID HAPPEN THAT NIGHT IN THE SEYCHELLES?'

Well, a good question I thought. What the fuck did happen that night in the Seychelles? I wonder how my life would have changed had I told him the truth that night in the darkness of the car in the middle of the bush with my best friend sitting next to me.

'Oh, John!' cut in mum. 'Drive on, for Christ sake. It's dangerous here.'

Pop ... the moment was lost, and into the darkness we drove. Silently. The question disappearing into the night like a firefly extinguishing its light. My father now had to take his doubts to his grave, eating at him like a cancer.

For years, Woody must have been brooding over this question. One could imagine it chewing up his brain like some kind of parasite, and not once did he have the guts or the gall to even ask me if I was alright? If I was damaged goods. If I was suicidal from the incident two years earlier on those paradise islands.

It made me laugh. Your own father cannot even speak to you. His rigid, prissy Edwardian attitude forced him into looking the other way. His silence spoke volumes. His anger and bitterness said it all. I knew that he knew. Deep down, I knew. Not only did I know that he knew, but I also knew instinctively he knew that I actually enjoyed it. Whatever 'it' was. The genie was out of the bottle. It absolutely killed me and no doubt it killed him, too.

So what did happen that night?

Two years earlier: May 1978. The call came through shortly after lunch, when all the kids were settling down for our obligatory half-hour siesta.

'WOOD! Phone call.' I leapt up and dashed across the dorm to the phone in the hall. No one ever called. It must be important.

'Hi Poops, it's mum.'

'Hi mum – everything okay?' WHY does she call me Poops?

'Oh yes, super. I'm calling to tell you that we want to take you out of school early this term, we're going to the Seychelles.'

'The Seychelles?' I screeched ... nothing in the whole world sounded more exotic than the Seychelles. My mind reeled as I tried to place it on the map.

'We're going with the Trembling-Johnsons.'

It was my dad's nickname for the Tremlett-Johnsons. Sue Trembling Johnson was a terribly sophisticated and glamorous lady of a certain age. I didn't know her particularly well and it did surprise me that we were going holidaying with them and not our usual rabble. But it also excited me no end that we were to travel with such a classy couple. And Sue spoke fluent French, surely a bonus in the Creole isles.

That afternoon I pored over maps of the Seychelles in the school library, exotic, fascinating names such as Mahé, La Digue, Praslin and Silhouette Island. The archipelago is situated off the coast of Africa on the equator. Everything would be a first for me. Crossing the equator, flying in a Jumbo, Coco de Mer, cocktails and who knows what else? What more could a 15-year-old want? Well, be careful what you wish for. I was soon to find out.

The islands were everything, if not more than I had dreamed of. People say that it is only the easily impressed who get to visit and write about the Seychelles. Well, maybe that is me. Easy and impressed. Isolated, mountainous and covered with a thick blanket of coconut palms, towering granite boulders thrust up from the earth's core and surrounded by the most gloriously aquamarine coral sea. Jacques Cousteau, part of whose documentary, *The Silent World*, was shot in the Seychelles, said he had never been anywhere else with such clarity of water or diversity of marine life.

The Reef Hotel on Mahé was the epitome of glamour. Or so I thought. This was the 1970s after all. Women still dressed in gowns at dinner. Men in slacks and smart sandals, hair slicked back with BrylCreem, smelling of coconut oil and glowing with health. The ocean crashing down on the reef only a few hundred yards from the dining room. Hot, lazy days spent exploring the islands, driving around the hairpin bends in a Mini Moke, diving off deserted beaches, drinking warm, sticky rosé, and picking the sweet flesh from grilled lobsters. It was all so idyllic. That was until the submarine came into port.

HMAS Orion was an Oberon-class sub belonging to the Royal Australian Navy. Built in the 1960s in Scotland, but only recently commissioned by the RAN, it was the height of Australian sea power in the day. With a crew of 56, she was a tight squeeze, and certainly caused a stir when she pulled into port in Victoria, Mahé. The sub had been at sea for six weeks out of Singapore and the sailors were feisty, tough, rowdy and fun. More importantly, they were staying at the Reef Hotel. My little hormones started bouncing. All my Sundays had come at once.

At first, it looked like the hotel was having a Freddie Mercury convention. Back then, the handlebar moustache was de rigueur for any man in the army or navy. This was, without a doubt, the precursor to the 'clone' look that was to take over the gay Castro neighbourhood in San Francisco a few years later and made so popular by Zanzibar's most wicked export, Queen frontman Freddie Mercury.

But here in the Seychelles were men, real men. No clones. Real moustaches, real sailors, real uniforms. I was 15. Well 15 and two-thirds to be precise, and was quite taken by their charm and rough-and-ready manner. Over the next few days friendships blossomed. Here I was on holiday drinking beer with these tough Aussie men and rather proud that they were falling over themselves to buy my glamorous, platinum blonde mum a drink. I really think even my dad was just a little proud too and rather enjoyed having some drinking companions.

For much of the day, I would lie on the chaise longue by the pool dreading the moment when I was expected to stand up. I cursed myself for ever wearing budgie smugglers, as the Aussies called Speedos. Our friendship with the crew finally paid off when, one day, the officers invited us on to the submarine to have a look around. My lasting memory of this was the tight fit between bunk beds. Once lying on a bunk, the bed above you was so close that you were unable to turn over. Your nose almost touched the metal bed above.

'It's a very tight fit,' I remarked to no one in particular. They all laughed.

'You'll be surprised how many people you can fit on to one of these bunks, mate,' one sailor commented, winking at me. My knees nearly buckled. Hello sailor?

Over the next few days, we gradually got to know these men well. '*Good buggers*', my dad said, not for the first time. My age and my naivety are quite apparent when I read back over my diaries from that period.

They are real beauts. Really fantastic chaps – one would not think that they would go out of their way for us, but they do. We all had a ball of a time and got drunk.

Hmm. Well, it gets more interesting.

In the evening all the sailors tried to get me pissed. They were amazed at how much I could take.

Really? And what were my parents doing when their 15-year-old was getting quietly slaughtered with a bunch of old salts?

Well, that was all about to change. Dramatically.

We were finishing dinner. The bar, only a few yards from our table, was heaving as usual with sexy women and sailors. My mother was looking particularly gorgeous in a floor-length cream gown shot with silver and complemented with matching killer silver heels. I could not have been more proud of her as she walked across the floor. Every head turned. But unbeknown to us, one head turned for me. John was relaxed and smoking his cheroot, gazing out at the phosphorescence in the ocean.

'Do you mind if I go to the bar and have a beer with the lads?' I asked. *Lads*, I thought? How dare I. Trying to be big stuff was not becoming. That said, age limit was not a barrier here and besides I was extremely precocious.

'I dunno, Pete,' said my dad.

'Oh, do let him,' chipped in Sue.

Then, leaning towards me, she whispered in a conspiratorial manner.

'Let me give you some advice, dah-ling. In this life we only have one chance. You must always make an impression.'

She paused for effect, then, hand on my knee continued.

'It doesn't matter whether that's a good impression or a bad impression. Just damn well leave an impression.'

My dad chuckled.

'Okay, mate, off you go.'

My mother absent-mindedly nodded consent. Sidling up to the bar, I ordered a SeyBrew, the local lager. I leaned back against the bar, terribly grown-up, and took a couple of swigs of the ice-cold beer, when one of the sailors I did not know came up to me and introduced himself as Arnie.

Arnie had the ubiquitous moustache and regulation crew cut. He was tough, rough and had a certain amount of louche charm.

'Look, mate, do you want to come back to my chalet for a beer?' he asked, the Aussie drawl stretching out the word beeeer.

How strange, I thought. I already have a beeeer. Why on earth ... then the penny dropped. FUCKING LORDY CHRIST! This dude wanted to fuck me! This macho man. This 29-year-old sailor wants to shag me, a 15-year-old. Nothing in my short, sweet life had prepared me for a proposal such as this.

We do stupid things as children, and I was just a kid. But to be fair, I was driven, pumped with complex hormones that had never been put into active duty, and I was in paradise. And there and then, without as much as a backward glance at my stunned parents sitting just a few feet away, I stood up and followed this sailor out of the bar, across the gardens, past the tennis court – where he waved knowingly to some other sailors playing a set – and down to his chalet.

My initiation into the real world was about to begin.

As soon as we entered the chalet, Arnie locked the door. Thinking on my feet, I unlocked it. Arnie relocked it. I shrugged. Then Arnie turned off the lights. I turned them on. He turned them off. This was becoming a bit scary and predictable, I thought. Oh well, my escape route was now gone. I waited for my eyes to get adjusted to the gloom. Thank god there was a full moon. Did this chalet even belong to Arnie? He would not touch the bed. I watched quietly as he lay a reed sunbathing mat on the floor and gestured for me to lie down.

He then proceeded to do absolutely everything one can ever imagine to me. Arnie threw the book at me. The book of O. The Sensuous Man. The Sensuous Woman. The A-Z of How To Have Sex. Seriously. I HAD NEVER EVEN BEEN FRENCH KISSED BEFORE. This was not a learning curve. This was a rocket shooting through the ceiling.

I thanked god for the book my mum kept secreted away in her side table at home: *The Sensuous Woman* by 'J' (Joan Garrity), a precursor, I expect, to the bestseller that took the world by storm, *The Joy of Sex*. I had never had any sex education from mum, so instead I would pore over this book learning how to kiss, how to satisfy a man, how to do the 'butterfly lick'. In short, how to arouse the male of the species.

Ironically it had been written for women and, of course, written in 1968, making it rather sexist and dated, even going as far as saying that only ten-year-old boys were off limits ... thank god! But for me it offered an entire education. The reality is much further and stranger than the truth.

Lying there on that uncomfortable reed mat, covered in Ambre Solaire suntan oil and gritty sand, all I could think was 'this man has a seriously long, aggressive tongue. Blimey – how in the hell am I going to tell my mates about this one?'

The ordeal did finally come to an end. I call it an ordeal with a handful of salt. It was educational, interesting, uncomfortable, terrifically enlightening, somewhat technical and frighteningly exciting. After about three hours, there was a hairy, heavy, sweaty man falling asleep on top of me. RAN[63] Arnold was spent and it was time for me to leave.

To be bestowed this sudden adult knowledge was confusing. The world began to close in around me, slowly, like a heavy weight. Secrecy bound tightly together with abject terror, knowing that my parents would be waiting for me. I walked slowly, back across the now dark hotel grounds to my room that adjoined my parents. In my chest my heart pounded. The light was still on. And they were absolutely FUCKING furious.

---

[63] The Royal Australian Navy (RAN) is the naval branch of the Australian Defence Force.

'WHERE THE BLOODY HELL HAVE YOU BEEN?' shouted my father. 'You have made us SICK WITH WORRY. You selfish little shit.'

Well, I had my doubts as to whether his worry concerned my safety or his pride. But this was no time to pick an argument about the merits or disadvantages of parenthood. An angry John Wood was a beast not to be tampered with.

'I was drinking with the sailors. I told you that,' I replied rather sheepishly.

Then, as if to make it any easier, I added in the names of two officers whom my parents had taken a shine to.

'We went down to the tennis courts with Robby MacDonald and Bob Ross and we were all having beers. It was just good fun.'

My father grunted, my mother shook her head.

'For three damn hours? Sounds bloody suspicious to me.'

And that, my dear reader, was that. The episode was over. Never mentioned again until that notorious night on the road home.

Truthfully, this initiation into sex had an enormous effect on me. The age difference was one factor. What he did was naturally (or unnaturally, depending on who you are) another factor. Yet the hardest part of all was the beginning of a decade or more of lies and bending the truth to friends, family and loved ones.

When my buddies spoke of a 'clamp' or a 'grope' with a girl, I knew far better. I could still smell his breath, slightly tangy from beer, as his tongue found its way down my back and beyond. When my friends spoke of a kiss with a girl, I knew of a kiss that was hard, eager, strong. Probing and masculine and deep.

Shocking and exciting. The taste of salt from his sweat and suntan oil. Not just a wet, shy kiss. But something from a person who knew exactly what they were doing and what they wanted.

When a pal shyly spoke of 'feeling up' a girl, I knew only of strong fingers, probing, hardened by work on a ship. Rough military flesh. I also felt guilt. Awesome, inexorable guilt. And waves of stupidity. Anger. I displayed immaturity by not thinking ahead that hot night. I felt trapped and I needed a scapegoat.

Betrayal is easy. Too easy. It is as old as mankind. RAN Arnold was going down with me. Of that, I was sure. It hurt me. I was not the kind of person brought up to betray another man. A part of me felt a kind of love for Arnie. But I was trapped. The morning after the event, following a breakfast eaten in silence, I decided to tell Robby MacDonald and Bob Ross. Everyone is capable of betrayal. But beware the children. My hormones were stronger than my common sense. I was still terribly muddled, yet never once did I think I was being wronged by Arnie. It was the natural order of things. I knew that what had occurred was the right thing. But I was teetering on a ledge and I was an extremely dangerous animal. Leaving a note in the pigeon hole of the two officers, I told them I had been tricked. Not forced. Not raped. But in my naivety lured into the room by Arnold.

The HMAS Orion set sail that day. A note left at reception written by Robbie simply said: 'Be strong. Good luck.'

The desire to be loved was far stronger than the desire to be secretive. But there was a vacuum. Nothing to lean on. No one to talk to. A void. I had to tell someone. I needed to tell someone. I tried to tell my mother, but lost confidence. I wish I had told Madeleine, my cousin. She would have understood. She was always pushing gender-bending books, films or music at me like Al Pacino's *Cruising* or David Bowie's cross-dressing antics. But a story like this would cause such upheaval and horror at boarding school, it simply did not bear thinking about. The first of many stories emerged from my mouth.

Keep it real. Don't ever get caught out. Do not betray yourself.

Arnie became Annie. Yes, she was 28 or 29. Yes, she was married, going through a divorce. Yes she did everything to me, and sorry, I won't list them here, although I suspect the anal part must have set a few alarm bells clanging. And so it came to pass that Pete Wood became the first of his group of friends to get laid, and indeed it would be many years before some of those chaps ever did some of the positions that Arnie, sorry Annie, and I performed on that balmy moonlit night in Mahé.

I managed to stay in touch with Arnie. In a way he became my first real boyfriend. It was doomed. We communicated through letters. Kind, sweet messages mostly, with little or no real depth. In the beginning, when Arnie wrote to me I was excited by these illicit letters, but I expect, as is so common with youth, I was quickly losing interest in the man. Or else I was lying to myself.

Got a letter from Arnie – the Australian queer – fuck it!

He sent me a postcard of Sydney Harbour Bridge and some posters of Olivia Newton-John in *Grease*, which according to my diary is '*definitely the best film I have ever seen*'.

And this is the truth. I wish I could see it four times. It is the only film that I have ever actually flipped over. Jesus by God, I could scream about it.

Rather strange, but so appropriate in so many ways. God bless Olivia, (and John ... oh, and Arnie as well, I suppose).

And still, to this day, when I smell Ambre Solaire I feel dizzy and a little nauseous.

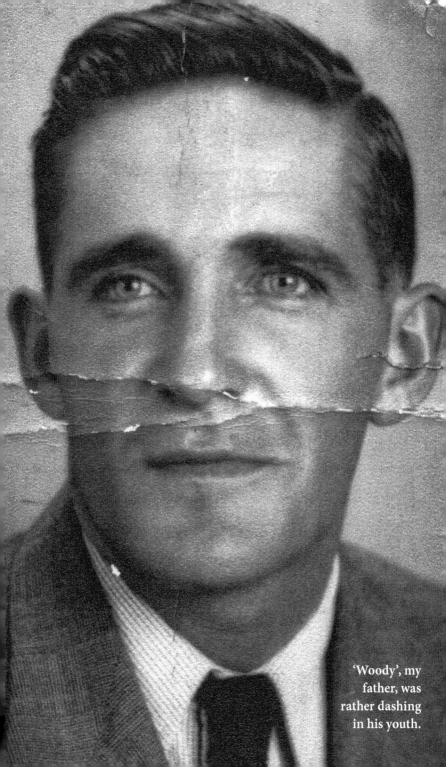

'Woody', my
father, was
rather dashing
in his youth.

ABOVE: My mum, circa 1970, wasn't bad either.

RIGHT: Mum and Woody, M'sitwe Farm.

LEFT: Lib and Woody with Mandy and Duncan, Salisbury.

BELOW: Mum with Mandy and Duncan, Durban, South Africa.

ABOVE: Mum and Woody at the Umvukwes Derby.

LEFT: A little worse for wear.

BELOW: 'Real beauts' – Sam Marnie and Norrie Spicer at one of the many M'sitwe parties.

LEFT: Mum and the author at M'sitwe Farm, circa 1965.

BELOW: The author with a rogue leopard culled on the farm, circa 1966.

The Zambezi hunting bags in the early 1960s were astonishing: *(FROM LEFT)* Norman Travers, Tom Salthouse, John Wood.

Zambezi Valley hunting camps: *(FROM LEFT)* Billy and Scott von Memerty, my aunt Sue, Flo von Memerty, Libby, Duncan. That's me at the front, standing inside the foot of an elephant and bawling my eyes out.

RIGHT: Mum's sister, Sue.

BELOW: My aunt and uncle, Susan and Andrew Ray.

BOTTOM: Mum in the Seychelles.

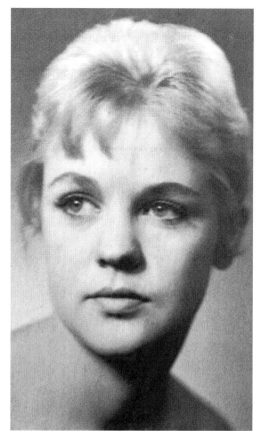

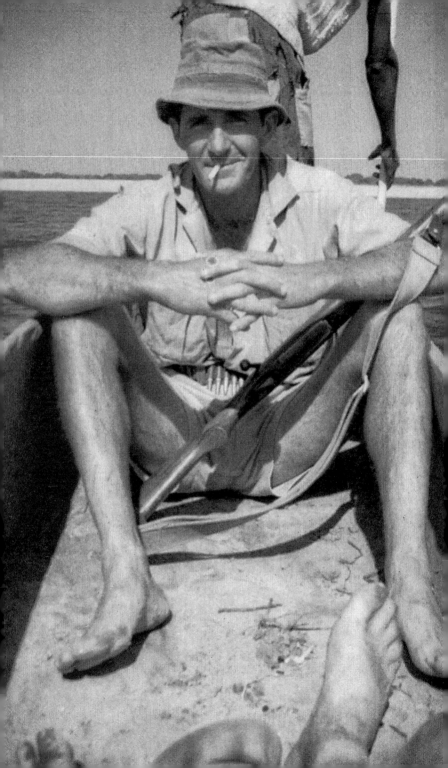

ABOVE: Duncan and Woody, Paradise Island, Mozambique.

LEFT: Mum with her sister Sue, Victoria Falls.

FAR LEFT: Woody in a dug-out canoe on the Zambezi River.

FAR LEFT: On board HMAS Orion.

ABOVE: Just 15 and ready to explore the world – La Digue, Seychelles.

LEFT: The Woods hit Europe – Duncan dressed to kill.

BELOW: Duncan and Woody, M'sitwe Farm – complete with leopard skin hanging on the wall.

ABOVE: The old house at M'sitwe in the late 1990s.

RIGHT: Workers prepare bales of tobacco for auction.

BELOW LEFT: The former scene of many a glamorous M'sitwe Farm party.

BELOW RIGHT: N'yau witch doctors were regular M'sitwe visitors during Christmas.

134144 Trooper
Wood P.W. of
the Rhodesian
Light Infantry.

ABOVE: The old house in 2005 – at least the bougainvillea was still flourishing.

MIDDLE: Derelict and forlorn – M'sitwe Farm, 2005.

BOTTOM: The pool as it was on the author's last visit to M'sitwe.

LEFT: An imprint of the leopard skin could still be seen on the wall years after the Wood family had departed the farm.

ABOVE: Peter Wood, author of *Mud Between Your Toes*. | BELOW: M'sitwe Farm.

8

The Birthday

July 1978

'You do realise that there is a war raging around us?' my father said. He raised an eyebrow waiting for my response. I was not to be dissuaded.

'Of course I know that, John,' I said. 'But my 16th birthday's important.'

My dad shook his head. I waited for him to answer.

'Look, you can have the party, against my better judgement I might add, but we can't have kids driving on those roads in the dark. I don't want to be responsible for someone getting their legs blown off.'

He paused for effect, Took a drag of his smoke, then continued, 'And the townies will have to stay the weekend.'

YES! I thought. Perfect.

'Thanks, John. I promise we will be careful.'

The Victory Block was known as a 'hot area' or 'the sharp end'. Living in the sharp end, any sharp end, was both terrifying and also something to boast about at school. Many of the kids at boarding school lived in the sharp end, whether it was Sipolilo or Centenary, Mount Darwin or the Eastern Highlands. When the V Block became the sharp end I was secretly delighted.

'I have to say, Pete, this is one of your more hair-brained schemes. I mean, look what has just happened to the Moorcrofts,' John reminded me.

I could hardly forget. The Moorcrofts had been on my mind all day. I kept quiet for the right amount of time to allow it to seep in. On the evening of 21 July our old family friends, Mona and Sid Moorcroft, were coming home from the club late, despite the curfew. Driving over the ridge that separated their farm, Berry's Post, from the native reserve, they noticed a glow on the horizon, reflecting off the low, overcast sky. Stopping the car, they stared in horror, Mona reaching back instinctively to see if the two kids, Ian and Michael, were still sleeping.

Ahead of them lay a path of destruction. Their life's work appeared to have simply gone up in smoke. Across the beautiful verdant Berry's Post valley, their house was ablaze, the fields of cotton smouldering, the compounds and barns glowing red from the embers. Realising the imminent danger they were in, Sid quickly reversed the car and sped back the 20 miles to our farm to alert the district.

That night, few people in the V Block got much sleep as the agric-alert came alive with worried farmers trying to make sense of it all and wondering who would be next. Early the following day, after the Rhodesian Pookie anti-landmine vehicle had given the all-clear, the Moorcrofts and my father drove back to Berry's Post, at least, to what was left of it.

What they saw gave them chills. The house, built in a Spanish style, was part-home, part-fortress with the main sleeping quarters inside a crenelated tower. Despite the three-foot walls and reinforced doors, the rambling dwelling had been razed to the ground. Not even a pot or pan in the kitchen had survived the inferno. Their entire crop of cotton and tobacco gone up in smoke.

More horrifying, perhaps, were the dead, bloated dogs and cattle lying about, the cattle having been hamstrung and left to bleed to death. Not even their dear Jack Russell, Lowly Worm, had been spared. This was the stuff of nightmares and every farmer in the area knew that it could have been any one of them.

Quietly, Sid walked down to the airstrip, instinctively knowing what he would find. There, still smoking, was the burned-out fuselage of his beloved Cessna Whisky-Vix. The hangar had partially collapsed and was riddled with holes from the AK-47s, the plane slumped to one side and bathed in a surreal light from the bullet holes piercing the smoke. The Moorcrofts were left with nothing.

My diary entry on my 16th birthday – 21 July 1978 – notes:

The fucking terrs had burned the house to the ground. There wasn't even a pot or a pan left. The dogs and cattle killed. Even the aeroplane gone. They have nothing left. Even Lowly was killed. Jesus I still cannot believe it. It's unreal. Mum has been on radio duty all night. This war is getting beyond a joke. I wish all of us friends could leave and start a new life. I'm still young but I know I'm born for Rhodesia and cannot leave it. It is so close to home. These past two months have been the most hectic months of my life.

First it was David Ward. Now it's them. What are they going to do? I don't blame them if the Moorcrofts want to leave – they have the same amount here than in any other country – that is NOTHING! NOTHING! Every night I pray for my relations and friends, but look what happens? Is there a god? I seriously doubt it.

Now I am just waiting for it to happen to our family. If it does, please God let it be me. I am not afraid of dying, but I am afraid of losing my own friends, relations, happiness and my farm. The place where I grew up. Can't those fucking terrs be stopped? I am losing faith in this government and this country.

Jesus – what a birthday!

And now I wanted a party. A date was set for 27 August 1978.

Phone calls all day. I hope to God we get enough birds to come to this dance. At the moment I have got 13 girls and 20 boys. Mum is away on radio duty. There were 2 ambushes on the Mazoe road which makes it harder for people to come.

The dynamics of organising such a do were clearly not easy, but neither was it impossible, and after countless phone calls I finally managed to get most of the teenage kids from Umvukwes to come. After all, most farmers were used to this kind of thing. The big question was whether the townies could make it. And the townies had the seriously cool chicks. Would their parents agree to let their kids bugger off to the most volatile district in the country along roads that clearly were not safe?

We made a plan and after much persuasion my mother managed to calm the city folk. Those from Salisbury were to be ferried over the day before in my parents' car and a Hertz rental. My mother allowed my friend Foxy to drive. One was expected, by law, to be over 21 to drive a rental car. But Foxy, being the only one of our gang who had a driving licence, left my mum with little choice. In the greater scheme of things it did seem a risk worth taking despite Foxy's age. He was just 16. And so we set off in convoy for what thankfully turned out to be an uneventful journey out to the farm. There were eight kids in the convoy of cars, including the girls.

My father was not the best company that night. He was not used to his farm being overrun by a mob of teenagers. He had little patience. He wanted us out of his hair.

'For Christ sake, Pete, take them camping or something. Just get the buggers out of the damn house.'

'Well, I can't take the girls, John. It's way too rough and ready.'

'Okay, leave the women here. They can stay in the cottage. Just tell them I don't want a bloody racket from their music.'

It seemed like a good enough compromise.

I decided to go camping down by the Nyarowe River. It was risky, but simply the best spot on the farm to camp out. I knew, as did my father, that M'sitwe Farm was a popular haven for guerrillas, many of whom used the farm for R&R. The Nyarowe was a natural route taken by insurgents moving from the native reserve to the mining district of Mutorashanga, where they could blend in with the crowds, get laid or just get shit-faced on Chibuku. And now I was to take these urbanite kids into the bush to camp out, armed only with a .22, a pathetic weapon at the best of times and quite useless at night. And to my ever-lasting chagrin, I was eventually labelled 'Pete in the bush with a .22'.

Getting out of my father's hair was one thing. Yet unknown to any of us, other than my dad of course, the police had approached my father the night before and told him that they had 'intel' from captured terrs, better known as tame terrs, that our house was due to be attacked over the weekend. The very weekend of my party. My father had blanched. While it was too late to cancel the party, he felt it would be prudent to quietly speak to some of the local farmers and a few key members of the community to join him at our house on Saturday night to keep guard, as it were.

It is doubtful that any of them really knew how tough it would be to control 70 drunken teenagers.

After a breakfast of fresh pawpaw from the garden, followed by eggs, bacon, fried eggplant and *boerewors*, we set off in the Land Rover towards the Nyarowe River on the north-western boundary of the farm. Konda had already packed the camping equipment, much to my father's annoyance.

'Bloody spoiled kids – as if Konda doesn't have enough to do already,' he muttered as he threw down his napkin and strode off to the veranda to pick up his hat and head down to the tobacco grading sheds.

John had a point, and insanely irritating as it was, often he was correct. Of course, we had no inkling as to why he was really so agitated. No sooner had we heard the rev of his pick-up truck halfway down the hill then my mother went over and turned on the wireless, Kris Kristofferson's gravelly voice crooning about *Me and Bobby McGee*.

My father, being quite unmusical, would always insist on silence in the house. 'Listen to the sound of Africa,' he would say. 'You might learn more from that than the bloody racket you play.'

'Right. Are you kids all packed for the camp?' asked my mum.

'I need you out of the house. I have lots to do.'

Of course, apart from the sleeping bags, groundsheet and tent, bacon, eggs, cast-iron frying pan, enamel tea pot, a small bag of mealie-meal and my mum's delicious marinated kebabs, known locally as *sosaties*, speared on to thin bamboo skewers, we had also managed to stash a crate of Castle Lager and several packs of my father's favourite 'Country Club cheroots'. Not forgetting that useless .22.

Our group was, except for me, entirely made up of my townie mates; the others being Foxy, Spike, Sean Elliott and Chris

Freemantle. Piling into the vehicle, we set off driving past some magnificent euphorbia trees, their cactus-like branches stretching up to the skies. A gang of noisy women from the compound stood arguing like a flock of parakeets in a feeding frenzy. Colourful *doek* wound tightly around their heads, snotty babies strapped to their backs. They were dividing the spoils of their hunt, fat field mice freshly dug from their burrows. They stopped their chatting and stared sullenly as we drove past. These pampered *murungu* must have seemed otherworldly to them, laden as we were with our mass of spoils for just one night.

Shortly the dense bush of *mufuti* and mountain acacia, *mahobohobo (Uapaca kirkiana)* and *mazhanje*[64] trees began encroaching on all sides of the narrow road. This was the bush I loved so much. Huge, granite *kopjes* rose above the tree-line along the way. A flock of guinea fowl suddenly burst from the safety of the long spear-grass lining the side of the road. Their loud staccato clucking clearly audible above the roar of the engine as they flapped their wings comically, trying to escape the careering vehicle. Golden streaks of light from the late morning haze created a delicate pall of dust hanging gently over a fallow field of pale, yellow grass.

The morning dew still sparkled on the blades of spear-grass and cobwebs. To our left I spotted some grey vervet monkeys, their black inquisitive faces masked with white fur, their fluorescent blue balls and scarlet penises proudly displayed between their legs as they scampered across the cattle dip with its crude thatched roof sagging with age.

As we slowed to drive over an ant hill, we could hear the haunting

---

[64]Large-leafed trees bearing a delicious yellow fruit popular with baboons, monkeys, and humans. *Uapaca kirkiana* or sugar plum is a species of plant in the *Phyllanthaceae* family. This is one of the most popular wild fruits in the zone where eastern Africa meets southern Africa.

chant of the herd boys as they rounded up their *mombe* into the chase, singing, 'Dip! Dip! Dipdipdipdipdip! Dip! Diiip!' Occasionally, a panicked beast would need a helping hand from one of the herd boys. Balancing along the narrow walkway and gripping the cow by one horn, they would then drag it through to the shallow end of the dip. The younger calves and heifers were generally more trouble and often needed a painful nip from a herd boy to urge them to make the leap. Running up behind the animal, the boy would grip its tail, twisting it up against the back of the beast, and then quickly sink his teeth into the tough ox-hide. Often this meant having to contend with a very shitty rear-end. These cattle boys lived among the *mombe* and knew each one personally.

Across the pastel expanse of grassland, broken only by the occasional ant-hill or clump of pigweed, I saw the evergreen tree-line along the Nyarowe River. Beside the river, a towering granite hill rose up from the valley; at intervals along its south face you could just make out the rows of stone walls built by bushmen hundreds of years earlier. I turned the Land Rover off the road and bumped over the ruts and contours, now overgrown with thorny saplings and blackjack bushes. A tiny duiker antelope sprang, startled, from the undergrowth and darted off across the field. In unison, the dogs jumped from the back of the vehicle and gave chase, barking madly. The duiker would be much too quick for these tame domestic animals, but at least it gave them some exercise. For minutes after we had lost sight of the dogs we could still hear the high-pitched yelping of my favourite companion, Bella, echoing along the river valley.

Of all the dogs, Bella was the smallest but made up for it with a fierce hunting spirit. Her antics always made me laugh as she ran through the bush, her little head bobbing up and down in the tall grass, trying to see where she was going. In stark contrast to the rest of the farm, the vegetation along the Nyarowe was almost like a rainforest. Huge, gnarled roots exposed to the air after years of seasonal flooding, giant banks of dead reeds wedged up against cliff faces and broken tree trunks, debris from the last rainy season. It was paradise down here, just a few miles from the house as the crow flies. It was the dry season, but this river flowed all year round, fed by streams up in the Great Dyke. Here on M'sitwe, the river was magnificent, plunging over the rocks and waterfalls, sweeping away bulrushes and dead branches in its wake. Ancient, delicate, yellow *Ansellia africana* leopard orchids clung to the trunks of mountain acacia trees. Bursts of scarlet from the flower of a kaffirboom tree (*Erythrina lysistemon*), its 'lucky beans' scattered around the base in a carpet of tiny shiny black-and-red dots.

Lugging our camping equipment, we walked for about half an hour along the river bank, admiring, as we went, these beautiful exotic blossoming flowers above our heads. Across a silent pond illuminated with mauve and yellow water lilies, a monitor lizard quietly slipped into the river, disturbing a bright orange dragonfly in its passing. The air down here had a mysterious aura to it, perhaps it was the smell of the rotting undergrowth and the hanging lianas, or the ethereal light filtering down from above, highlighting the millions of fine strands of cobwebs stretching from tree to tree like a gossamer canopy.

Presently, we came across my favourite camping spot, a wonderful site nestled among superb shade trees on a flat piece of ground above a waterfall that crashed and bubbled between a narrow granite face to form a superb natural rock slide, known locally as a 'foofy slide'. There was something creepy about that pool. Perhaps it was just too deep and too green for my liking. I always imagined the cold evil eyes of a crocodile slipping quietly beneath the surface to lie in wait for a victim.

The dogs returned from their adventure, tongues lolling from their frothy mouths. Bella, a miniature German schnauzer, was covered in sticky blackjack seeds and burs.

'Come here, you silly bugger,' I commanded. 'And is someone going to go hunting for scoff?'

Everyone had a duty at these camps. The group split up, with one gang setting off with the rifle to bag a few bush doves for dinner. They were going to walk along the river as far as 'Ndegi', which in Swahili means aeroplane or bird. Ndegi is a large arable field where a trainee pilot from the RAF came down during the Second World War. The remains of the aircraft could still be seen strewn across the bush. Southern Rhodesia was one of the safest training areas for the RAF during WWII. For some, anyway. Not this poor bugger.

With a sharp whistle, the dogs took off after them. They would be gone for the best part of the day, so the rest of us set about collecting firewood and assembling the tent amid much cursing and laughter. We each cracked open a bottle of Castle Lager, deftly flipping off the top with another bottle. A couple of shots echoed down the river canyon. The hunters must have been in luck. There would be fowl for dinner tonight. We all settled down to a long and languid afternoon of teenage banter and laughter. By the time the lads returned, two miserable grey bush doves and a guinea fowl hung limply from Spike's waist, dried blood smeared across his khaki shorts. We had the fire crackling nicely, the tent erected and food stashed in the crook of a tree to keep it safe from the dogs, badgers, jackals and ants.

'What twats. Is that all you could get for the pot? Thank Christ for bully beef,' I snapped.

We decided to sleep outside under the stunning Milky Way, the tent there just in case of rain, which was unlikely at this time of year.

'Man, we can't eat these,' I said. 'There's fuck all meat on them.'

We tossed the doves over to the dogs, who attacked them as if they had never had a decent meal in their lives.

Lighting yet another Madison, I laughed, 'Fucking dogs – you'd think we never fed the goddamn things. Okay, who's for another beer?'

The mood was peaceful as the sun dipped and hit the peak of a nearby *kopje* illuminating it in an ethereal golden glow. The war was suddenly very far away. The horrors of what happened to the Moorcroft farm a few days earlier seemed like a distant memory. Someone passed around another Country Club cheroot. The cheroots were reserved only for special occasions. We sat back and looked at the waterfall cascading down the rocks into the deep pool.

'You know the Nyarowe has a more sinister side, don't you?' I said to the group. I simply couldn't help myself. I continued to my now rapt audience.

'I mean, it being the main artery where the terrs often head for R&R.'

I had their attention.

'Shit, man. It's pretty damn chilling to think that somebody might be watching our every move,' one of them said.

The others looked around at the dense surrounding bush. I laughed, trying to sound casual.

'Oh, come on. It's unlikely that even terrorists would compromise their position by murdering us. After all, they're here to hide out. Not to expose themselves.'

They remained unconvinced. The guerrillas would often hit

farmsteads and then disappear as silently as they had come, crossing the Nyarowe River on to the 13,000-acre M'sitwe Farm and thus fading into the bush like ghosts or shadows.

'Weren't your neighbours attacked recently?' Spike chipped in.

'Oh, yeah,' I answered. 'But that was a few weeks ago. The terrs would have scattered by now. Seriously, don't worry about it.' My mind drifted back to the last half-term exeat break from school. My dad and I were sitting on the veranda beneath a lush jade vine. It had just gone dark. The air was cool and we were watching the antics of a pair of long-tailed widow birds grubbing on the lawn before they headed off to roost. My dad was enjoying his whisky and soda and I a Castle Lager, when the agric-alert burst into action.

'God dammit,' muttered Woody, 'I wonder who the hell it is this time?'

'Control, control! This is Victor-Charlie One-One. Repeat, Victor-Charlie One-One. We are under fire, over!'

That was the call sign for Muir-of-Ord Farm. Ron and Val Grossmith were being attacked. Ron and Val were a stoic, semi-retired couple living ten miles or so from our house, but as the crow flies it was only a few miles across the valley in front of us. Suddenly the world in the direction of the Grossmiths was lit up with a spectacular firework display as tracer bullets and RPG rockets whistled and soared through the night sky. I clearly remember being more fascinated than terrified, thinking how amazing the colours were and how strange that we could not hear the explosions.

We continued drinking while listening to my mother on the radio speaking with Val, checking if she was okay, offering encouragement but ultimately helpless. This was their battle, and, despite their age, Ron and Val would simply have to weather the storm. While Val calmly filled magazines with 7.62mm rounds, Ron kept up a heroic barrage of bullets, finally scaring off the attackers. Only cosmetic damage was inflicted, a rocket straight through the sitting room, and several smashed windows. But the psychological damage would remain for much longer.

I shivered and looked at my mates lounging around the camp site.

'Come on, you guys – last one in is a nincompoop!'

Laughing and shouting, we stripped naked and dived into the cool, green water of the Nyarowe.

The blood-red sun set over the granite *kopje* across the river, occasionally highlighting the eerie ancient rock walls surrounding the steep cliff, now guarded over by tiny furry hyraxes or dassies, silent sentinels perched on these battlements in the sky. As dark descended, and the rock surface changed from gold to indigo and then black, the bush around us began to take on an eerie murkiness.

In Africa, there is no twilight. Suddenly it is dark. Dark as only Africa can be, with a sky as vast as eternity and the Milky Way, with its Southern Cross painted like a massive peppered smudge across a giant black canvas. We huddled down around the fire, feeding it sticks and wood, the sparks exploding into the night sky. And like all teenage boys, we began talking about what comes naturally – girls and sex. Girls and sex, sex and girls, and more sex.

The alcohol began to kick in. The heady, damp vegetation and the warm glow of the fire added to the atmosphere. We were still naked from the swim and our pink skins glowed in the firelight. Inevitably, we began comparing boners. Who was the biggest. Who was a Roundhead. Who was a Cavalier. Measuring and summing up. Of course, at school we all cavorted around starkers, but this was something else. I was not unaware of the silliness and seriousness of my predicament. I stared around the fire at the group of boys, peachy skins glowing in the firelight.

'Well, this is all terribly grown-up,' Elliott said. His sarcastic tone was lost on me.

Freemantle giggled. There was an embarrassed silence. At that moment Bella broke the spell by bolting into the camp. Our night was about to change.

The dog was shaking with fright. Something was up. She cringed next to me, her body trembling, spooked. Anxiously we looked around, peering into the inky darkness, at the same time scrambling for our shorts.

'Quick! Put out the damn fire!' Foxy commanded.

All conversation ceased. The sudden silence seemed to ring in my ears. I heard one boy struggling with the bolt of the .22, trying to load a round in the darkness. We were drunk and flustered and much too young. The round jammed in the chamber, rendering the weapon useless. Bewilderment spread across our faces.

'Look,' I whispered, 'it might be nothing...' but as the words tumbled from my mouth, a flaming torch caught all of our attention down on the opposite bank of the river.

Moving silently in between the riverine trees, disappearing behind a rock or bush, this sinister apparition would reappear, always drawing nearer. It seemed like an eternity as we held our breath waiting for it to show itself again.

'There!' Spike whispered, 'it's getting closer.'

'Fuckin' weapon! Why does it have to jam now? Fuck, fuck, fuck,' groaned a voice in the darkness. It was Elliott.

But his voice had echoed across the canyon. Almost immediately the torchlight went out. Now the shit was going to hit the fan. We had been compromised.

'They've heard us. Bugger it...'

'No shit! Let's get the fuck out of here!'

There was nothing to it but to move away from the camp, and move away pronto. Like shit off a shovel, to coin a phrase from my dad. But where? Trying not to panic, we all crept off into the thick bush in silence. Our eyes wide like the bush babies that lived in the trees near the back of the house.

Every time someone trod on a dead twig, the crack made our hearts lurch and our sphincters tighten.

'Shit, ouch, shit. Goddammit, there are thorns!' Freemantle squeaked.

'Stuff the thorns – hurry up,' Spike hissed.

We quickly decided the best plan would be to make our way through the dense bush and eventually hit the road a mile or so further on. Then it would simply be a mad dash back to the house and safety. The Land Rover was out of the question. It was right in the path of the enemy. And, of course, they might have laid down landmines. Dirt roads were constantly mined and had become an absolute curse.

An owl hooted somewhere in the distance, and some nocturnal

animal dashed across our path in the gloom. It was a porcupine, rattling its quills to keep us at bay. We huddled together, the two people on the outside constantly moving and muscling into the centre like some mad modern ballet or a blind Irish dance troupe, as if being in the middle would afford extra protection. As if being in the middle made you safe. No one wanted to be on the outside, exposed.

We continued along the road in silence, bumping into one another, skin against skin, trying our best to become invisible. After ten long minutes we reached the road. As we emerged from the relative safety of the trees we glanced up to the sky. To our horror, the moon was full and the sandy road made our bodies stand out like beacons in the darkness.

'Bloody hell!' Spike exclaimed. 'We look like flippin' sitting ducks.'

Against the white sand of the road and the full moon, we were indeed sitting ducks.

'Let's take our clothes off,' Foxy suggested.

We looked across at him.

'Are you stark raving mad? What the fuck are you talking about? This is hardly the...'

'No, man!' he whispered. 'Look at us – our skins are white. The road is white. The goddamn, fucking moon is white, twat face!'

We needed no further persuasion. Too terrified to venture back into the bush, we decided on the only coherent action. We stripped off. Bundling our shirts and shorts under our arms, we were relieved to see that our fish belly white skins blended into the light-coloured sand of the road.

'Fox, you're a daft bugger,' I said smiling in the darkness, 'but a clever daft bugger.'

'Somehow I don't think they do this in the army,' a voice commented in the gloom.

I stifled a giggle.

'Shhhhh.'

Without another word being spoken, we took one last hysterical look at each other and moved off down the road. Bump, bump, shuffle, shuffle. You could smell the fear, but not the irony. Naked together, once again.

The situation must have been a rare sight to encounter.

But the night was not yet finished with us. To our utter horror, in the distance, sudden flashes of light exploded across the sky in the exact direction of the house.

'Jesus! What the fuck is that? The house is being attacked!' I gasped.

'How d'you know?' Freemantle barked.

'It could be fucking lightning.'

'Look at the stars you toss pot! There's no goddamn rain for miles!'

'Jesus H Christ. Stop bitching you two! We can't go back. We can't go forwards. What the fucking hell do we do?'

Again the flashes lit up the night sky. But there was something amiss. Something surreal about these unearthly flashes of light.

'Surely, if we were being attacked, we would hear the shots?' I suggested.

'After all, we are only a mile or so from home. The sound would carry, even if the wind was against us.'

I tried to concentrate. When the Grossmiths had been attacked, we heard nothing. AKs tend not to make much noise. More like a pop, pop, pop. The FN on the other hand made a fucking racket. We would hear the FN wouldn't we? Think clearly. Make a decision for these terrified teens.

'We go forwards,' I said. 'Keep to the plan. Watch out for landmines. Keep your eyes peeled guys.'

I explained that with there being no sound coming from the homestead, we might just be imagining something. We pressed on. No one was interested in arguing. Walking into a firefight seemed infinitely better than going back to the dark, creepy camp site. With an occasional furtive glance backwards, we managed to keep our eyes peeled on the road ahead for any tell-tale signs of upturned earth that may hide the danger of a mine.

After half an hour, we reached the bottom of the security fence surrounding the garden. I realised something was wrong.

'Shit. The security lights are off and the house is in total darkness.'

We crouched behind the garage wall and waited. Five minutes. Ten minutes. The silence was deafening. Even the chorus of frogs copulating by the pool seemed to have shut up. Eventually, I started to call out to my father.

'John?' No response.

Again I called. 'JOHN!' No response. Finally, I heard my father's voice. He must have been keeping out of sight behind the veranda wall. What the hell was going on?

'Is that you, Pete? Are you guys alone?' he called.

'My god. He thinks we are being held hostage,' I whispered.

It was a ploy used occasionally by terrorists to lure farmers to their imminent death.

'Ja. We are alone,' I called.

Still he did not reveal himself. I tried to laugh, make light of the situation, trying to get him to believe me. Foxy decided to change the game and spoke to my dad in Afrikaans, hoping this would do the trick.

'Nee John. Ons is alleen. Ek sweer.'[65] No doubt this added to his confusion. Woody did not speak a word of Afrikaans. I glared at him in the darkness. Foxy shrugged, it was worth a try. After what seemed an interminable period of time, my father walked out to the gate. The FN semi-automatic held out at an angle in front of him, ready to fire. I cannot remember a time when I have been so relieved to see him.

'What the bloody hell is the matter with you kids?' he said, unlocking the gate.

'Why have you returned from the camp?'

Stammering, I explained our predicament. He glanced at the other kids, looking at their naked bodies without so much as a raised eyebrow and laughed.

---

[65] 'No, John. We are alone. I swear'.

'Bloody kids. There was a big bush fire down there last week, you twits. It was probably just a burning tree stump catching in the wind. Honestly, Pete, I had no idea you were such a townie these days.'

Needless to say, with a backward glance he quickly hustled us into the house and locked the security fence. Between that crazy moment of sheer exhaustion, elation and downright childish giggling, we scrambled to put on our clothes. I asked him about the security lights.

'Listen, you lads,' he ventured, 'the flashing lights you saw was due to a power failure. The Electricity Supply Commission in Mutorashanga was simply testing the power.'

Every time the power came back on, the lights would flash out across the dark bush.

'Nothing to be alarmed about. Now get to bed. It's late.'

He shook his head and walked back to his room. His explanation all made perfect sense, and having sent the other four kids to bed, my father took me aside and sat me down.

'Look, Pete,' he explained, 'I'm not sure what that was you saw. I will take a walk down there tomorrow and have a look. But after you left for the camp I had a call from Special Branch. They were confirming information that our house is due to be attacked tomorrow night. I thought it best not to panic you chaps. In fact you probably would have been safer at the river anyway, that's why I sent you down there.'

I didn't tell my friends about this for weeks.

And my father, thank goodness, didn't ask why we were all naked.

The next day, the household kicked into party mode. Afternoons in Africa are generally so quiet that for those more used to city life it can be almost unbearable. Not even the bush doves call, nor do the go-away-birds warble out their sad 'go-way, go-way'. The sounds of the farmyard die down, the tractors are parked in the shade, the farm boys asleep in their compounds. Only the distant click-clicking of the bamboo grove down at the sheep pen breaks the monotony as the tall, smooth branches expand in the heat. Or the occasional snap of a monkey-bread pod as it heats up and explodes, spraying seeds over the ground.

But on this particular afternoon, the homestead was a hive of activity. From the pool area, there were intermittent splashes and shouts as the kids swam and played, or lounged under the thatched *rondavel* by the water's edge. Inside the house, cooled by the smooth, polished Sinoia slate floor and high ceilings, a constant flip flop of heels could be heard as my mother moved from one end of the long L-shaped veranda to the other, arranging vases of roses, chrysanthemums and Gypsophila, shaking out tablecloths and laying them on trestle tables, delegating staff and moving furniture in the dining room, where the dance floor would be.

Vinyl records were carefully being stacked in order of play next to the old Bush stereo. Five fast; one slow; four fast; one slow; two fast; two slow. Towards the end of the evening the music would all be slow shuffles allowing the teenage couples to become more intimate. Most of the music came from my cousin Madeleine. Her mum, Sue, managed to get all the records for free from Gallo, where she worked. My own collection was questionable, not entirely surprisingly given my father's loathing for anything musical.

Madeleine's room was adorned with posters of Bowie, The Stranglers, The Sex Pistols, Debbie Harry and, for sentimental reasons, some older ones of a gloriously back-lit Peter Frampton and The Bay City Rollers in their bizarre striped socks and fantastic high-heeled boots. Her bed was always strewn with well-worn copies of *Smash Hits* or *Melody Maker* sent out from the UK by her dad. Walking around Mad's room was like a trip through 1970s British music.

Down at the guest cottage the girls were busy with curling tongs, making up, trying on clothes. There were skinny midriffs, hipsters, bell-bottoms, heavy blue eye shadow, gypsy tops and halter-necks. Despite the international sanctions, Estée Lauder and Revlon still managed to get through. Most farmhouses in those days had their own bar stocked with 'lethal' Rhodesian gin, vodka, scotch and mixers. Not for the kids, of course.

For tonight, a selection of farmers from around the district would descend on Woody's bar and ride shotgun, should any trouble occur. The bar itself was built by my father from the hard black indigenous iron-wood trees that dotted the nearby bushveld – the same wood used to make the flutes for bagpipes. The walls of the bar were festooned with trophies. Cape buffalo and sable antelope skulls loomed over the sofas, their arched horns resplendently proud, while bushbuck, impala and zebra skins lay strewn across the floor. On the bar, a set of ivory dice in a furry box made from a dried reedbuck scrotum and a silver-inlaid ice box made from a hippo's foot, sat centre stage in rather grotesque fashion. On one wall, a beautiful glossy leopard skin was stretched and pegged. Another old rogue shot several years earlier after it had started killing calves. Behind the bar, a pair of giant warthog tusks and a menacing baboon skull.

Of course, the bar was not entirely a man's world. My mother had still managed to create a feeling of comfort by arranging vases of dried flowers cut from the bush and garden. There were pampas, bulrush, dried calabash, Chinese lantern and papyrus. The shelves were stacked with beautiful reference books on Michelangelo, Titian, Van Gogh, JM Dent & Sons' beautifully bound *History of Fashion*, *Encyclopaedia Britannica* and, of course, stacks of untidy photo albums mapping our lives in shambolic detail.

This was a bar designed to both amuse and interest but, above all to fascinate. Many an hour was lost lying on the sofa reading the books and leafing through the stacks of old albums, excitedly examining the gorgeous torso of Michelangelo's David, or guiltily tracing my fingers along the veins running down the arms of Moses. There were certificates from the Pioneer Society proudly proclaiming us as 'Grandsons of Pioneers'. There were framed photos of my brother in the army, a creased black-and-white of my father standing next to a dead elephant, my mother trying to look like some movie star. My sister all made-up like a Charlie's Angel.

An old musket rifle hung above the window, and above another window the skin of a python that we thought had swallowed a piccannin some years back. We were wrong. The bulge fortunately turned out to be a small reedbuck. On the coffee table were old editions of *Harpers & Queen*, and a catalogue about Palace House, Beaulieu, Hampshire, where my mother would constantly remind guests that her cousin, Fiona, was *the* Lady Montagu. And always along the walls and behind the pictures scuttled the geckos, huge and fat from an endless diet of insects that were attracted to the lights in the evenings.

In the spacious kitchen and out at the back of the house, Fred was issuing orders to the staff. Fred was in his element. He loved the drama of these parties. The time to show off his skills. His knowledge. He also got to catch up with some of the other cooks, such as the Moorcrofts' chef Manuel, who was over to lend a hand. Manuel was originally from Mozambique and brought with him the extraordinary flavours of Portuguese cuisine. Much of this rubbed off on Fred. They both knew all my friends and occasionally during the day would pop their heads round the corner to say hello, have a chat or ask for a Coke. Fred, like most long-serving staff, was well-versed in my parents' moods, their movements, their habits, but more importantly, he had witnessed the work that had gone into this hard, unforgiving farm, and had watched it prosper.

Like many good head chefs, Fred was an important figure both among his peers and their employers in the district. When he answered the phone, he would take on our surname and announce, 'Hello, Fred Wood here', much to the amusement or confusion of the caller. We were not to know that this use of the master's surname originated in the slave quarters of the British West Indies. Macarena, the Haringtons' nanny, had learned her English from Jean Harington, and spoke such perfect Queen's English that callers would often mistake her for Jean.

Fred was overseeing the food and drinks for the party. A huge zinc tub out the back near the boiler was filled with blocks of ice, cool drinks and beers. A bottle opener tied by nylon twine hung from the handle of the tub. A large Virginia ham, boiled in spices and ginger beer, was being sliced on to large platters, salads were being tossed, and trifles and crème caramels were being turned out on to glass trays. Small dishes of home-made beef and buffalo biltong were being delicately sliced into small snack dishes to be taken down to the bar, as were roasted monkey-nuts and far-far, a curried Indian snack. Meanwhile, the silverware and crockery were getting a final polish before being taken out to the tables on the veranda and placed between luscious centrepieces of tiger lily, roses and frangipani.

Towards late afternoon the first convoy of cars began arriving, bringing with it a fine cloud of red dust. Because of the danger of being ambushed on the roads, people always arrived and departed together. The first to come were the adults assigned to guard the house, a collection of friends and neighbours. Each with their own histories. All with their own stories.

There was Robbie Walmsley, nephew to Beatrix Potter, who had lost an entire, irreplaceable collection of his aunt's first-edition memorabilia when his thatched house burned down. At the bar was Tim Harington, whose family were the Arbuthnots of Scotland. Even a town was named after them. And of course Tim's wife, Jean, who used to work for the British Secret Service. Bill Francis arrived with my pals James, William and Annabel. James was my naughty partner-in-crime buddy and Annabel was my secret crush. So secret, not a soul knew. Bill was arguably the most successful farmer in Umvukwes and was also the chairman of the Rhodesia Farmers Association.

It was a beautiful time of day to arrive, with the garden looking at its best. Wide, verdant, rambling lawns of Australian evergreen and kikuyu grass stretched down past the security fence to the drive. Hot pink bougainvillea tumbled over the gateway, mauve jacaranda trees shaded the vehicles from the fading sun. The heady smell of moon flower and jasmine, rambling rose and orange and mandarin blossom filled the evening air. Banks of bizzie lizzie and petunia tumbling from baskets around the patio. It all looked so benign.

By sundown all the guests had arrived, making their way across the lawn to the veranda and the bar. Excited chatter, laughter and greetings echoed across the house while rifles and revolvers were stashed behind the bar, hidden but close enough should they be needed.

The party got off to a good start. The adults got sloshed. The kids got close. The music slowed. The lights in the sitting room were dimmed. The noise in the bar continued unabated. Eager mouths and hungry fingers probed the teenage flesh on the dance floor. Then my father snapped.

It began as a slow, deep rumble, increasing in volume in just a few seconds. From across the garden near the cottage, I could hear the commotion begin, and very quickly reverberate across the lawn and into the house. Silence quickly descended. The needle of the record player rudely screeched across my Linda Ronstadt LP. The rooms, one second ambient and dark, were now unceremoniously thrown into bright light. Confused, dazed and inebriated kids caught unawares. A couple of rather plain wallflowers were standing in one corner with wide eyes observing the hoo-ha. Surprised parents poured out of the bar, weapons cocked. Their eyes darting around to see what was afoot.

My father, unfortunately, had walked in on two teenagers entwined on the double bed in the cottage. His outrage in having discovered this disgusting carnal act of indecency, together with the knowledge that we might expect an attack from the terrorists at any moment, was enough to bring him crashing to his senses. My father was someone who did not particularly enjoy music, children and – very possibly – sex (in that order), and this was the perfect time to end off, round off, and cool off. His voice bellowed across the lawn and continued unabated for a full ten minutes, by which time any chance of recreating the atmosphere previously being enjoyed by all had long since evaporated. Several weeks of careful planning down the drain in a matter of seconds.

'Bloody disgusting brats! Fornicating under my very own roof. They should be SHOT!' was one phrase many children would take home with them that night.

'Oh, for god's sake, John, calm down.'

It was Mona Moorcroft, one the few women who had any power over him. Alas, tonight he was not for turning. Adults rounded up their charges in hushed groups and, thanking my mother for the wonderful evening, departed en masse to their homes. For many it meant 25 or 30 miles on dirt roads. It seemed a better option to brave the landmines and ambushes rather than face my father's wrath.

As soon as it started, it was over. My father was never one to hold a grudge. Besides, it was way past his bedtime. With a final grumble, he marched off to his bedroom and flipped off the power, plunging the entire house into darkness.

Most kids from Salisbury were to remain the night, and very soon muffled laughter or murmured conversation could be heard from distant corners of the building as friends and new-found lovers recapped the night's activities. At no stage had any of the children been told about the imminent attack, and it was to my mother's utter horror that the following morning she was to walk outside and find several kids fast asleep beneath shrubs and bushes in the garden. Images of an RPG rocket screeching towards the dance floor, or the white-hot tracers searing across the garden at the sleeping children was enough to give her nightmares for a long time. And yet, for now, notwithstanding the drama from the previous night, the party was a roaring success and would be talked about for many months to come. Perhaps the gods had favoured our happy gathering that night, yet they were in no mood to tolerate us the morning after.

After breakfast, my mum and the kids from the city piled into the two cars and departed for Salisbury. Once again the farm was plunged into silence, so heavy it seemed to weigh down upon us like a gravitational field. Nursing a sore head, I went into my room for a nap. I caught myself drifting deeper and deeper into sleep, trying to claw my way back up to the surface; the book I was reading slowly falling to thc floor beside me. A suicidal bluebottle buzzed around, continually crashing against the glass pane until finally dropping with a thud to the window sill. A final buzz or two, then still.

As the world closed in on me, my brain began to pick out the distant sounds of my mother's voice, initially dreamlike; a voice that at first seemed so far away it was difficult to discern what was being said or even the tone. But very soon the anxiety and panic in the voice started hitting home. Crashing through layer upon layer of sleep-induced fog.

'John! John! Come quickly … there has been a terrible accident!'

My immediate reaction, naturally, was to believe that they had been ambushed. The sudden guilt, the anxiety and the horror is impossible to describe. This had been my party. They were my friends. Of course I was responsible. We had assured all their parents that we would take good care of them. My dad and I rushed outside to meet my mother. My father taking control, calming, dependable, solid. In the panic and commotion, the story began to unfold.

Foxy had taken the lead in the rental car. His passengers were my cousin Madeleine in the front seat, her friend Beverly in the back with Spike and Shaun. On Bev's lap, was Bella the schnauzer, who had unexpectedly, come into heat and was going into town to get laid by some pedigree mate. Two minutes behind, came my mum with the rest of the guests. As she drove over a rise in the road, she instantly saw the rental car pulled over to one side.

'Oh, for god's sake, surely they don't want to spend a penny so soon?' she grumbled.

Then her heart lurched.

'Christ. They've been attacked.'

From all four doors, kids were falling out. Smoke or steam rose from the front of the car in a thick cloud. Children fell to the ground, faces contorted in confusion and shock. From my mother's vantage point, it did indeed look like an attack, but where the hell were the terrorists? Where was the flash of AK-47s? The bush around either side of the road was fairly barren – very little space for any ambusher to hide. This was the dry season. The grass had been chewed down to the roots by the cattle. Could it be a landmine? For the next 20 seconds no one spoke until she pulled her car alongside and discovered the real story.

The front end of the Datsun seemed to have crumpled like paper and disappeared up and under the front seats. A huge white concrete culvert protecting a storm drain had been sliced diagonally in two by the impact. Taking in the situation in an instant, noting the blood pouring from Shaun's face, Foxy sitting on the ground in shock, Madeleine and Beverley appearing to be okay, albeit dazed, her terror immediately turned to anger.

'What the bloody hell has happened?' she demanded.

It was a perfectly straight road. What could possibly have gone wrong? Clearly it was an accident, but why for god's sake? In broad daylight on a straight road. And in a rented car being illegally driven by a 16-year-old. A quick head count ensured that no one was missing or dying. She put her first aid to work. Shaun had bitten straight through his tongue, causing severe bleeding, but little pain. He would have a lisp for the rest of his life, which would prove to be a great pull on the ladies.

Foxy had broken his nose on the steering wheel, managed to give himself a nice shiner and was more in shock than anything else. Beverley had a gash in her face that would need stitches and Spike had a cut on his leg that would leave a scar for life. Fortunately, all farmers' wives did first-aid lessons each week and my mother was able to patch up the bleeding without much fuss. It was the shock that worried her most. Shock, she knew, was a killer.

Grabbing the rifle Shaun had been holding, and piling the kids into her car, she turned around and headed back to the farm at break-neck speed, at the same time trying to make sense of what had just occurred.

'Now,' she demanded, 'what happened? You had better have a damn good excuse. John is going to be furious.'

Foxy, in a state of shock and unable to comprehend anything, let my cousin Madeleine, who seemed to be the only one in a sensible state of mind, tell the story. It was no secret that Foxy had fancied Madeleine for several months, writing to her, calling her, and generally making a nuisance of himself, as any love-struck teenage boy would. Madeleine had indulged him for many reasons. He was my best friend, and Madeleine adored me. She was flattered by his attentions, he was generous and amusing, he was charming, clever and erudite, and we were a part of a teen gang who hung out together.

But Foxy had a problem. His vanity. So vain, in fact, that when driving the car that day, under-aged, hung-over, with little driving experience under his belt and with Madeleine sitting next to him, he refused to wear his glasses, which, to be fair, were rather naff and nerdy. Yet the passengers did notice his erratic driving.

'Dammit, Fox. Where are your specs?' Shaun asked.

'You're driving like a drunken bum,' Spike added.

'Okay, okay...' Foxy concurred and leaning across the passenger seat, he fiddled in the glove compartment for his glasses. He never saw the culvert, never noticed the car rapidly moving towards the side of the road. The vehicle hit the concrete barrier at 50 miles per hour, flying 25 or more feet through the air, and landing on its nose, the force of which rammed the engine up and under the driver's seat. The car was a write-off. The kids were simply lucky. As was Bella.

Back at the house, first-aid kits were pulled out, bandages, Mercurochrome and cotton pads were tossed aside as soon as they became saturated in blood. A sprained ankle was bound tightly. A silence descended while each person was laid on a bed or sent on a chore. Calm was finally being restored to the group of shocked teenagers. Well, everyone except my father and Foxy.

'Where's that sodding kid?' he roared.

'I am gonna bloody KILL HIM!'

This was my father in full fury, and it seemed the windows rattled with his deafening voice. Nearly an hour had passed since returning to the house, and it was only now that someone inquired whether anybody had seen Foxy? It dawned on us all that not only had Foxy disappeared, but so too had the gun. My father was not a malicious person, by any stretch of the imagination, but he demanded justice where justice was due. He had remained calm throughout the hour following the accident. But now things began to change. Rapidly.

'Christ,' I said, looking up from bandaging a wound.

'I hope Foxy hasn't gone off and shot himself.'

He had been in shock. Unhinged, almost. Fortunately, as soon as my father realised that Foxy was missing, and had taken the gun, he changed tack and quietened down. For the next ten minutes we could hear my father walking around the house calling in a softer voice.

'Look, David. Please show yourself. I am not angry, just worried. Come on out now.'

Like a hunter, my dad stalked the house. Cupboards clicked open, then closed. Bed spreads were gently lifted. Doors squeaked open, then closed again. Minutes passed.

'Fred! Wa'naz ipi David?'[66]

'Ai'kona baas. Kabunga lapa cottage?'[67]

Everyone strained to hear that crack of the rifle.

'Please, Foxy,' I called. 'Don't do anything stupid.'

My initial shock was now turning to anger as I digested the events. What the fuck was he up to?

'Fucking Fox. Such a show off. He could have killed you guys. He could have killed Bella. What in god's name was he thinking?'

At that moment we heard my father's voice steadily talking from one of the spare rooms in the cottage.

'Come out now, David. Just come quietly. And please put that gun down immediately. Nothing will happen to you. You are not in any trouble.'

From out under a bed, Foxy emerged, stealthily, shamefaced, but alive. Ashen white. Without another word my dad took the rifle and walked calmly back across the lawn and into the main house.

The party was over.

---

[66] 'Fred. Do you know where David is?'

[67] 'No boss. Maybe in the cottage?' (Fred knew everything).

9

The Lunch Do

Farm life is governed by strict routine. The rainy season and the dry season, the fortnightly dipping of cattle, the weekly traipse to the club on Thursdays and, most importantly, the afternoon kip.

Another routine that never seemed to change was that of lunch. Always promptly at 12.30, Monday to Sunday. Occasionally, god forbid, this hallowed routine might be broken by the uninvited arrival of the fertiliser salesman turning up just before the bell, much to the annoyance of my mum and dad. One particular salesman had an irritating habit of timing it so perfectly that you had little choice but to invite him on to the veranda for a drink, then some lunch, often throwing the kitchen into disarray and leaving my father in a bad mood for the rest of the day.

Sometimes, Jehovah's Witnesses might be sent packing with a flea in their ear. My father would watch silently like a viper about to strike a mouse as the pair from *The Watchtower* would piously stroll up the lawn towards him, an armful of pamphlets clutched to their chests. Having defended themselves against the dogs, they now had my father to contend with.

'Well, you're wasting your time here, so you can get back in your car and bugger off,' Woody would say, looking around as if fire and brimstone were erupting beneath his feet.

'And another thing, I know I'm going to hell, AND I'M BLOODY WELL LOOKING FORWARD TO IT!' he would yell after them as they skedaddled down the hill to their Morris Minor.

He would stride after them shaking a fist and glaring at them in his best Charlton Heston 'down from the mount' look. They were never to know that it was not religion but the interruption of his lunch routine and his much loved pre-prandial G&T that angered him the most.

While my dad poured himself another well-earned Gilbey's and relaxed back in the shade of the ancient bougainvillea, mum, on the other hand, never stopped.

My mother has the most extraordinary energy I have ever known. I would watch her rush to the bottom of the garden to give instructions to the garden boy, then back up to the house to answer the phone, then back across the garden again to prune a shrub or deadhead a flower, then back into the sitting room to pull out some invoice or bill from the dried buffalo scrotum my father used to keep all-important bumf in, and always-but always stopping along the way to bend down and pull out a weed. On and on, never stopping. Weeding, dead-heading, weeding, dead-heading.

One of my strongest and most enduring memories was sitting next to Woody in the shade of the veranda, watching mum in her striped Capri pants dashing around or bending over pulling up weeds from the lawn.

'Christ, that woman just never stops,' Woody would muse.

'How she still has such a fat arse is beyond me?'

He would shake his head and stir in another gin.

Yet *she*, as he rather disparagingly called her, always had time to sit down and talk to me about the history of art, music, fashion and theatre. She was, and is, my inspiration. Where John taught me the importance of punctuality, truth and honesty, how if you look after the pennies, the pounds will look after themselves (something I was woefully inadequate at), mum taught me every colour of the rainbow and nurtured my creative side.

She played us old, scratchy recordings of Laurence Olivier in *Romeo and Juliet* and Gielgud in *Julius Caesar*, weaving us stories of the tragedy and the wonder of Shakespeare. She pulled out books on the great Renaissance painters, explaining the soft light employed by the Dutch masters, the ghastly horrors of Hieronymus Bosch, to the fascinating and seedy life of Toulouse-Lautrec and the Moulin Rouge, the madness of Van Gogh, the fleshy Rubenesque curves, and Da Vinci's genius. And above all she taught me how to connect with the world. How to embrace life. How to be a human being. How to love. I have fond memories of those school holidays spent on the farm, learning to paint and draw from my mother and learning about the bush and about Africa from my father.

At 12.30pm on the dot, Konda would ring the bell for lunch.

'Jesus,' Woody would mumble, 'he's always on bloody time. I still have half a drink to finish.'

Of course, Woody would be the first to complain should Konda be late.

For most of my life on M'sitwe, the kitchen was ruled over by these two extraordinary men called Fred and Konda. Fred was older, the cook. His wife was nanny to all three of us kids and we absolutely adored them. Fred was sent out by granny Wood to look after my dad when he was a bachelor living in a grass hut at the bottom of the hill.

Unsurprisingly, Fred and Nanny knew everything there was to know about us. All my childhood, Fred was always there. He was part of the fabric of the family. Servants often stayed with one family for life. We had Fred, the Moorcrofts had Manuel, my gran had Gresham, the Francis family had Jennifer, the Haringtons had Macarena. This was how it was, the same cook boys and maids all our lives.

Konda was a huge blue-black man from Malawi, or Nyasaland as he liked to call it, with sinewy muscles stretching down his workman's arms and across his chest. His biceps were massive and hard as steel. When Konda tightened the top on the tomato sauce, no one could ever open it again. It took inverting the bottle in hot water to expand the top, tying a rag around it and twisting with all your might. Rarely did we succeed.

'For god's sake Konda,' my mother would groan. 'Can't you just close a bottle normally?'

Despite his strength, Konda was always terribly gentle towards us kids. In all my years I never heard him raise his voice. This beautiful trait often drove my father bonkers and it was not unheard of for John to hurl an ashtray at the retreating statuesque figure of Konda in frustration.

Fred and Konda loved us kids, of that I am certain, and they often felt compelled to protect us against my father's short temper, once even grabbing my siblings and me, tucking us under their arms and dashing down to the bottom of the garden to safety.

Both servants had been sacked a few times. Life without Fred or Konda soon became untenable. The simplest thing in the world became a nightmare. Tomato sauce bottles aside, it was often the mundane tasks that finally defeated us. I have often watched my mum open packets of cereal or biscuits like a wild animal, ripping the packaging apart then pawing down the innards. Surely this comes from a lifetime of having a cook to do all the opening for her or a houseboy who loved tightening bottles with the strength of Samson. It fascinated me to watch a trivial task become an epic display of tearing, pulling, and gnashing of teeth. The outcome would inevitably end in tears with Post Toasties flying across the room in every direction followed by a rather curt, 'Oh, shit. Where the hell is Konda when you need him?'

Within days, either Konda or Fred was quietly and without fanfare, reinstalled to his rightful place. At most this might have raised my father's eyebrows as he buttered his toast.

Life in the Wood household went back to normal.

In sharp contrast to the home-grown lunch, but no less regimented, is the 'lunch do'. People would drive for miles over dusty, corrugated roads on a Sunday, arriving like clockwork at 11.30 am. Lunch parties would go on until late at night and cost a small fortune. John always set up the bar under the jacaranda, barking orders at the staff like a sergeant major while mum did the flowers and food, all laid out on long tables on the veranda. Fred would be prepping, marinating, stewing and stirring for days in advance.

These lunches were occasions that also allowed the dozen or so nannies from the different farms to meet up and catch up on gossip. Laying out colourful blankets under the shade trees away from the main party and out of earshot of the guests, they would sit and crochet doilies, hats and tablecloths, turning a ball of dull string into a work of art. Stretching their legs out in front of them, they would drink sweet Tanganda tea from chipped enamel mugs and chat in loud voices, their small charges running around and rolling in the dirt with abandon.

These epic lunches were a 'Who's Who' of landowners in the Umvukwes district. If you did it, you did it properly; and if you did it, you did it big. Many farmers in the area had frightfully glamorous lunches, that required re-training staff to manage and understand the quirky ways of their *murungu* bosses, often with questionable results. John Strong, a local pig farmer, had to teach his cook boy to spit-roast a suckling pig. Since John's knowledge of Shona was limited and the cook's knowledge of English even more so, he had to go into the kitchen and act out how to stuff the animal. Never having been great at charades, John grabbed a bunch of dates in one hand and an apple in the other, and attempted his best to explain.

'Now, Phineas, watch what I am doing carefully,' he commanded in his plummiest accent. 'First you put the apple in its mouth,' he dramatically mimed, illustrating the task by pointing to the apple and directing it to his mouth. 'Then you stuff the dates up the arse,' he continued, again acting it out and patting his backside just in case the cook wasn't sure.

And so, the scene was set, the stage lit, the guests having arrived in all their finery, the cut-glass decanters twinkling off their jewelled earrings, and the fine South African Roodeberg going down a treat. At the given hour, and the donging of the gong, the guests took their seats in what was one of the finest dining rooms in the district. And then it happened, the moment they were all waiting for. TA-DA!

The huge double doors swung open and in came a rather startled, if not bemused Phineas with an apple in his mouth. As the Strong family matriarch, Joyce, pointed out in her best West End pronunciation: 'I didn't DARE ask where he put the dates.'

Another memorable event was the wedding of the gorgeous Leslie Chance to Mark Cutter, held in the garden of Leslie's parents, Betty and Martin. It was on their stunning farm, Nyarowe, which overlooked the purple and mauve hills of the Great Dyke. Les had broken away from tradition by asking a young, hip priest to conduct the garden ceremony, rather than Father Basil French, who was adored in the district, but did tend to be somewhat traditional when it came to ceremony. Clearly, there was a certain amount of rivalry between Father French and the young usurper. My diary on Saturday, 23 September 1978 states simply:

The priest was young and Father French did not approve because the young one said things like 'Well Mark – now you've got her' instead of 'I Now Pronounce you Man and Wife'.

Father French had the cheek to say, 'Leslie – you do realise that you have not been married in the eyes of God?'

Leslie's wedding attracted the crème de la crème of the farming communities, from the Victory Block to Umvukwes, Centenary and Bindura and beyond. Scattered across the lawn, chatting and gossiping and catching up with old friends was a colourful fascination of hats that would have made Ascot proud. The constant jangle of bangles as glasses of Pimm's were raised to lacquered lips. A posse of loud dames would be followed by an overwhelming pong of too much scent. It was a stiflingly hot day and my mum couldn't help noticing that our neighbour, Jean Harington, was wearing a jacket.

'What on EARTH are you wearing a blazer for Jean – aren't you hot?'

Jean was wonderfully funny and never really fazed by anything. Tall and willowy, she was a natural clothes horse, but because of that, or despite, she didn't particularly bother as much as her fellow farmers' wives about fashion. She wore her clothes well, but without ceremony.

'Well, Libby,' she explained with a laugh, 'just look what Macarena has done.'

She removed her jacket and revealed a large hole the size and shape of an iron right in the centre of her back.

'It was just such a jolly expensive dress, it seemed such a shame not to wear it.'

This was not surprising coming from a lady who ordered her daughter Joanna to drive all the way across Salisbury to return a newspaper to the vendor, all because Jean had already bought one earlier. At sixpence a paper, I suspect the petrol was slightly more pricey than the *Rhodesia Herald*.

All this dressing up for lunch occasionally had its disadvantages. Child drownings in Rhodesia were an epidemic. When I was three years old, once again at a lunch do, at Martin and Betty's, I decided to go for a swim. All the grown-ups were on the veranda enjoying their drinks and the breathtaking views across to the Dyke. I was paddling around in the shallow end of their pool about 50 yards away. Inadvertently, I got to the slope descending into the deep end and started to slide down, deeper and deeper, inch by inch, until my nose was just below the water.

Incredibly, my mum sat at the table watching this scene with a morbid fascination thinking, 'God, I wonder if he will make it? And I have false eyelashes on. Bugger!'

Betty, a former Springbok champion athlete and the only person I know who used to train-surf on top of the carriages in her youth, finally leapt from the table, shattering trays of drinks, upturning tables and vaulting the beds of petunias, sprinted across the lawn, dived into the pool and saved me. A couple of weeks later, I saw Betty in the village and I went up to her and said, 'Betty, I can *thwim* now.'

She looked at me over her glasses and said, 'Well I should bloody well think so with a mother like that!'

One learned to swim or sink at an early age and a few weeks later I was having lessons with a Mrs Gimble at The Settlers Inn pool in Raffingora. Standing in the shallow end holding me tightly, her ample bosom acting as ballast, she would take me through the tedious motions of breaststroke and crawl.

'Now, dear, think that you are a frog,' she would command, 'don't worry now, I am holding you, so don't be scared.'

Both my mum and I had neglected to tell poor Mrs Gimble that I could now swim, and I doubt if she ever did fully recover when later, at the bidding of my mother, I suddenly sprinted across the lawn and dived straight into the deep end. That was the end of Mrs Gimble's swimming lessons.

More often than not, these lunches were always followed by a long and winding drunken journey home through lonely countryside, over rocky roads. My father had an alarming habit of suddenly braking the car and staggering out into the moonlight to have a piss in what we imagined to be the most likely ambush spot on the entire journey. I have no doubt he did it deliberately.

At midnight, the canopy of crenelated *kopjes* towering over the road were frightening and forbidding. Creepy, twisted limbs of the *msasa* trees. Dead, leafless branches like the withered talons of an old witch doctor reaching out over the vehicle.

'Look at those stars!' he would growl, flailing his arms above his head, his pee frothing in the dust at his feet.

'For god's sake, John – get in the bloody car!' my mother would bleat as she glanced over at us kids cowering in the back seat.

'What's wrong with you all? You're just a bunch of bloody weeds! Sissies! Where in the world would you see such a magnificent sky? This …' he gestured, waving at the expanse of the Milky Way, the Southern Cross, Orion's Belt, 'is what we are fighting for!'

'Oh god,' Duncan would groan. 'Here we go again.'

After what seemed like an age, cupping his hands around the flame, he would light a fag, lurch back into the car and take off, the lonely beams of the headlights picking out the hundreds of iridescent moths and insects along the road. The occasional nightjar, soaking up any remaining warmth from the sandy track, suddenly startled into life by the engine and blinded by the light, would flap its wings in panic before smashing into the grille. Splat.

'I must remember to get Fred to pick that dead bird off the radiator tomorrow, otherwise the whole car will stink,' mum said absently.

Distance was never an issue in Rhodesia, even for the early settlers. My great-aunt Isobel Herbert had bought her first car, a Model T Ford, by the age of 20. To keep cool, it had a thatched roof, which at the best of times was a comical sight. A pretty young girl driving through town, cloche pulled tightly over her brow and looking like a runaway panto prop, must have brought the traffic to a grinding halt. Isobel's daughter, Fiona, later married Lord Montagu of Beaulieu, who owned the largest motor museum in Britain. One wonders if a thatched Model T made it into the collection.

One fateful day, after a trip to have lunch with friends who lived way out towards Marandellas, some 80 miles away, Isobel was all set to drive back to Salisbury when, to her horror, the car stuck in reverse. Not to be outdone by her 'Tin Lizzie' she simply reversed all the way home, thatched roof bouncing above her and shedding straw along the way. Of course, she had to visit St

Anne's hospital to have the crick in her neck sorted. Isobel was not timid by any means and like a good old Rhodesian girl, she took the hardships thrown at her on the chin.

While 80 miles in reverse in a Tin Lizzie might have been extreme, a 25 mile journey for us kids seemed to take forever. It was made all the more difficult when stuck in the back of the car with an irascible father. First, he would begin with mum, nagging at her and bickering, us kids motionless in the back, pretending to be asleep. Psychologists might have had a field day, but back in the early '70s, when men were men and my father was a man among men, this was simply par for the course.

We dreaded those journeys back from the lunch dos and I still shiver when I think about those awful, tedious drives home. To the outside world, my dad was charming and one of the funniest guys around. But to the inner circle, his alpha male traits were quite overwhelming. Thirty odd years later, I still bump into people who confess that they were terrified of my father. Christ, I think, you should have tried living with him.

Mum tried her best to stand up to the old bugger. Invariably she lost, and on a few occasions was actually thrown out of the car in the middle of the bush in the middle of the night.

'Get out and walk, you bitch!' he would scream, slamming on the brakes and shoving her out.

It was soul destroying. Peering back through the dust-streaked window we could see the rapidly diminishing figure of our beloved mum, dressed in stunning clothes, false eyelashes and bouffant hair. It was a forlorn sight that remains embedded within me to this day. African nights can be pitch-black and it must have been terrifying. But mum being mum, she would pick herself up, dust herself down, and walk the ten miles or so in the dark, often through country that was teeming with dangerous nocturnal wildlife, not to mention some very dangerous people. By morning she would be at the breakfast table, behaving as if nothing had happened.

On one such occasion, I couldn't bear it and as soon as we got home I jumped on to the motorbike and sped off into the night in search of her. I found her trudging down the lonely road, shoes in hand, laddered stockings, mascara smudged down her face. She looked like Blanche DuBois or some other tragic Tennessee Williams character. It must have been a pretty strange sight to see a woman dressed to the nines clinging on to the back of a Suzuki 125, panda eyes, stilettos slung over her back, and hair, still stiff from a ton of spray, stuck up at a jaunty angle.

One upside to the bush war was that the conflict put a stop to this. Even my father realised that he would never get away with it by then, but he never let her off too lightly and she was still in for a hammering once they got home.

'You're just a drunken bum!' she yelled at him one night, tossing her head, hoping he was too pissed to get out of the sofa.

Before she knew it, he was up like a bolt of lightning, chasing her across the veranda to give her a clip across the ear. Mum gave as good as she got, but John was stronger and frankly could be quite the bully. Mum always felt that intrinsically he hated women. He really was a man's man.

Some days my mum was let off the hook and so it was my sister Mandy or me next in the firing line. Mile after mile on those bumpy roads, getting nailed by Woody, every single fault you could imagine was barked back at us in that car. We were trapped and defenceless. We began to dread those journeys to the club and to lunch dos knowing what was in store for us later. I used to see other kids at school hugging their fathers or even, god forbid, talking back to them. It seemed like another world. I was jealous, and for most of my teenage years I loathed my father. He instilled in me a cold terror that tended to freeze me in my tracks.

One night, after a wonderful long lunch at Honk and Gina Hyde's at their Pembe Chase farm in Umvukwes, Mandy and I were trying to sleep in the back of the car. Occasionally, pretending to sleep got us some respite. On this occasion, John was arguing with mum about us kids. Bitching and moaning and teasing apart every fault he could find. It was miserable. Neither Mandy nor I will ever forget the words that came from John's lips.

'I can't help it Lib, but I just can't stand Mandy and Pete.'

It was quite a thing to say about your kids, but at least now we knew where we stood. Mandy and I silently looked at each other then went back to pretending to sleep, squeezing our eyes tight to stem the flow of tears. Woody breezed into breakfast the next day as if nothing had happened.

'What the hell's wrong with you lot?' he asked, raising a signature eyebrow.

'You all look like you're about to bawl. You bunch of miseries. Lib, pass the toast.'

He really was a nasty drunk. You didn't dare question him nor would you analyse the previous evening like some perfect American family. Nothing was ever said about those hurtful words until after my dad's death, when Mandy and I began to pick apart the life we lived with this maddeningly hard, yet colourful man. A man who expected us to shake his hand every night before going to bed, 'and shake like a bloody man, not some drippy Pom handshake!'

This was a man who made us watch news bulletins on the war in Vietnam and Kampuchea, 'because it will do us good', before allowing us to run off and play. A man who insisted on being called John and not dad because 'dad' was just sissy. A man who outlawed any form of music in the house. Ever. Yet still I loved him and tried desperately to please him and in his own strange way, I think he tried his best to love us, hard as it might have seemed at the time.

Apart from Cyril Hall, who was of Scottish descent and played the bagpipes every morning, most, if not all, managers and assistants employed by my father were solid, hard-working Afrikaans *volk*. The first manager we had was Mr Van Huyssteen, a simple, resolute man with a large brood of wild and unruly kids. Even to a child such as I, the difference in class was palpable. Our homes dripped with chintz and bone china, our lawns rolling across to the swimming pools, our manicured garden borders and hunting trophies proudly displayed on whitewashed walls. Our strict routine and silent lunches.

Cut to the Van Huyssteens place. Noisy and fun, corrugated-iron roofs, often with a pumpkin or two growing on top, or an old car tyre thrown on to the roof to stop the tin blowing off in the rainy season. Furniture was practical and threadbare, clothing home-made and built to last. Shoes were rarely worn except when going to the Dutch Reformed church in the Sinoia. There were naked dips in the water tank to cool off, and visits to the veggie garden to pick mulberries and Cape gooseberries to be made into jam.

These large, homely Afrikaans women had the best vegetable gardens I have ever seen. And always the most delicious aromas and smells coming from the Aga stove in the kitchen: sticky sweet *koeksisters*[68] dipped, still hot, into Lyle's Golden Syrup;

---

[68] South African doughnuts, from the Dutch *koekje* meaning 'cookie'.

wild honey gathered from the farm; roast yams and pumpkins sprinkled with exotic spices such as coriander, star anise and cardamom, brown sugar and a hint of dried hot chillies; and the welcoming waft of baking cakes and scones with lashings of granadilla[69] icing sugar.

Lunches down at the assistant's home were worlds apart from those at the big house. Noisy, happy, unbridled assaults upon our senses, Afrikaans food never seen in our house. These were rural folk with uncluttered lives. When my dad told Van Huyssteen that Kennedy had been assassinated, the response to my nonplussed father was, 'Oh, is that why there is a road block on the way to the club?'

Then again, this worked both ways, and when one day Mr Van Huyssteen rushed up to my father and revealed in a shocked hushed voice that Jim Reeves had died, my father's response was, 'Oh really? Does he farm in Umvukwes?'

While most farm assistants were good practical workers, there was always the odd exception to the rule. One chap was tasked to build our guest cottage at the bottom of the garden. Somehow, he managed to put every single door in upside down. Perhaps more surprising was the fact that they were never removed and put back on correctly and all my life we invited guests to stay in this shambolic cottage where all door handles lifted up rather than down. Oddly, the loo handle also went up instead of down – quite an accomplishment. The loo leaked constantly and my father's solution was to build an elaborate brick structure around the lavatory to stem the flow, ensuring that having a pooh was an experience akin to sitting on the Peacock Throne with your feet dangling in mid-air.

But quite possibly the most memorable thing concerning that

---

[69] Passion fruit.

guest cottage was the wildlife. I always felt so sorry for our guests from town. These hapless city slickers would arrive with a look of wonder and excitement as they unpacked their suitcases. But their euphoria was always short-lived and they would emerge next morning at the bell for breakfast, 8am on the dot looking wild-eyed and somewhat bleary.

'Good morning. Sleep well?' we would all chirp.

It was an in-house joke. Few townies could ever get used to the African night chorus and drama going on around them and above them. They would lie in bed petrified as the large picture mounted on the wall opposite would slowly move from one side to the other as if a poltergeist was present. Eventually, the head of a giant gecko would emerge, its tongue darting furtively as it tasted the air. We knew that if the ten-thousand frogs singing and croaking all night outside their window did not keep them awake, then the nightly Waterloo between the nine-foot mamba and the nest of grey African squirrels in the ceiling certainly would.

In truth, the noise from this battleground was rather disturbing, even for a hardened African. Flakes of paint would drift down on to their faces as guests lay mesmerised listening to the squealing, scratching, squeaking, sliding, and occasional silence. It was that toe-curling final silence that really got to you. Why the squirrels chose to live in the ceiling near a black mamba is questionable, but perhaps losing one youngster to the mamba every few days was a small price to pay in the greater scheme of things. After all, the fluffy rodents had the run of the garden during daylight hours and gave our dogs hours of unbridled fun chasing them across the lawn.

And it wasn't always the squirrels that came up against snakes. Mum had her share of run-ins. The garden was a paradise for cobras, pythons, boomslangs, puff adders and the inevitable black mambas. Mum was fearless. She believed they would always get out of your way.

'Anyway,' she would say, 'they have as much right to live here as we do. And they get rid of the rats. You know, I've never, ever seen a rat in our house.'

And for the most part, she was right. Besides she had the Jack Russells to alert her of any danger. Despite that, she occasionally did come face to face with a snake, once even cutting one in half with the secateurs.

We didn't have much of a menagerie compared to most other white African farm kids. I did have an aviary full of lovebirds brought up from the Zambezi Valley in woven straw baskets. They were beautiful but vicious little buggers, and if ever we tried to introduce other birds to the aviary we would soon find the newcomers on the floor, their legs brutally snipped off by the jealous rosy-faced parrots. So much for love. We finally released them into the wild and for years we would see the odd pair flying around the garden like brightly painted missiles. But I suspect most were eventually taken by kites or hawks.

Some of the wildlife was seasonal. The swallows returned every year to the cottage. Each season building their mud nest in the corner of the porch. The greater striped swallow (*Cecropis cucullata*) has a beautiful steel blue upper and a pale orange rump that shines and flashes as it ducks and dives over the fish ponds gathering insects, twigs and water. That corner of the cottage belonged to them and we would wonder how far they had migrated and whether they would still be there long after we were gone.

One day the cattlemen brought in a tiny orphaned serval[70].

---

[70] *Leptailurus serval* – a medium-sized African wild cat.

These beautiful spotted leopards in miniature, were rare in that part of the world. Leo was loved to death, quite literally. The poor animal was smothered, fed prime steak, coddled, cuddled and finally, at the young age of 18 months, laid to rest at the bottom of the garden with the rest of the dead pets. No one told us that wild cats needed roughage. Apparently they need feathers and hair mixed into their food. But more than likely, Leo died of cat flu, pure and simple.

We did have another orphan, a wild piglet. Again he did not last long. I strongly suspect his habit of rooting up mum's beloved flower beds sounded his death knell. The saddest wild pet we had was a baby baboon. He never recovered from the shock of being plucked from his mother. Fortunately, we had the sense to take him back to his troop. If memory serves me right, the little blighter was accepted back into the troop despite having been in our captivity for several days. A happy ending for at least one creature in a long line of disasters.

Snakes were a part of growing up back on the farm. But it was my sister who seemed to attract them the most out of everyone in the family. Hers was the coolest and darkest of all the rooms in the house, so it was a mystery why these cold-blooded creatures gravitated to her room.

On her bedside table, Mandy had a Spanish doll, possibly about 18 inches high with a massive, green, ruffled flamenco dress.

One winter holiday Mandy kept complaining to mum about a ghastly smell coming from her bedroom. Konda was brought in to clear the cupboard in case a mouse had crawled in and died. Nothing was discovered. The smell remained for the holidays. Then one morning Konda came rushing through to the veranda, his face ashen.

'Madam, madam,' he called, 'come quickly.'

My mum looked up from the bookkeeping, annoyed to be disturbed.

'It's the big doll, madam. The doll is dancing. It has come alive.'

They both rushed through the house to Mandy's bedroom and there, sure enough, the flamenco doll was dancing, swaying as if it had a life of its own. And then suddenly, to their combined horror, from beneath the ruffles of the dress emerged a glistening African rock python, hungry from six months hibernation and just inches from my sister's head. Pythons are a protected species and a quick phone call to Dave Dolphin, a local herpetologist, put paid to the danger and the smell. But that doll was never the same again.

Mandy was still not entirely off the hook. As boarders we all had black tin trunks with our names stencilled on the top. For days before we returned to school, these would stand open in our room as we packed a term's worth of uniforms and sports gear. The trunks would then be locked and chucked on to the back of the Land Rover and delivered to our school hostels. The hostel matron would be the first person to open the trunk to unpack the clothes. One start of term my mother took a frantic and disturbed call from my sister's matron.

'Mrs Wood. What on earth do you think you are trying to do!' screamed the matron at my unsuspecting mother. 'Are you trying to have me killed?'

'Now, calm down, Mrs Reoch,' cautioned my mum. 'What do you mean I'm trying to have you killed?'

On opening the trunk, the matron came face to face with a very angry, very venomous puff adder that must have slipped in between the jerseys and hockey skirts to hide. She was lucky to have escaped with her life.

Often during the Christmas holidays, *n'yau*[71] would come up to the house, much to the excitement of all. This was the only time that strange masked men were given carte blanche to walk around the garden as if they owned the place. The *n'yau* were fascinating characters, some with eyeless masks made entirely of guinea fowl feathers, others made from colourful strips of cloth suspiciously similar to the patterns from my mum's missing blouse, while others preferred rather sinister masks in the form of animals and weird ungodly creatures, often based on their totem or animistic protector.

This wild spectacle was always accompanied by drummers and dancers and hordes of kids screaming and singing. It was wonderful. Bags of sweets and loaves of bread would be taken out of the kitchen and distributed. It was a carnival atmosphere that was to mirror something far more serious many years later when my parents were evicted from the farm.

One particular year, the *n'yau* and their entourage had been and gone, the dust had settled and I was lying by the pool warming myself on the slate when my brother bellowed from the veranda: 'SNAKE!'

Alarm bells rang. I was blind as a bat and required glasses, which naturally were by my bed. Where else would they be? And where the fuck was the snake? Was it near me? Was I in danger? Panic ensued. I scrambled and sprinted across the lawn towards the house and to the source of my brother's voice.

'Cobra!' shouted Duncan, pointing to the blurred coil right in front of me.

Too late, my momentum was carrying me forward. I had no

---

[71] A Mashona witch doctor or soothsayer.

time to stop. I was almost on top of the hooded snake. I had no choice, the cobra was now in full attack mode, rearing its gorgeous head towards me and in that moment, I managed to perform a flawless grand jeté. It was a perfect leap, toes pointed outwards, legs tensed, arms akimbo. Just like Gary Burn, the accomplished Rhodesian ballet dancer, who I had seen perform live. Up, up and slowly over as the cobra struck, its deadly fangs missing my feet by an inch. I was over and out of danger. The cobra made a dash for the prickly Parkinsonia tree and to safety.

Duncan gave me a withering look and turned to take the rifle back to the gun cabinet when suddenly another blood-curdling yell came from the sitting room, followed by the vision of my mum tearing across the floor screaming, 'Snake!'

What? Another snake? Are you kidding? Rushing into the sitting room, we were greeted with the sight of the Christmas cards on the mantelpiece fluttering to the ground, and there, entwined among the ornaments and cards was a massive eight-foot black mamba. This time there was no escape for the serpent. Unfortunately, it managed to entwine itself around the legs of the TV.

'Duncan, don't you dare shoot it in the sitting room,' shouted mum as she peered over his broad shoulders. 'You'll bugger up the telly.'

That must have been the only black mamba ever to die a rather undignified death by 15 pellets from a Diana airgun.

As to why the snakes were so active in the house at that time: perhaps it was the drumming? Maybe it was the time of year. Or maybe just coincidence. Hell, who knows, maybe it was witchcraft. Well, that's what I like to believe.

The last big lunch do I ever went to was in early 2001. It was the wedding of Paul Francis to Catherine Greenshields, scions of two notable families from the Umvukwes district. Trouble had been brewing for some time in the farm areas. War veterans, spurred on by Robert Mugabe, were beginning to occupy farms around the country, often in a very violent manner. People were rightly very twitchy and decidedly nervous. Some could see the end. Others buried their heads in the sand.

If we had to go out with a bang, then this lunch do was a suitable occasion. This was a high-society wedding with all the trimmings. The setting was the magnificently manicured Greenshields farm overlooking their dam at sunset. As the couple tied the knot some 15 to 20 mares led by a single white Arab stallion galloped across the shallows of the water, a spume of spray behind them catching the late afternoon light like a billion diamonds, scattering Egyptian geese in their path. The sight was both haunting and beautiful and perhaps was the very moment that an era came to an end.

Later that night, at the reception held in the gardens of their impeccable home, I found myself standing at the makeshift outdoor urinal having a pee, when a tall, well-dressed black man walked in and stood next to me. Not thinking much of it, I continued to relieve myself. But then I noticed that he was not doing the same. I glanced nervously across at him. I hadn't seen him at the party.

'Are you here for the wedding?' I politely inquired.

'No,' he responded firmly, though not impolitely. 'I am here for the farm.'

Concerned that he was a CIO[72] agent, I quickly zipped up and

---

[72]The Central Intelligence Organisation is the much-feared national intelligence agency, or 'secret police', of Zimbabwe.

fled back to the soiree. Weeks later, this farm, along with most of the others in the district, had been occupied, the landlords and tenants unceremoniously evicted. I have no doubt the man at the urinal now lives in that beautiful house.

The age of the lunch do was over.

10

18 Harrow Avenue

As the farm lorry reversed up the drive to take her furniture to her new home, she looked back in panic at 18 Harrow Avenue, soon to be torn down for bijou town houses. The pre-war house, built by her husband at a time when homogeneous red-brick semis were all the rage, had Bauhaus styling.

Not that any of the old biddies along the street knew what Bauhaus was. For them this was a shock. To the liberal-minded, it was exciting and modernist, even radical. The clean, straight lines, the flat roof, the simple portico all designed in clear-cut Weimar lines. Now standing dark and empty, the walls bare of the fine paintings and rococo mirrors, the delicate claw-footed side tables purchased from Woburn Abbey, or some equally ancient pile, packed away together with the Murano glass ashtrays. Chipped and cracked Royal Winton and Wedgwood and the faded Sanderson chintz carefully stored in crates or sold at the flea market. The bay windows would no longer cast their inviting light across the garden. The house was still splendid if somewhat tired, having done its duty serving the past four generations of kids, all of whom loved it, yet none of whom seemed to have respected it.

In the far corner of the plot, an ancient jacaranda tree with the last of the season's mauve blossoms scattered across the lawn, was marked with a crude white X, ready to be torn down and cut up for firewood, an ignoble end for a noble tree. The garden stretching for acres, all uprooted, the moon flowers, guavas, avocado trees and flame trees gone. The things of her old world now a thing of the past, and a dreary future at Rose Friars Flats offering nothing but nosy neighbours hemmed in by ugly, utilitarian, suburban red-brick bunkers.

'Rose Friars,' she thought, what an awfully twee name.

'You know it's for the best mum,' my mother couched, peering across at her mum.

'I mean, it's only a matter of time until you get murdered. Oh, Gresham, do be careful with that box. Those things are expensive. Anyway, mum, this Mugabe lot don't give a fig about law and order. And an old woman living on her own, well...'

'Yes, I know, Elizabeth,' she snapped.

When angry, my gran always called mum by her full Christian name. She sighed. My gran was a sentimental old thing, but having to be wrenched from her home so suddenly was a shock.

'I would have been happy to have died there,' she said. A stubborn look set upon her face. She shook her head and stared straight ahead. 'And anyway, I had my dogs to protect me.'

'Oh, for god's sake, mum. Those soppy dogs would do nothing. Don't be ridiculous.'

My gran raised her hands in front of her in mock surrender, 'Alright, enough Elizabeth.'

She turned her head to the side to hide the tears. Even the smell of the place seemed to have changed, she thought. The wood smoke from the bonfires at the back, or from Gresham the cook's small home behind the house, now extinguished. That constant, heady smell of roses and lavender long gone.

My gran, or Ganty as she was known by her pack of grandchildren, lived in a house that had begun to crumble around her like some ageing grand dame. The dog hair and the cracks in the walls were invisible to her. The ceiling peeling back in one corner, where a fresh crop of mushrooms grew, seemed not to concern her. The creaking sprung floors and shabby kitchen appliances, not to mention the pre-war electrical cords, had become a hazard. On closer inspection, the Spode and Wedgwood displayed around the sitting room, were held together with Trinepon glue. Slowly, the heirlooms disappeared to maid Sophie's house in Harare township, or to the antique dealer down the road. Ganty had no concept of money and often parted with valuable antiques for a song.

So strange to think that this place would no longer exist in just a few weeks' time, the bulldozers having ripped the tree stumps from the ground, the verdant lawns torn up by their steel tracks. So many memories. Good, mostly. My aunt Susan and Lib growing up. Lib sneaking in on the back of the milk cart after a night on the town with Barry Norman, later to become the BBC film critic, and getting whipped across the back of the legs with a riding crop for behaving like a loose woman. Barry also lived on Harrow Avenue.

Lib recalled the time when Susan rushed up to the nuns at St Anne's hospital, screaming that Dinah 'was getting fucked!' I expect those poor nuns must have got the shock of their lives until they realised that Dinah was a King Charles spaniel. Ganty smiled at the thought. And what of those dogs? Always the dogs. Alsatians, sausage dogs, spaniels, corgis, schnauzers, mongrels and pedigrees, barking and snapping and rushing underfoot. And lord, the hair. Dog hair everywhere: on the garden furniture, on the sofas, on the beds. Few seemed to notice or care and those who did knew not to comment.

This fading grand dame was once the centre of the universe for so many people. It used to be such an elegant house, tastefully furnished. For us grandchildren, the highlight of the week was always Sunday roast. Cousins Mark and Madeleine and Duncan, Mandy and I, together with a posse of hangers-on, would descend for lunch cooked by the imperturbable Gresham, who gave us a clip around the ear if we got too unruly. My grandfather, known as Fluffy, would always make a hash of the carving. He would not have considered letting someone else take over. Ganty would become so frustrated, it was not unusual for a pudding bowl to fly across the room and explode in a spatter of jelly, strawberries and cream set against the Jackson Pollock print.

'Pass the potatoes please, Mandy,' one of us might ask, trying to ignore the green-and-red blob sliding down the wall.

While 18 Harrow Avenue hosted a plethora of fascinating visitors, my gran much preferred the company of animals to people. Birds of all colours and sizes flocked to the garden where they would religiously get fed. Bush doves and African green pigeons would trip you up as they pecked under the table. Flocks of blue waxbills, red-backed larks and yellow wagtails vied for attention. Canaries and budgies in countless colours hung in cages above our heads on the veranda.

'Who's going to feed the birds? My poor dicky birds,' my gran lamented as she was gently guided to the waiting car.

'Oh mum, that old house is just too difficult to run without an army of staff, not to mention dangerous for a woman on her own. Anyway, since dad died the place has been crumbling around you. You just don't seem to notice, do you?'

'I'm rarely on my own, you know, Lib,' she said. 'There are always people popping in to see me.'

My mother looked at her, exasperated. 'They're all bloody

pensioners, mum. How on earth can they keep you safe?'
Silence.

'Anyway, there's space for a small garden at Rose Friars. You will
love it.'

Of all my memories of 18 Harrow Avenue, it was without doubt
the garden that endures. Ganty could be seen from morning
until night kneeling on the lawn in her floral sun dress, cigarette
hanging from her mouth, a huge straw hat upon her head and
a trowel in her hand, gently planting seedlings. Hers was an
English country garden that attracted admirers from far and
wide.

Another vivid memory is the radio. Unlike life on the farm, 18
Harrow Avenue always had music and voices and sound. The
wireless was on from breakfast until the early evening news
bulletin on TV. An old black-and-silver Panasonic portable,
bound together with masking tape, followed us from one
side of the house to the other. The Rhodesian Broadcasting
Corporation was the only channel we could get, but the talent
down at RBC was just as good as at the BBC.

I can still hear the dulcet tones of Jill Baker reading the news,
or the wonderful BBC voices of John Parry, Geoffrey Atkins
and Allen Riddell, three characters whose crisp BBC accents
dominated the airwaves for more than a decade. These people
came into our lives and remained an integral part of our world
for many years.

Possibly the most popular programme was Sally Donaldson's
Forces Requests. Sally was a glamorous woman with lacquered
hair piled high on top of her head and large doe eyes. She
would travel with her team to the sharp end and interview the
troopies, the boys in the bush. *Forces Requests* was aired at the
end of the day. By then we were on our tenth cup of tea, having

migrated with the sun back to the other side of the garden where tables were set under a large shady avocado tree, and Gresham's wonderful lemon cakes or scones dripping with clotted cream and jam were served. Here, the ladies would chatter away while doing their knitting. Ganty might be working on some fabulous frock taken from a *Vogue* pattern. Most of Susan and Lib's clothes were fashioned by my gran, and they always looked chic.

The gossip beneath those trees and among the flocks of dicky birds would get so animated that Helen Martin, my gran's best friend, once knitted a baby romper suit with three legs. The mind does boggle. For hours we would listen to the animated conversations. They painted an exciting and exotic picture to this impressionable young lad.

Of all the stories, it was those about aunt Susie or cousin Fiona, Lady Montagu of Beaulieu, that I loved the most. My mum's sister was Susan Ray (nee Burnet[73]), a star of the London stage and Broadway in the late '50s and early '60s. Her husband, Andrew[74], was a film star. Quite different to my mum, Susan had a short Twiggy haircut and was dubbed the 'Brigitte Bardot of the UK' by the tabloids.

---

[73] After winning a scholarship to LAMDA when she was just 15, she rocketed to stardom at an early age, taking the London stage (and later Broadway) by storm. Her first play at the Haymarket was a leading role in *The Flowering Cherry* starring Ralph Richardson and Celia Johnson. 'In physical allure,' noted one reviewer, 'Miss Burnet reminds one of Brigitte Bardot and from a thankless role she draws more than it intrinsically contains.' The play ran for 400 performances and later went to Broadway.

[74] Andrew was a child star and at the age of ten played the title part in the 20th Century Fox film *The Mudlark* with Alec Guinness. Among many theatrical achievements, Andrew starred as George VI in the West End play *Crown Matrimonial*. He also took it out to Rhodesia, and had Susie play the late Queen Mother. So successful was his depiction on stage of the stammering George VI that he was cast in the same role (though then Prince Albert, Duke of York) in the television series *Edward and Mrs Simpson*.

Ganty had a suitcase full of clippings from the British press. A photo of Susan rushing out of the stage door, wedding dress hoiked above her knees as she ran from a matinee performance to get to her wedding on time. Susan again, in fishnet tights photographed by the tabloid *Daily Mirror*, captioned 'Saucy Susan'. Susan and her kids, Mark and Madeleine, were flown secretly to the UK to be on the set of *This Is Your Life*. Andrew's father, the comedian Ted Ray, was the star of the show. This was the reality of Sundays at Avondale. Gossip, not necessarily about the neighbours, but about Joan Collins, Susan Hampshire, Ralph Richardson and Celia Johnson. It was like a fantasy. Only it was real.

At the height of her career, Susan lived in the UK with Andrew and the children. They were often in our thoughts, but separated by bush, savannah, oceans and the teeming streets of London. They were with us through the LPs, usually sent by Madeleine, or the jewellery clunking on mum's wrists, bartered for by Andrew at some South Asian market. They were there in the British magazines and papers scattered around the house with pictures of Fiona, Sue and Andrew at some glam event. There were curios from Kathmandu and theatre reviews from the West End, and best of all there were letters from Susan, her distinctive handwriting curling across the flimsy blue aerogrammes, her stories and messages so clear and so close she might have been in the room with us. For Christmas presents, usually arriving nearer to Easter, there were the St Michael's M&S jerseys and Pears soaps and Black Magic chocolates. Luxuries which to this day still remind me of them.

The left-hand drawer in my mum's dressing table was an Aladdin's cave of fabulous things from the London of her past. She lived there when she was 18. This was hallowed ground, and we were not meant to be rummaging through it. I doubt if my dad even knew about it. When you opened the drawer, you were engulfed with a scent that teleported you right into the narrow streets of Soho and the West End. Here were autographed programmes from plays and musicals, invitations to Al Burnett's risqué Stork Club, the symbol of London cafe society, where movie stars, gangsters, celebrities, showgirls and aristocrats all mixed freely. Or the flashy London Casino with its saucy, neon dancing lady, her legs forever kicking up in a *can-can*.

There were menus from restaurants such as Rules on Maiden Lane and J Sheekey in Covent Garden. I would press the menus against my face and smell them. Some had a faint scent of Chanel or Miss Dior. Like watching a Fellini film, I would lie back and read each page and dream. I noted the hairstyles. The fur stoles. The eyeliner. The lacquered lips. I imagined tables of diners fogged in cigarette smoke, sipping champagne from a cut-glass coupe held elegantly in tiny, gloved hands, the bubbles fizzing up their noses. I imagined the conversations about ashrams and jokes about cranky directors or eccentric movie stars.

The theatre programmes often contained names of famous actors, many of them signed, 'To Libby with love'. There was even an old vinyl record from the BBC staff labelled 'London Calling Libby'. My mum spoke of Chelsea and Earls Court, which were the *it* places in the late '50s. They were the domain of those on the fringe of society, where the heady excitement of high-bred, often impoverished toffs mixed freely with East End criminals and beat generation poets, artists, actors and their entourages of managers, party animals, drug dealers and molls.

Fiona, Susan and Andrew were part of it all. It must have been intoxicating. Having decided that the hedonism of London life was no place to bring up kids, Susan returned to live in Rhodesia. She and Andrew had a huge influence on me, as did their kids Madeleine and Mark. Susan virtually became a surrogate mother to me during those many weekends spent at 18 Harrow Avenue.

When Susan moved back to Rhodesia with the kids, Andrew would occasionally visit us. We loved him unreservedly. We knew of no adult in the country who behaved like Andrew. My father, naturally, loathed him. He represented everything my father hated in the liberal Brits. Although we all thought John secretly had a sneaking respect for Andrew. Uncle Andrew was a bohemian, hippie, erudite, pot-smoking, kaftan-wearing provocateur. Many a time, my dad would drive down to the sheds and see Andrew in a flowing robe sitting in the lotus position in the middle of the workers compound meditating, the village quietly going about their business around him. I am sure he did it just to annoy my dad. He got up my father's nose and the rows that ensued were legendary.

'Let me call a taxi,' Andrew would exclaim as he walked out of the sitting room after some blazing political row.

'Andrew, don't be bloody daft,' my mother would reply.

'Anyway, you can't get a taxi around here. We're a hundred miles from anywhere.'

'Then I shall find a bus,' snapped Andrew.

This would be followed by roars of laughter from the sitting room. These set-tos rarely lasted longer than the next scotch. I believe Andrew was a threat to my dad. He stood for freedom of expression, free love, The Beatles, weed and LSD. His funny stories and famous friends won us over. People sat engrossed as Andrew held court and told tales in his wonderful English accent about this famous person and that, about Kathmandu and Morocco and the hippie trail, about ashrams and gurus and music we had never heard of. Andrew epitomised flower power and this rubbed off on many people who knew him. To this day, my mum is still very much a boho chick with jangling bracelets and beads and flowing tops and tunics. I never tired of Andrew's antics and prankish behaviour. He was kind and gentle towards us kids, who had never really known tenderness from a man, other than our granddad.

Yet Andrew was a raging liberal. His own leftist tastes even got him thrown out of Rhodesia by Ian Smith's government, becoming one of the few people I knew who was a PI (prohibited immigrant). He even became a member of Mugabe's ZANU-PF party after independence, although later in life he agreed Mugabe had lost the plot and that the Zimbabwe dream had been a spectacular failure.

Andrew and Susan's political leanings rubbed off on their kids too, and many Sundays spent at 18 Harrow Avenue would degenerate into a shouting match, with Mark and Madeleine on one side and my siblings and me on the other. In retrospect, our naivety regarding the Smith government was pretty spellbinding considering he had declared UDI without even bothering to hold a referendum, but things were different back then. Yet once all is said and done, kids were dying on both sides in the war and it was horrific and far too easy to judge with hindsight.

For the most part, Susie kept her politics to herself, although she was far more liberal than my mum, and once famously refused to shake the hand of prime minister Ian Smith, instead embarrassing the man by reminding him of the affair her grandmother, Bella-Kay, had conducted with his father. She loved Africa and although she returned to England for a few years to try to save the marriage, her heart might not have been in it. Life in the UK was not all it was cracked up to be. Constant strikes, lengthy blackouts, frigid winters, three-day working weeks and very little money were a fact of life.

One time, when Madeleine was just a baby and Susan was returning to another bleak English winter, her nerves got the better of her. These farewells were fraught with sorrow at the best of times. Susan and mum clutched each other, bawling uncontrollably as people do when they have no idea when they will ever see each other again. At the last minute, Susan unexpectedly thrust baby Madeleine into mum's arms and dashed towards immigration.

'Take care of her for me, Lib,' she sobbed as she rounded the corner. 'Please. I can't do it. It's just too hard over there. I just can't cope.'

'Susan, for heaven's sake. Come back,' mum called in desperation. She looked down at the beautiful, violet-eyed babe in her arms. 'Oh, Susie. What on earth have you done?' By the time she looked up, her sister has disappeared from view.

Rushing upstairs to the balcony, she called after her sister as she was about to board the BOAC flight to London. 'Susan...'

'Bring her back to me safe and sound, Lib,' called Susan. 'It's the only way I will be certain to see you again!' And with that she was gone.

My gran and mum became surrogate parents to dear Madeleine, although I am told that it was the nanny, Sophie, who really took over. After waiting for a year with no sight of Susan, my mother flew back to London with the child and, as promised, reunited the child with her mum and dad and newly born brother, Mark. Leaving Madeleine behind in this day and age would simply not be tolerated, but I see this as a divine act of love and understand entirely how Susan was thinking. Families split apart by whole continents back in the '60s rarely saw each other. All too often, departure meant forever.

Both Andrew and Susan died relatively young, Andrew taking his final bow by having a heart attack on his agent's floor in London, and Susie of lung cancer a few years later. I miss them terribly. I still occasionally hear someone laughing or chatting on BBC radio, and it sounds just like Susie, and all these memories come flooding back. Stories about Kenneth Williams[75] and his camp entourage. Diana Dors[76] and her alleged sex parties in Sunningdale. The notorious East End gangsters, the Kray twins, who knew Susan and Andrew through Diana, and how the schizophrenic, gay twin, Ronnie, sent Susan a lace hankie every year for her birthday, no matter where she was living. The fact that he even knew her address was alarming enough.

There are stories about cousin Fiona, who married Lord Montagu of Beaulieu, a man not without his own skeletons, and we would sit and listen with delightful abandon about all their shenanigans. Fiona was every bit the lady. She was tall and willowy with big hair. At Christmas she would send cards with pictures of her and her family wrapped up in furs, with Palace House, Beaulieu looming behind them. Even the envelopes had their own unique post office stamp.

Susan and Andrew and Lady Montagu were not the only stars in the family. From our side of the pond, we finally got two members of our family into the movie industry. Their cameo performances rocketed them to stardom in 1987 in a blockbuster movie still being watched a quarter of a century later. These accolades belonged to my brother's two Scottish terriers. They were flown around the country in all the style that a star is accustomed to. These two small cheeky black dogs (whom I am certain had given the odd black worker a nip or two in their time) were the two Scotties owned by Donald Woods in Richard Attenborough's epic *Cry Freedom*.

---

[75]Kenneth Charles Williams (22 February 1926-15 April 1988) was an English comic actor. He was one of the main ensemble in 26 of the 31 *Carry On* films, and appeared in numerous British television shows and radio comedies. Williams was also godfather to my cousin Mark.

[76]Diana Dors was an English actress. She first came to public notice as a blonde bombshell in the style of Marilyn Monroe.

Well, we can't all hog the limelight, can we?

Things might have gone to our heads, but as with all things in life, there was always someone who managed to calm things down, to bring things back down to earth and teach us humility and kindness and not to be a snob.

That person was Fluffy.

My grandfather, Fluffy, was the ying to Ganty's yang. My granddad Gordon 'Fluffy' Burnet was, as his nickname implied, possibly the softest, kindest man I have ever known. Generous to a fault, funny and utterly endearing, he was the antithesis of my father, or indeed any of the other alpha males among our circle of friends.

In his youth, in the early part of the 20th century, he would spend his holidays hunting, shooting and fishing along the untamed rivers of the Zambezi, Gwaai and Shangani. He told us tales about his treks on ox-drawn wagons to the foothills of the Mazoe Range to shoot leopards, once climbing hand over foot up a steep granite cliff only to come face to face with the very leopard he was tracking. He spoke of herds of sable antelope where farmland now existed, of falling asleep on the banks of the Sanyati River only to awaken just before a croc was about to take him.

His adventures enthralled us kids, and yet this gentle man was not a hunter by nature. He was a thinker. An intellectual. His extraordinary brain won him a coveted Beit scholarship, a forerunner to the Rhodes scholarship but restricted only to residents of Rhodesia and Nyasaland[77]. The outbreak of World War II prevented him from going to Oxford and he spent most of his life working in the Rhodesian Parliament library, a posting

---

[77] Now Malawi, Zambia and Zimbabwe.

my father always felt was a cop-out. He was adored by everyone, both black and white, and his funeral was attended by both Ian Smith's party and Mugabe's – something quite unheard of at the time. In another age, perhaps we might have heard the captivating shout, '*Bayete!*'

Fluffy drove a clapped-out Opel station wagon that groaned and farted its way up the school drive, much to the hilarity of the boarders and the utter humiliation of us kids. Fluffy didn't care. And, in truth, neither did we, but kids are impressionable and I am ashamed to say that on occasion we hid away in the dorm or ducked behind the seat when driving past the rugby fields. We were lucky to have a grandfather who taught us to appreciate the plant life in the garden and in the veld. We would often spend Sunday mornings on thieving missions to places such as the botanical gardens and even people's homes.

'Look at the colour of that geranium. Let's get a cutting. Hurry, before anyone sees you.'

In a trice, the cutting was stowed away under a rug in the boot, ready for replanting in the rockery. My gran loved the English garden flowers, eventually creating a paradise abundant with flora pilfered by her grandchildren from many an unsuspecting housewife.

Fluffy was an eccentric and sloppy dresser. He was doddery at times and was a man of limited means. His wealth came from kindness and generosity and us kids loved him beyond reproach. Later in life, I would see or hear something that took me back to those fabulous farting drives in the Opel down the avenues, dogs yapping in the back, hairballs everywhere, Fluffy constantly saying, 'Oh, heck...' as he missed yet another turn or nearly hit an approaching car. 'Silly old coot!' the irate driver would shout.

When he died, a great wrench was felt within the family. A chasm that could never be filled took his place, particularity for my sister, Mandy, who saw Fluffy as a surrogate father. I will never forgive myself for not going to his funeral. I have no idea why I didn't go. I was working on a farm at the time and surely my boss would have given me the time off. It made little sense. It seemed such a strange choice to stay away from the final send-off to a man who had spent his life giving to everyone.

Perhaps now I can salute both Ganty and Fluffy. I am what I am because of them.

BAYETE!

11

Woods Hit Europe

On 29 May 1979, Rhodesia became Zimbabwe-Rhodesia. For us, this hybrid country meant fewer restrictions and the lifting of sanctions. It also meant, marginally, that travel outside southern Africa was finally permitted for those carrying Rhodesian passports. I say marginally because all that actually meant was Greece, Switzerland and Spain.

The ascension of the Spanish Bourbons and deposition of Ioannidis of Greece meant relaxation of some rules, and Switzerland, well, was just being Swiss. To the rest of the world *over there* (namely, the UK and USA), we Zimbabwe-Rhodesians still represented a repressive, racist regime. It also meant that flights to Europe had to take a very long, circuitous route right around the bulge of Africa in order to avoid hostile airspace.

My brother Dunc and I were absolutely delighted when my dad very kindly suggested that a trip to Europe would do us some good. Coming from my father, who was an avid anti-*over there* kind of chap, we strongly suspected that we were either going to be used as drug mules, foreign exchange embezzlers or diamond smugglers. Either way, it was going to be character-building.

I think that my poor, long-suffering brother would have much preferred to have gone with his ex-army mates on a booze-fuelled road trip across America or any other country *over there*, instead of getting strapped with his rather drippy younger brother. Okay, I was never drippy, despite my father having yelled at me once when I was seen walking around the house with my hands clasped in front of me.

'You look like a goddamn priest. For god's sake, walk properly.'
I never made the same mistake again.

So, while his army pals, UK passports in hand, disappeared in a
cloud of Cadillac dust down Route 66, lesser beings such as we
Rhodesian passport holders headed for the liberal backwaters of
the Aegean, Costa del Sol and the less-than-liberal Swiss Alps.
In short, Duncan got lumbered with yours truly.

So it came to pass that on 4 August 1979, having never left
Africa and armed with our US$800 allowance from the Reserve
Bank of Rhodesia (US$400 apiece), two huge expandable
suitcases donated by our gran (last used on the Union
Castle[78] to Southampton back in 1952, according to the many
stickers plastered over them), laden with two dozen extremely
semi-precious stone eggs that our worldly wise travel agent,
Pam Spicer, said we could trade for money (the very same
eggs that accompanied us to Beira a decade earlier), and
rather awkwardly dressed in, wait for it, brown slacks, cream
jacket and fucking '70s kipper tie, we left the continent of
our birth for the first time. Did we really think people still
travelled like that?

We embarked on the 22-hour SAA flight from Salisbury via
Joburg and then around Africa, a fuel stop in Lisbon and on
to Rome and finally Athens. Naive, idiotic farm kids with
zero knowledge of what had happened socially in the outside
world since sanctions began in 1965. In 1979, Europe was at
the tail-end of flower power, hippie, pot-smoking free love. I
had recently finished James Michener's epic novel *The Drifters*
and imagined myself as some cool, worldly-wise traveller ready
to lay my head and my heart on the lap of some LSD-addled

---

[78] The Union-Castle Line was a prominent British shipping line which
operated a fleet of passenger liners and cargo ships between Europe and
Africa from 1900 to 1977.

Torremolinos angel. Disaffected and directionless, according to the magazines of the day. And here we were.

Disembarking from the plane in our jackets and ties, we must have looked quite a sight, drenched in sweat from the mid-summer Greek heat and no doubt the laughing stock of the hordes of young, long-haired people hanging out at the airport. Even the phrase 'hanging out' conjured up illicit images of sex and drugs in my naive brain. I thought these hippies were all on pot. I didn't realise that people actually rolled up Turkish tobacco using something called Rizlas.

I thought I could see dishevelled groups in frayed cut-off jeans on every street corner injecting themselves with heroin, when in fact all they were doing was counting their drachmas for an ice cream or souvlaki. Almost immediately on landing, and clearly quite mesmerised by the activity around us, we left one of our bags on a bench. Sadly, it was not the bag containing the stone eggs, and so lugging the massive trunks behind us we began our trip into what can only be described as total farce.

My diary is short, brief and to the point.

Sunday, 5 August 1979

Athens is absolutely fantastic. PORN! The works.

It was in Athens that we saw *Midnight Express*, not the best of films to see when on vacation so close to Turkey. Nevertheless, it would not be illicit drug smuggling but carnal porn that would come back to haunt us. Having never seen pornography before, (well, not openly displayed like this smut sitting snugly beside *Women's Wear Daily*, several Greek newspapers such as *Eleftherotypia* and *Kathimerini*, and the *International Herald Tribune*) and terrified that it might all disappear before our goggle eyes, we quickly stocked up on copies of *Playboy*,

Penthouse, Mayfair, a keyring of a man fucking a woman doggy-style, a small Priapus with a very large member and, for me, a quietly sneaked-in copy of *Playgirl.* I was in heaven. I nearly passed out the first time I took a peek at all the naked men.

Of course, the stone eggs were still there like a bad smell, unsellable and unloved.

Dunc and I did the islands. Lugging our cases on to the Metro, on and off ferries from Piraeus to Poros and Spetses, on buses and trains, donkey carts, up and down flipping hills, and on to flat roofs where we hung out hoping to look like the other European hipsters, but failing in spectacular fashion. Our worn Veldskoens, shorter-than-short boxers and checked shirts stood out like the Lighthouse of Alexandria on a foggy night. You could spot a southern African a mile off.

From Greece, we fled to Switzerland, staying at the Hotel Tourelles on the banks of Lake Geneva, then on to the ski resort (out-of-season) of Leysin, where we were turfed off the bus for flicking a cigarette butt out the window. Still lugging those stone eggs, we traipsed from shop to shop (lists of which had been given to us by Pam the travel agent) and were not only met with a negative response, but with a look of total bewilderment.

One Swiss shopkeeper went as far as to take us to his cramped store on the Quai de Bergues on the shores of Lake Geneva, where he heaved open a large trunk filled to the top with sparkling, semi-precious stone eggs. The limp light spilled across the dusty oval-shaped stones. He ran a long, bejewelled finger over the top of the eggs, revealing their blues shot with gold, rust, amber and turquoise, then wiped his finger clean on a linen handkerchief. The stones looked like a nest of arachnids or evil, winking alien eyes.

He shook his head. 'I have no idea who in Rhodesia gave my

name to your fellow travellers, but I simply cannot get rid of the awful things. What did I do to deserve this?' he complained with a shrug.

And with that, he let the lid crash back in a cloud of dust as a bony hand guided us out of the shop.

In revenge, we both pissed in the pristine lake, hoping to pass on some bilharzia[79] to the dull, squeaky clean Swiss. A very sad photo shows Duncan sitting on an enormous suitcase by the side of the road, a spectacular chocolate-box Alpine vista in the background. All we were missing was a hat box.

From the glory of the Alps, we moved on to the shithole that was Malaga. The sea was filthy back then, with visible sewage floating around, fat women with massive, hideous *dugs*[80] hanging down to their waists, and awful, rough sand on the beach, so unlike Mozambique. My dreams of playing a Hemingway character lounging on the *playa* squirting Rioja from a wineskin into my mouth were dashed against the Torremolinos promenade. So, naturally, we did what all drunk teenagers do. We tried to get laid. Our victims, as my diary recounts, were two German women.

Wednesday, 29 August 1979

We met the birds who had been making eyes at me on the beach earlier. They are German – quite nice actually. We never got a fuck out of them because in our broken English we never knew how to go about it.

Well, I guess we all have excuses. Mine was a magazine nestled

---

[79] A chronic disease caused by infestation of blood flukes passed on through the urine. Bilharzia is endemic in Africa.

[80] Afrikaans farming term meaning the udder, teat or nipple of an animal.

under the beryl, tourmaline, iolite and heliodor stone eggs in the bottom of my case. In frustration, Duncan and I decided to do what all self-respecting hippies did. Shoplift. Something I had never done before and never did again.

The target of our thieving was, not surprisingly, porn. Sadly, our suspicious demeanour and slinky behaviour got us caught by the store owner within seconds, sneaking between the aisles like evil ham actors in some pathetic panto. My life flashed before my eyes. I imagined *Midnight Express*, filthy Spanish jails, a life of drugs, hard labour and buggery. Duncan punched. I ran. Behind us the shopkeeper yelled, 'Ladrón, ladrón, ladrón! Stop thief. Theeeef!'

Christ, he wasn't giving up. Fortunately, I managed to sneak between some racks of clothing in a market and cowered down between the tie-dyed kaftans and rosaries until the moment had passed. I was never going to make a good thief.

Nor a smuggler, for that matter. On our return to Salisbury airport (those bloody stone eggs still in tow, jacket and tie now stowed away) we were detained by customs officers and searched.

You need to understand the kind of person that worked for Rhodesian Customs and Excise back in the '70s. They were, generally speaking, boors and Boers. With absolutely zero tolerance or sense of humour and with faces like slapped arses, tiny pencil moustaches, beady eyes and lascivious looks, they discovered one contraband item after another, holding them up in utter horror. *Playboy*, *Penthouse*, keyrings, statuettes. Even a goddamn ballpoint pen that when shaken allowed the bathing costume of a woman to fall away. Hard-core or what?

'En wot do we hiv ya?' the man would utter in a voice containing less warmth than that of a serial killer.

With sweat pouring down my back, and with much irony, I stared in disbelief at the poster above their heads. It was of elephants around a waterhole with the slogan, 'Rhodesia is Super!' Is it? I thought back to the poster competition I had won so many years ago and stifled a laugh. The word 'super' seemed to sum up the mood. Who in their right mind calls a fucking country at war 'super'? Why is a country super when even a bloody joke keyring is considered illegal? I watched and waited with morbid fascination as they got nearer and nearer to my *Playgirl*. How in god's name was I to explain this one to Duncan? A mistake? It must have slipped in on its own? It wasn't mine? I bought it by mistake, it belonged to the Germans, sorry about the dog ears.

By now, the inventory on the Formica table was beginning to look eclectic to say the least:

- » *Playboy* x 1
- » *Mayfair* x 2
- » *Penthouse* x 1
- » Keyring, silver (pornographic) x 1
- » Statuette, plastic, white (pornographic) x 1
- » Alcohol (ouzo), Grecian pillars, 500ml
- » Doll, Spanish, 18-inches, green
- » Flick knife (did I not mention that? Oh well ...)
- » Stone eggs (various) x 20
- » Kipper tie x 4

And then it was over. They pushed my case at me, my dirty secret undiscovered. I was palpably relieved, although the worst was yet to come. Those small-minded customs officials had the gall to write to my father explaining that his two sons had been peddling in carnal contraband. Well, if ever the shit hit the fan, it was then. My dad did not know what 'carnal' meant. To his mind it concerned people fucking dogs. What sort of disgusting bastards had he brought up? Is this what you get from those years at school? Peddlers in porn? All I could think was, 'Little do you know.'

It was way beyond him and we were way beyond explaining to him that in fact these were not magazines of weird and disgusting bestial activities. He gave us a look of total incomprehension and revulsion before slamming shut the Land Rover door and speeding off down to his tobacco. My final humiliation came when my dad made me write a letter to those customs officials apologising for my lack of judgement and could they possibly forgive me for going astray. I will never forget that moment and I expect those idiot officials laughed about it long and hard as they flicked my keyring back and forth.

Ironically, when my dad went to the Seychelles, his mates asked him to bring in some girlie mags. The last time my father had read a *Playboy* was in 1965. I still laugh at the memory of him burning the magazines at the back of the house having realised that porn in the late '70s had progressed to a rather more, how shall we put it, 'carnal' art form.

I still have those wretched stone eggs.

12

Horsey Bit

It was to be another of those Umvukwes horsey events. A gymkhana at the club followed by a paper chase on the Francis farm.

We were on our way to the club and then on to Galloway Estate, which was the starting line for the paper chase. I was daydreaming in the back of the car – gazing out the window as farm after farm drifted past. Wide, flat, irrigated fields. It almost looked like England.

Umvukwes was always much cooler than M'sitwe, being a couple of thousand feet higher in altitude. As rocky indigenous forest gave way to a more undulating countryside, huge swathes of rich, fertile, land fell away on either side of the narrow tarmac road.

This was the breadbasket of the country with centre pivots irrigating the fields of wheat and mealies 24-hours a day for as far as you could see, broken only by the occasional rocky hillock, dam or plantation of gums. Plough discs screwed to rusty posts and painted in bright colours indicated farms with mostly English or colonial names – Sandford, Epping Forest, Birkdale, Forester Estate, Galloway Estate, Frogmore – huddled together with local names such as Pembi, Dahwye, Nyarowe, Mandindindi.

We arrived at Umvukwes village. This small agricultural town was teeming with people, mostly farmers doing various chores. Unlike most people in our area, I rather dreaded the Christmas hols, if only because it meant paper chases, gymkhanas and riding clubs, all of which we felt obliged to take part in. Horses. Always horses. They seemed to be the bane of my life. When I was at Umvukwes Junior School, term was always punctuated by riding lessons at Fluff John's on their farm called Blighty. Admittedly this gave us nippers a chance to get out of lessons.

I thought back to those days spent on Blighty, which was in a beautiful part of Umvukwes, overlooking the Chiweshe native reserve. Wild, rugged and mountainous. Passing through the winding eucalyptus-lined roads to the farm in the rattling Umvukwes school bus, our school insignia – a bright red-and-yellow flame lily – painted on both sides. We used to sing and eat the nibbles provided by the 'mum-in-charge', some of them more in charge than others. To me, riding lessons were tedious, and frightfully strict once you were mounted.

Out of the saddle, however, it was quite a different story. The afternoons were spent roaming about the Blighty *kopjes*, and exploring caves and marshy *vleis*[81]. Throwing off our shoes we would run through pink seas of feathery cat's tails and get our jodhpurs covered in the twisted spines of spear grass. These were salad days and while there was little love lost between horse and me, I did enjoy these adventures in the bush. There was little discipline and few grown-ups to tell us what to do. The Umvukwes horsey set were perfectly happy to have their kids careering off in the bush. But woe betide anyone who might maltreat a dog or horse. I expect the animals were loved far more than we were. It was not uncommon to see an old, fat and farting Labrador receiving far more attention than junior.

When we were younger, we were sent to the pony club on nearby Vigila Farm, owned by Felicity von der Heyde. My distrust of the steady steed and my even greater distrust of strange people

---

[81] Low-lying, marshy ground, covered with water during the rainy season.

became apparent during these week-long events that seemed to drag on forever. I would count the hours until I was once again free to enjoy my holidays on M'sitwe, horse-free. Pony club was, for me, pony hell.

Kids of all ages, often from frightfully posh families, used to arrive from all over Mashonaland, driving up with their smart horse boxes and even smarter horses. With plummy accents, they would yell orders to their grooms and make snide remarks when our clapped-out Datsun pick-up with Heath Robinson bamboo rails would shudder to a stop to offload the irate and dusty Pedro and Piccolo. Even our horses got in on the act by kicking or nipping the mares from town, often resulting in one of us copping a sound whack from a riding crop.

In hindsight, these pony clubs were a lot of fun, if you removed the whole horse element. The food was always sensational with tasty buffets laid out on corrugated iron trestle tables in the tobacco-grading sheds. The older kids slept in a tented village in the garden, while we younger ones had to contend with dossing down in the creepy hallway of granny Von der Heyde's house, her huge gilt-framed portrait staring at us wherever we went, and her grandfather clock terrifying us on the hour, every hour throughout the night. That is until Tracey McGrath kicked it and it never ticked-tocked or donged again. Sadly, I remember little of the actual lessons taught during those weeks, except a vague memory of trying to get our wild, rough-and-ready farm ponies to obey during dressage. A thankless task, made slightly funnier by the fact that our friend Larry Norton's pony, Star, was just that bit less tractable.

As we pulled into Jack & Jill's Hair Salon, I was brought out of my daydreaming. The salon was owned by mum's friend Jill Robertson. The pink paintwork and flower boxes always looked out of place adjacent to the shabby, untidy garage. That day the salon was bursting with blue-rinsed ladies getting ready for the night ahead. Jill bounded over to us, curling tongs in one hand and a salad in the other. 'Hi,' she leaned in the window and handed me the salad.

'Drop that off at the club, will you. I'll be here for yonks. Those bloody Malvern House women need hours of pampering,' she said (Malvern House being the local old peoples home).

Along the road Fred Youngman, the butcher, was leaning against his counter chatting to a couple of farmers. Fred used to take a particular pleasure when slicing down through a block of cheese with a wire cutter. An evil glint in his eye, perhaps inducing fond memories from his time in the special forces during World War II when he had to creep up behind the enemy and garrotte them silently in the dark. The wire would glide through the cheese, and send shivers down our spines. He waved cheerfully as we drove past.

'Christ! That last lot of rump was as tough as Henderson's arse,' barked my dad. 'Next time we should buy our meat from the Farmer's Co-op.'

Good luck to that, I thought. John had worn false teeth since his twenties. He came from a school of thought where you pulled a tooth rather than fill it in, resulting in a mouth that collapsed in on itself like a failed soufflé. On one trip down to Johannesburg with all his buddies to watch a Currie Cup rugby final, the hotel maid chucked out his falsies when she cleared his tea tray. It resulted in the entire long-suffering staff of the hotel donning rubber gloves and masks and rifling through the revolting bins until they found the nasty gnashers.

During breakfast that morning, in front of a room full of diners, the maître'd swanned across the room to my father's table bearing a huge silver salver, and bowing down in an overly dramatic way, he lifted the lid with a flourish and announced,

'Your teeth, sire.' A quick wash and they were back home in Woody's mouth.

'Do you think Pedro got up to the club okay?' I asked mum.

'Well, we would have heard if he hadn't. We sent the truck up yesterday.'

I thought of poor Pedro stabled with those other horses. If Pedro disliked the pony clubs, he utterly abhorred gymkhanas. This was the moment when he would wreak retribution, and havoc, paying us back for the indignity of having to do dressage. This quiet, sweet little bush pony became an absolutely uncontrollable, stubborn and thoroughly spiteful nag. Not surprisingly, I generally came last at all the events, often ending in tears of shame, and a good kick to Pedro when no one was looking.

'All you're good for is the knacker's yard,' I would grumble, stroking his fat tummy. 'Glue. That's what you will be made into. Glue.'

Pedro would respond with a loud rattle of farts. These constant failures prompted the gymkhana committee to eventually come up with a booby prize for the losers.

'And, of course, ladies and gentlemen,' the compère piped over the tannoy for everyone in the greater Mashonaland area to hear. 'As you know, no one's a loser. So the consolation prize for the pole-bending race goes to, wait for it, drummers please ... Peter Wood.'

'Aagh shame,' one could hear the murmurs from the sidelines as I shambled my way through the bales of hay to collect a rosette. My father would quietly pour himself another drink in the beer tent and mutter to the barman, John Carr, about all these bloody expensive riding lessons he spent on us kids.

We drove past the utilitarian green government clinic and mortuary. Whitewashed breeze blocks on either side of the drive created makeshift seats for the long-suffering queue of people waiting to be treated. The clinic was open to everyone of all races and was generally teeming. The institutional building was run by a charming, imperturbable man called Doctor Scott, and like all bush doctors he was a jack of all trades, having to perform everything from basic ops and sutures, to full-on amputations and autopsies.

'I bury my mistakes,' he was fond of telling us.

He also loved sport and would turn up at the Umvukwes Junior School rugby matches where he could often be heard bellowing from the edge of the pitch.

'Go on, Umvuks ... kill 'em! Go on ... gouge his bloody eyes out! Just kill 'em!'

'Who on earth is that ghastly man?' visiting parents would ask.

'Oh, him,' one of the local mums would reply casually. 'That's Doctor Scott. Business must be bad.'

When I was about five years old, I was out riding with my mum. I always rode Pedro, who was incredibly gentle with kids. Nearing the end of the ride a snake on the track spooked the horse, causing him to bolt. I fell off and broke my arm. It was only a greenstick fracture but it hurt like hell and I bawled my eyes out all the way to the clinic.

After about six weeks, it was time to have the cast removed. Arriving at the clinic without an appointment, we asked the nurse where the doctor was and were directed outside. Like an apparition from a horror movie, the doctor emerged from an out-building, which we later realised was the morgue, his usually spotless white coat flecked with blood and some grisly pale gunge. And in his hand he held a circular saw, bloody with bits of gristle and bone stuck to it.

'Oh, hello, young man,' he said, quite oblivious to the fact that he looked like Vincent Price in *The Tomb of Ligeia*.

'So, you need your cast taken off, do you? Well I'm damn busy right now. Oh, to hell with it, let's just do it with this. Won't take a minute. I've been using it to open up the skull of a man who died of some hideous disease,' he said as an aside, and with that held down my arm and using the whizzing bloody electric saw, began to cut off my cast.

I think my poor mother nearly fainted. I loved every second of it.

'Talking of casts,' he went on, oblivious to the trauma around him, 'last week I had a black chap in here going crazy. He had boiling water poured over his arm and we bound him up. But for weeks he nearly went mad. You see, his arm just never stopped itching.'

'Was that from the burns?' my mother asked, trying not to notice the whizzing saw getting closer to my skin.

'God no,' Doctor Scott said. 'Apparently, some flies had laid their eggs on his burnt skin. It was the maggots, you see. Maggots. Can you imagine? Now, young man, hold your arm still. I don't want to cut you. Anyway, as I was saying, the maggots had hatched in his arm and were eating him alive. But to tell you the truth, Libby, I have never seen such a good job, ever. No scar, nothing. Those bloody worms had eaten all the dead skin and left the bugger with the most beautiful new skin, like a baby. Aha! There you go – clean off.' He patted me on the head.

No one was off limits to the doc. My father once had an operation for his piles. Anything related to that part of the body or any of those bodily functions was a no-go top of conversation for the prim and rather proper Woody. Drinking quietly in the corner at the bar of the club with his mates, Bill and Ben, Doctor Scott appeared at the door, looked around to see who was present, then roared 'Evening, Woody. How's your backside?'

Every eye in the pub turned to John. All you could hear was the clicking of Dawn Fussel's double-stranded pearls. Mortified, John turned away and mumbled something under his breath. Scott was not one for giving up that easily.

'You should have seen him with that cotton wool up his jacksy,' he continued to his captivated audience.

'My god. He looked like a bloody bunny girl.'

Friday, the steady barman, was still chuckling to himself half an hour later.

Often, it was not possible to get a patient up to the clinic, and so we had to take things into our own hands. Early one morning, there was a knock on the kitchen door. Fred rushed through to the dining room.

'Madam. You had better come. Big problem. *Maningi shupa*[82].'

There, standing outside the back door, seemingly without a concern in the world, was Mishek, one of my father's cattlemen, with an axe sticking out of his head. A long-handled African-style 'demo' axe wedged in his skull. Yet, there he was standing as if a tomahawk in your head was just another of life's irritating trials, akin to a thorn in the foot or a stubbed toe.

---

[82] Chilapalapa term meaning 'big trouble'.

'Sorry, madam,' he apologised, 'but my missus caught me with another woman. Aayeee, she was very angry. I need some *muti*.'

'John,' my mother called, 'you had better come and see this.'

My father had been schooled in the Scottish doctrine where you ate hard-knocks for breakfast, and poked holes in new-born lambs, if they were born without arseholes. He took a deep breath and told the man to brace himself. He grabbed the axe by the handle and slowly, began to ease it out. Wedged very deeply, the blade made a truly gruesome sound as it was worked out of his skull. 'Eeee, aaar, eeee, aaar.' With a final tug, and a sickening sucking sound, the axe came out.

'Give him a couple of aspirin, Lib,' said Woody, handing the axe to the startled cook before returning to his now-cold breakfast.

'Oh, and tell him we're dipping the cattle this afternoon. No bloody excuses.'

Mishek lived to see another day, and was there to dip the cattle, despite the splitting headache. He and his wife divorced.

Konda was another man my father would describe as 'rough as a goat's knee'. He had been over to the Haringtons' compound one Sunday getting plastered on Chibuku beer, a thick, gruel-like home-brew. Returning home on his bicycle, he went off the Haringtons' rickety bridge on the M'sitwe River. It was a terrible fall of some 30 feet on to jagged rocks.

Incredibly, Konda survived, but his right foot was almost severed. With the stoicism and bravery of a warrior, he picked himself up, and carrying his broken bike, limped the five miles back to the house with his foot dangling by a thread. Not once did my mum hear him complain or cry out or even whimper as she hurtled over bumps in the truck, going, as my father would put it, like shit off a shovel to the clinic. Once there, Doctor Scott lovingly sewed the foot back on. Konda's rehabilitation took several months, but he was back at work, slightly wobbly and still uncomplaining.

The locals weren't the only ones who were tough. Despite all her girlie traits, mum also seemed immune to pain and as tough as old boots, once impaling herself on a garden stake, the bamboo stick going straight through her calf muscle. Shouting for Shine, the garden boy, who immediately fainted on seeing the blood, she clambered into the truck and took off for Umvukwes, with a newly revived Shine trying to stem the flow of blood. As the journey progressed and more and more blood was lost, she began to veer from side to side, driving like a drunkard, coming in and out of vision, finally getting to the clinic just in time. Much to the relief of poor Shine. A few stitches from Doctor Scott and she was on her way back home to finish the pruning. Shine took the rest of the day off.

Snake bites, axe wounds, even the odd ear bitten off by an angry wife, all this was normal on the farm. It amazed me that we only had the most rudimentary first-aid box. Aspirin, Mercurochrome, Band-Aids and a large brown bottle of cough *muti*.

'Oh, John,' my mum said as we approached the pink stucco Anglican church, 'I need to drop off *The French Letter*.'

St Andrew's Anglican Church had been presided over for as long as I could remember by the indomitable Father French. Its Virginia creeper-clad clock tower dominated the village and pastoral skyline. Father French was no ordinary priest. Born in the UK, he came out to Rhodesia to take his place in the Umvukwes Parish long before many of us were born. He had married a retiring, small dormouse of a lady called Grace, who I have absolutely no doubt ruled the roost behind closed doors.

Father French was flamboyant and loved the ceremony of it all, walking down that aisle adorned in his embroidered dress of cassock, surplice, academic hood and a tippet. The young boys from the Umvukwes Junior School, as choristers, always led the way, holding aloft the cross and the candles while the top of Grace's head would bob up and down behind the large organ near the altar banging out hymn after hymn. Father French's booming voice would echo around the church and rebound off the walls, rattling the colourful stained glass windows commissioned by Barbara Warren in memory of her late husband Wallace, whom she had little time for when he was alive, but immortalised in death.

Not surprisingly, Father French totally immersed himself in the life of the district. He joined in the dramatic society plays, light of foot, deep of voice and large of frame. Like all district priests, he officiated at the many christenings, farm weddings and funerals – especially funerals during the height of the bush war. Being an ex-army chaplain, Father French was often the first to be told by the army if there had been a tragedy in the district, an ambush or worse the death of a beloved son in the war.

This was the time of fuel rationing and not even god could intervene in that respect. Frenchie would cover the entire Umvukwes, Centenary, Mount Darwin, Sipolilo and Raffingora districts, some 17,000 square miles, always rocking up on his clapped-out BSA motorbike, which could be heard farting from miles away. With his faith in the lord in one hand and faith in the engineering of the Birmingham Small Arms Co. Ltd. in the other, he could be seen careering over rutted roads and gullies, quite impervious to landmines or ambushes and usually dressed in a muddy, black oilskin coat, wellies and a black waterproof hat, looking every bit like a benign Paddington Bear.

He was always the first to console a grief-stricken family, so his appearance at your front gate was not necessarily always welcome. Once, one of his visits backfired when he turned up unexpectedly at Martin and Betty Chance's farm. Poor Betty got the fright of her life as she was sure that her son Gordon, who was away on active duty at the time, had been killed. Ducking her head like the Pink Panther, Betty leopard-crawled across her sitting room floor and then ran around the back and hid behind the pawpaw patch in the veggie garden as she could not face Father French.

He never made that mistake again and always phoned first before going to see anyone, except for one memorable occasion when he pitched up at our house on M'sitwe in the aftermath of a rather drunken party thrown by my parents. Frenchie was greeted by the sight of Sam Marnie, a man of many talents, drinking being one of them, lying fast asleep, snoring on the veranda floor, Castle Lager bottle still gripped firmly in his hand. An almost naked Norrie Spicer, who suffered from alopecia, his hairless, lily-white reputation covered in a rather disturbingly tight leopard-print budgie smuggler, was lying on his back, blowing a four-and-a-half-foot copper trumpet held tightly between his toes.

Unperturbed, Father French stepped over Sam's prostrate body, turned down the volume of Lulu singing *My Boy Lollipop* – 'You make my heart go giddy-up' – and joined in the revelry for about an hour. On leaving, he got up, made the sign of the cross, and said, 'Bless you my children and I will pray for you all,' and roared off on his bike.

Father French sent a monthly newsletter to the parishioners titled inappropriately *The French Letter*[83], in which he recorded births, deaths, christenings, and, of course, all the local gossip. You could run but you could not hide, literally. Mum had the

---

[83] British slang for a condom.

only Roneo[84] machine in the district and would print the *FL* every month.

It was customary for Church of England children to be confirmed when aged ten. Like the Anglican Church the world over, this involved a confession, or as they like to call it: the sacrament of reconciliation. For a ten-year-old, having never had to confess to anything before, this was puzzling. Rather than anonymously stepping into a confessional box like the Catholics, we were presented with a text book filled with all the 'sins' of man written in neat columns down the left-hand side. All one had to do was tick the box next to the appropriate sin. How clean. How English. Henry VIII had a point.

I read down the list. 'Blimey, I have no idea what these sins even mean, let alone whether I have ever committed any of them.'

Most of the boys finished their 'ticking' suspiciously quickly and ran out to play among the gravestones. Rather than burn in hell for all eternity, I felt it was wiser to confess to everything and seek reconciliation later. And so I ticked all the boxes. Every single one of them. When Father French came up to me to read my now very long list of sins, I recall the twinkle in his eye as he peered at me over his reading glasses.

'Adultery?' he said raising an eyebrow. 'Well, well, Peter Wood, in that case I absolve you of all your sins.'

Over Christmas, the paper chase used to be the event of the season. Based loosely on the English fox hunt, but with no fox, no hounds and certainly no blooding, the paper chase was, simply put, a point-to-point ridden through the bush over a 30 or 40 mile course. Hurdles, giant jumps made of fallen logs, ditches, rivers, dams and massive gullies were no obstacle to

---

[84] A stencil duplicator or mimeograph machine.

these crazed equestrians. They were exhilarating and fun and terribly dangerous at times. Anything from 20 to 50 horses took part, ridden by people of all ages.

Each leg of the race was punctuated by a tea break – actually a tractor-trailer loaded with ice-cold beers and plenty of grog. By the end of the last leg, many a rider was, to put it mildly, perfectly legless. The paper chase might take the best part of the morning followed by a sumptuous, boozy late lunch or *braai* in the gardens of the host farm. Horses aside, they gave everyone a chance to catch up and mingle without having to dress up.

'It puzzles me,' Woody said. 'I mean, the club committee insists that us rugby buggers shower before entering the bar. Yet these horsey types just charge in smelling of saddle soap and horse shit.'

We all have our pièce de résistance or, in my case, a swan song. That Christmas, Bill and Anne Francis were hosting a paper chase on Galloway Estate. Pedro was too old for this sort of thing, so I was rather happy to be left on the sidelines with a Castle Lager in my hand. I was old enough to know better.

'Hello, Pete,' a bold voice called. It was Alison Wyrley-Birch astride a huge palomino.

'Golly. Aren't you riding today?'

Alison had a commanding voice, one which few people could ignore. Several riders looked over. Before I could answer, she boomed, 'Of course, you must ride. Good heavens, Libby, why didn't you bring him a horse? Val, get the groom to saddle up Crackerjack. He's one of our polo ponies. You will love him. But be gentle on his mouth.'

Crackerjack? I visualised a small, friendly pony. I watched in horror as this war horse was led from the stable. It was a monster. Actually it was not a pony at all, more like a stallion in my eyes. I had little choice, what with everyone looking on. So, thanking Alison for being so thoughtful, I mounted The Beast. As he snorted, pawed the ground and skipped sideways, I knew that I was not the one in control. Crackerjack became Beelzebub and with a final snort, cantered in the direction of the other horses.

Dear Beelzy had one gear – flat out. Sensing my nervousness, he flattened his ears, flared his nostrils and took off. 'Be gentle on his mouth,' I thought. 'Be gentle on his fucking mouth.'

At first, all went well, what with the wind in my hair, the feel of a strong beast between my legs, taking the jumps in a stride, waving to the other riders as I rode gracefully past, laughing as I overtook them, watching them grow smaller, more distant. I felt a certain surprise, shall we say, as the other riders disappeared from view altogether. On the horizon across the field of Rhodes grass I saw the distant, hazy feature of a single copse of waterberry trees[85], growing less hazy, getting closer, sharper, growing bigger and bigger, the branches hanging down to a certain height. What height? Were they eight feet above ground? Seven? No, they look more the height of Beelzebub.

Funny that, I thought, as I crashed through the trees, the sound of snapping branches exploding all around me, thundering through like a juggernaut, unstoppable, the noise in my ears, the wind gone out of me. The Beast was now through the trees unscathed and I was tumbling across the ground head over heels, finally coming to rest with a jarring crunch and a groan against a termite mound. Beelzebub never stopped running and ended his days with a bullet to the head, although I am

---

[85] *Syzygium cordatum* – an evergreen, water-loving tree which can grow to a height of 25-50 feet.

reliably informed not because of me. I, on the other hand, had the misfortune to have to walk bloody and scratched into the après-lunch party, my new T-shirt emblazoned *Sex Lessons – First Lesson Free* now tattered and torn. My riding days were over, or so I hoped.

'Well done, Woody!' shouted someone from the polo set. 'Get this man a beer. Looks like he bloody well needs it.'

Being a glutton for punishment, I soon found myself once again in a situation involving horses, this time lots and lots of them.

When I left school at the tender age of just 17 to go into the army, I found myself in the uncomfortable position of being one of the youngest in that year's intake of soldiers. As with all armies, the first ten days involved a selection process for the different battalions and departments. My dream was to enter the Rhodesian Light Infantry, commonly thought to be cannon fodder but also incredibly brave and adept. They also had the best uniforms.

The selection process began at the Llewellyn Barracks in some godforsaken place near the Somabula Flats. There were hundreds trying out for different units and that year the RLI, as the Rhodesian Light Infantry was known, were taking only 25 men. Twenty-five men out of some 1,500 recruits. The elimination began.

'Who here is under 18?' the NCO barked.

Delighted to be helpful and look willing, I raised my hand with gusto.

'Then you're out,' said the recruitment officer, his face expressionless. I then remembered my brother's advice: never volunteer for anything in the army.

Too late. That was it. No choice. I was out. Just like that. No press-ups until you fall, no running until you drop. Out, in three short words. I was devastated. In a panic, I looked around me. There were only two choices left. There was the Signals Corps, a bunch of losers in my estimation and an ugly uniform to boot, or Grey's Scouts, the country's mounted infantry regiment. Horses.

So, with a sigh, I drew myself up and resigned myself to a full year surrounded once more by bloody horse shit. The room where the Greys were having their peptalk was the size of an aircraft hangar, crowded with some 400 men, all sitting upright, fists closed on knees, staring rigidly ahead as a commanding officer strode up and down the podium singing the praises of the Grey's Scouts.

Finally, after what seemed like the dreariest hour of my life, he turned to stare at us all one after the other, taking a moment to give it all the right amount of oomph, and delivered his punchline.

'The Grey's Scouts are the best regiment in this army with the finest and bravest soldiers in Rhodesia. So if there are any of you out there who think they don't have the balls to take this, stand up now and walk out.'

A breathless silence engulfed the room. Not a cough nor squeak nor sound. Then I stood up. And head held high, I walked. And walked. Eight hundred eyes followed me in my 'march of shame'. You could have heard a penny drop.

No sooner was I out of the hangar then everything came rushing back to me. The exhilaration of having listened to my instincts engulfed me in waves. No more horses. No more fucking horses. But then what? Hardly a soul stirred in the entire barracks. All the hangars were silent, their doors closed, their selection processes over. Not even a breeze stirred, even the wind seemed to have held its breath. An MP with his red beret rounded the corner.

'Excuse me sir,' I asked.

'I'm not a bloody sir, you idiot. I am a sergeant, you little twit,' he growled.

'Excuse me, sergeant,' I continued, 'but can you tell me in which hangar the RLI are having their selection?'

He eyed me up and down suspiciously and laughed.

'The RLI made their selection over an hour ago. You're way too late. It's the Signals for you, soldier.'

As a goodwill gesture, he waved his hand in the vague direction of a small corrugated-iron building, indicating that was where the RLI were, then he strode off.

'You're wasting your bloody time,' he called back.

I entered the hallowed halls of the RLI selection room to be met with my second stony silence of the day. Twenty-five lads in a row being lectured to by a fit-looking man covered in silver pips.

'What the hell do you want?' he asked.

All 25 heads turned to see who had interrupted such an important talk.

With a trembling lip, I stammered: 'I want to be in the RLI, sir. I left school to be part of this battalion, sir. I have only ever dreamed …'

'Oh, shut up and stop blubbering,' he said with an amused twinkle. 'Sit down. You're in.'

And so it was that I got into the RLI and so it came to pass that I became the last person ever to enter the 1st battalion of the Rhodesian Light Infantry.

Unknown to us, that very day Robert Gabriel Mugabe became the first black prime minister of Zimbabwe-Rhodesia, and the rest is history.

13

The Saints

There we were, ten of us, right on the cusp of becoming hardened commandos in more ways than one. With only a week away from our much-anticipated passing-out parade, I found myself sitting in a circle of boys on the polished concrete floor of our barrack room pumping away furiously at our members.

Every single one of us had the same thoughts thundering around inside our heads. At what stage during a circle-jerk does one ejaculate? Cum too early, god forbid, and that could mean you are a bit too keen, which, of course, I was. Arriving too late, on the other hand, might mean you are cock shy, something equally ridiculed in the barrack room. Besides, I was not yet proficient in *coitus reservatus*. It was a lesson in intense concentration, nerves of steel and an inner control that only comes with the joy of youth or Superman, which is one and the same really.

Daring to open my eyes, I spied the group of lads not yet out of their teens, at the peak of physical fitness, faces glowing with vigour and health and a slight fuzz of hair along their gritting jaw lines. Their taut, unlined faces red and speckled with beads of sweat from the effort, bodies hard from an exhausting 16-week training course that would begin at 4am each day and end close to midnight. Young men too tired to even get a morning glory, let alone the time to find release in the cubicles. If you had five minutes to spare, you slept: where you sat; on your bunk; wherever you were. You did not have sex.

'Jesus fucking Christ!' said Kurt. 'When was the last time any of you guys had a bone?'

The small group scattered around the barrack room, polishing boots or writing letters looked up in surprise.

'No, seriously guys,' he continued, 'when did you last have a fucking hard-on? Even a bloody morning glory?'

We looked at each. Some laughed in embarrassment.

'Dunno,' said Craig. 'Come to think of it, I can't remember. Shit, man.'

'It's true,' said another. 'Sheesh. I swear I haven't even had a twinge since we began the course.'

'Maybe it's the blue stone,' giggled one chap, referring to the legendary crystal copper sulphate that was allegedly put into the tea to prevent soldiers from having an overly active libido.

Then we were all talking in unison. Nodding and agreeing and very aware that not one of us had managed a boner in six weeks. At this age, we should have been having them several times a day, according to the text books. An embarrassed silence followed this revelation. We looked at each other, no one daring to notice the elephant in the room.

S-E-X.

'Fuck, man,' said Kurt, possibly the toughest and hardest (and the most handsome) of all the recruits. 'I'm seriously horny.'

His voice trailed. He pretended to rub an imaginary spot from his mess tin.

I lay back against my locker waiting to see how this would pan out. I knew instinctively that this was not the time to be a leader of the pack. I was the youngest and by no means the weediest, but I had secrets. I had better reason than anyone else to just fade into the amber sodium glow cast from the corridor light outside.

Nothing had ever prepared me for what was about to happen. Not at school, not on camping trips along the Nyarowe, and certainly not in the army.

'Let's all wank,' said Kurt. 'In a circle. Here in the barrack room. Now.'

It was simple and perfect and it came from the very embodiment of masculinity and heterosexuality. I was off the hook, albeit on the verge of fainting.

The complexities and nuances and etiquette of a circle-jerk were something none of us had ever discussed nor experienced before. Not even at school. Well, not me, anyway.

Naturally, there was the noise factor. This was first and foremost in our minds as we settled into our positions.

'Uggggg, uggghhhh, phhhwoaar...'

'Shut the fuck up, you toss pot.'

Stifled laughter. Most of us were seasoned professionals in the art of wanking silently. On the other hand, too loud meant you were having too much fun. Of course, too little grunting might also mean a suspicious need to prolong the session. And then there was the horror of being caught by an NCO or fellow recruit doing their rounds. Awkward. Very, very awkward. There were also technical issues not yet discussed. Quick thinking, knowledge about the diameter created by ten boys and a vague idea how far one can shoot, or more importantly, marksmanship, which was going to be fundamental to a happy, unembarrassed ending. As for timing, I think I came fifth.

How did it come to this?

In sergeant Charlie Warren's book *At the Going Down of the Sun,* there I was, in black-and-white: Trooper Wood P.W. sandwiched between Oberholzer F.J. and Hardwick W.A. One of just 33 men to have served with 3 Commando until the very end. This comprised an unlikely smorgasbord of hardened war veterans and the final 15 from our 26-man intake earlier in the year.

And what a year it had been.

Earlier in the year, I had signed away my civilian life. It had seemed so easy. I was in the bloody army. 134144 Trooper Wood P.W. Sir!

Well, I was not yet a trooper or 'troopie', the name given to a private in the Rhodesian army. I was a recruit. With a number. The troopie part would come much later after initiation and training, which was expected to last a staggering 16 weeks. I was young. I was exceptionally fit. I could run like 40 bastards. I was driven by a desire to prove to myself and my father and my country that I was fit to serve. I was also slap bang in the middle of an identity crisis raging through my head. My limbs, my nether regions, like some crazy, never-ending battleground. An identity crisis that was going to require nerves, concentration and suppression of every natural instinct (other than survival) that I could muster.

My timing could not possibly have been worse. The day I got into the army, Rhodesia simply ceased to exist. The humour of enlisting – voluntarily – into an army to fight a losing battle was not lost on me. Of course I was not to know, until several days after I enlisted, that Mugabe had won the elections. The military has a way of suppressing that kind of thing. Rumours filtered in but never seemed to manage to take hold among the thousands of recruits at Llewellyn Barracks.

If anything, there was just total confusion from how to make a fucking bed fit for inspection, or what exactly spit-and-polishing your boots meant (it means just that). I felt that I had stepped back in time to my first few days at boarding school. Nothing was familiar or recognisable. Young men seemed to be running everywhere with panicked looks upon their faces. And absolutely everyone was getting shat upon. My father instilled a terror in us through his timbre and use of English. But the army was a whole new kettle of fish. Pared back, it revealed a raw, ancient method of quickly reducing a man down to the last common denominator.

I got my first taste of drill. I realised for the first time that I had two left feet. I learned very rapidly that bunks were not to be slept in (but admired from below on the cold concrete floor). The stories about polishing bed springs is all true, that eyes were to stare straight forward regardless of who was screaming at you, that my mother was blessed like the Virgin Mary (the only curse not allowed in the army was, 'son of a bitch').

'You are fucking nothing. You are the lowest fucking person on earth. You are as low as shark shit. In fact, you little pricks, you are even lower than shark shit. You recruits are the sand that the sharks shit on. Brace up recruits, you little cunts. And what are you looking at, you little fucker? I'm going to pluck off your fucking arm and shove it up your arse and wave you around like a toffee apple.' They liked that one.

Of course, all this is yelled two-and-a-half-inches away from your face, the spittle spraying your forehead, the NCO's moustache tickling your chin, your eyes staring ahead, through the instructor, beyond, to an imaginary place, another world, another life. A life of boarding school, being a senior, like being a big fish in a small pool. Now reduced to the sand that sharks shit on. It was a terrible shock.

Everything was new to me. At the time I joined, the Rhodesian army was made up of more than 60 per cent black volunteers, many of whom had never seen a flush toilet, and they all mixed with us at Llewellyn. That alone was alien to me. But the ablution blocks were without a doubt some of the most disgusting I have encountered, what with thousands of recruits passing through them daily. The punishment for sleeping on top of your bed (not under the bed staring up at the wire springs) and thus not passing inspection, would more often than not lead to a vomit-inducing clean-up muster in the toilets.

Simply put, Llewellyn Barracks was a hell-hole. It was designed purely as a recruitment depot for all the different battalions of the Rhodesia Regiment. It was designed to bring those cocky high school boys to heel. Everyone from potential officers to grease monkeys came through that place.

If anything, it encouraged me to try harder. To run harder. To raise my arms to shoulder height during drill. To stamp my heel harder when saluting. To shout, 'Yes sir! or 'Barrack room, shun!' louder. Getting selected for the Rhodesian Light Infantry, commonly known as The Saints, was absolutely and beyond a doubt the most important thing for me right at that moment. Nothing else mattered. And not just the RLI, but 3 Commando: 'The Lovers'.

And a Lover I became. Against the odds, I was selected as the 26th recruit in a year when only 25 were being picked, so admittedly by sheer luck. We automatically became members of an elite group, singled out from the rest of the rabble. Make no mistake, we were still low-life, but now, safely back in our battalion HQ in Salisbury, away from the overflowing latrines and scared, sweaty crowds and smells, and small-minded, red-capped MPs, I could finally get some semblance of who I was, why I left school and why I signed up and wrote off a year of my life. It was also a time to reflect, to step up as a man and step back as a gay boy. Anything I felt about myself was gently placed on the back burner for a later time in life. Quietly simmering away, but unnoticed.

In the rural areas the war continued unabated, almost as if the elections had never happened. It was as if Mugabe, our sworn enemy, was not prime minister. It would take up to six months for the soldiers from ZIPRA and ZANLA to lay down their arms, and ahead of us there was a job to be done. I was embarking on a training regime considered one of the hardest, not only in Africa but globally, a course that was going to turn a soft, pampered schoolboy into a commando. A course that was no different to any of those taken by my predecessors. In fact, as far as the RLI was concerned, Mugabe had not even won. For the Rhodesia Regiment, it was business as usual.

The army is a very grown-up place. The polar opposite of school. The shouted abuse becomes commonplace, almost dull. The hours of parades, saluting, stamping, slow marching, presenting arms, inspections, leopard-crawling beneath barbed wire under live fire, and the aches and pains all become a means to an end. The hurry-up-and-wait attitude. You just suck it up. That sprained ankle? Move on, buddy. It is far better to stamp your foot when saluting and just bear the agonising pain shooting up your leg than to go to 'sick parade' and have to walk around the barracks with a white Second World War helmet with a red cross emblazoned on the front.

'You call that a salute? Stamp harder, recruit!'

'Yes, sir.' Sha-shoonk

'You call that a goddamn stamp? Stamp harder recruit!'

Yes, sir!' Sha-shttonk.

'If you do not give me a proper salute I will have you sent to the box[86]. Now, salute. Use your heel. Not your toes, you little drip.'

SHTTUNK!

'Hmmmph ... that's better.'

The agony coursing through your body keeps your comrades happy for now. If one recruit fails, all recruits fail.

It is the few stolen moments of fun, camaraderie, hilarity, real danger, and cocking around that tends to make life in the army bearable. And friendship. Love, almost. You are trained, day-in and day-out to work as a unit. A well-oiled machine. As a single man, you are nothing. As a group, you are unbeatable. A killing machine. If one man falls, you all go down with him. Or you pick him up, again and again, hating him, cursing him, wanting him dead for making you work harder. Tough love.

We were all there at some stage and we all fell. We were all picked up. Time and time again. You walk, march, salute, run, sing as a unit. You sleep side by side and you learn that your brother in arms is the most important person in the entire universe. No one else matters. No one. It is deeper than love. Stronger than desire. More intense than hatred. You will, quite literally, die for each other. It is as simple as that.

I loved the army for that very tenet, that they can take a boy and not just mould him into a man, but make him into an organism that works as one and will die as one. It also creates friendships

---

[86] A military jail.

that border upon love. A love that is complex and masculine yet beautiful in its simplicity. Homosexuality did not come into the equation. Tenderness could turn into a black rage within minutes, urged on by exhaustion and discomfort. Those that could not fit in simply went AWOL. If one weakness in the chain was discovered, it was better for the unit that the broken link should be extricated, encouraged to slip away quietly in the night. No one was looking out for them. No MPs would search for them. The guards were asked to turn a blind eye. It was simply survival of the fittest.

One of most horrible, psychologically fucked-up and degrading exercises during the training was, without a doubt, that of the bayonet drill, an exercise as old as the British army itself. Simply put, it taught young freshmen to hate the enemy as fervently as they could, and kill as many of them as possible.

Bayonet drill might sound dull and boring. It begins after breakfast and continues all day. Fixed bayonets, charging again and again at hessian sacks filled with straw and placed on poles. The men are encouraged to make horrible blood-curdling screams as they thrust and twist their bayonets into the targets. Charging, screaming, baring their teeth, staggering, falling, getting up, charging, screaming. And all the time, the instructors' grim faces bearing down upon you, smiling – more like a ghastly grimace.

'Kill him! Kill the fucker! C'mon you little fuckers. Charge! Tear his bloody guts out. Rip open that belly. Again! Do it again, you little bastard. Thrust – upper swing – into his goolies. Tear out his bollocks. Charge! Do it again...'

As the sacking disintegrated, new sacks were called for. More charging. More screaming. All around me, grown men were crying. On their knees. Unable to move further.

'Get the fuck up, Wilson,' we would shout.

One man down would mean all men punished.

'Come on, you cunt. Get off your bloody knees. Oh man. Here, give me your hand ... wanker.'

On and on. Again and again.

'Bite him. Stick your goddamn teeth into him,' the instructor would roar. 'Right, you lazy buggers. Do it again. Wilson ... you fucked up. Everyone back to the beginning.'

By evening, our voices had grown quiet, rasping. There was little to say anyway. Few people could get their vocal cords to work. Our arms had seized up. Our legs were jelly. We had casualties and we knew we would pay for it. Pay for not keeping our unit intact.

The first time it happened, it took us by surprise. Naturally, we had been told by other soldiers of the infamous barrack room parade. But nothing prepared us for it. The exhaustion from the bayonet drill earlier in the day, and then the sudden confusion of being woken at 2am by the instructors and corporals.

'Barrack room, shun.' Lights on everywhere. Distant shouting and screaming as your brain tries to engage. Then the sudden shock of having your bed, your locker and all of its contents thrown on top of you. And the worst part? Being told that you have half an hour to carry the entire contents of the barrack room, beds, steel lockers, clothes, equipment, the works, across the barracks to the parade ground a thousand yards away. We were to have an inspection, our beds made and our lockers tidied in exactly the same way and the same order as it should be inside the barrack room.

No one was ever really expected to pass barrack room parade. That was not the point of the exercise. It was to degrade you, bring you down a peg, to teach you to work as a team and then to build you up piece by shattered piece so that when they say 'kill' you kill, without thought, without guilt, without hesitation. We were pit bulls in training.

The second time we had barrack room parade, my youth finally got the better of me. The other lads were all two years older than me. They had that extra time to build up muscles and strength. Carrying my tall steel locker across the yard was, quite frankly, my Waterloo. Recruit Smit on the other end of the locker was helping me. My team-mate. My shoulder muscles went first. Then my thighs. I fell, again and again, bringing both the locker and Smit tumbling down on top of me. Time and again he helped me up. Time and again I fell.

'I can't do it, Smitty,' I called.

'Fucking get up, Wood. Don't you fucking dare think about quitting.'

'I haven't got the strength. I swear. My hands are cut to the bone from the fucking steel. I'm stuffed, Smitty.'

'Then we will all be fucked, you little wanker. Get off your arse. Now!'

It hurt. Smit was one of my heroes and a Prince Edward School old boy. His harsh words bit into me. From somewhere deep within I managed to haul myself up and with the help of Smit, carry the locker, the bed and of all his gear too on to the parade ground in time for inspection.

Then we had to take it all back again into the barrack room ready for morning inspection.

By reveille at sunrise, a Kiwi recruit who had been dragging us down in the past fortnight was gone. It could have been me. But encouragement and resilience had managed to give me a second life. For the Kiwi, the message was all too clear. He was a skiver. That was unforgivable. We surrounded him in the barrack room.

I don't know who took the first swipe. I do remember the terror in his eyes. The confusion, then the understanding. It wasn't even his war. But we punched anyway, like savages. Each taking two or three swipes. Then hanging back. Taking a breath. Then going in for more. It was awful. I wanted to shout out to stop it. I expect everyone else felt the same. These were not animals. These were my comrades. For our small band of brothers to survive, the Kiwi had to go. By morning he was reported AWOL and the savagery of the previous night forgotten. Quiet. The Kiwi had gone. We had done it. Naturally, it drew all of us closer. The smaller the group got, the closer-knit we became.

The RLI was nicknamed 'The Saints' or 'The Incredibles', and regarded, through astounding success with both internal fireforce[87] operations in Rhodesia and external pre-emptive strikes against guerrillas based in Mozambique and Zambia, as one of the world's foremost exponents of counter-insurgency warfare. The 3 Commando insignia became a numeral '3', emblazoned on a banana, with the word 'Lovers' above and the designation 'Commando' beneath, all on a green shield. I was never to find out exactly why the banana but perhaps it referred to the 'Lovers'.

As far back as I could recall, I wanted to be part of this fighting unit called The Lovers. I wanted to sing *When the Saints Go*

---

[87] Fireforce is a variant of the tactic of vertical envelopment of a target by helicopter-borne and parachute infantry developed by Rhodesian Security Forces during the bush war.

Marching In with gusto as we drove through the centre of town to the excited cheers of the schoolgirls. We hardly noticed the sullen faces of the black workers. In short, I wanted all the glamour and glory. But to get there I still needed to get to the end of training.

RLI training covered standard infantry counter-insurgency as well as conventional warfare, such as digging trenches, which we loathed. We had daily assault courses to get over. I loved these and found myself in the commando assault course team against the other Rhodesian battalions. We won. As well as commando training such as 'watermanship', rock-climbing, abseiling, unarmed combat, bushcraft, survival, tracking, demolitions and helicopter drills, we also, unbelievably, started to have fun.

One of the favourite training exercises was at the Ngezi Dam in the Midlands, a part of the country I was unfamiliar with. It was a relatively dry region, given mostly to ranching, but quite beautiful and very wild. The entire training troop would camp out at the dam. For us new recruits, it was exciting to see how an army moves and marches on its stomach. The canteens would produce outstanding grub, in the open under the *msasa* trees and among the granite rocks.

Much of the training involved water sports, kayaking and canoeing and, of course, swimming. It surprised us that the instructors would keep hurling thunder flashes into the water around us. These heavy duty fireworks could burn underwater and let off a ripping bang strong enough to rupture a kidney. We believed they were doing it to give us some form of battle realism. We were wrong. This we would find out the hard way.

Recruits would pair up and form bivouacs by digging shallow trenches, stretching our groundsheets over as a roof. There was enough room to squeeze two men inside. It was cosy, to say the least, and spooning one another was quite acceptable behaviour. It was nearly winter and the mornings could be very cold. One group of seemingly rugged lads decided to pitch their bivouacs on a spit of land 100 yards or more away from the main group. By daylight, it looked like a good position, but that night the boys were woken to a grim surprise. At first, they heard a slithering. Followed by a scraping. A strong fishy odour permeated the bivouacs. It seemed to be coming from all around their tents. One chap finally had the sense to peep out of his bivvy. And there, just a couple of feet from his head, was a huge black crocodile. Then his eyes adjusted, and saw the rest. Ten, maybe 20 crocs had chosen this spot to sleep, or hunt.

At first the screams sounded distant, like a dream. Then they began penetrating our sleepy heads. We all jolted upright, a mass of tangled guy ropes and tarps and sleeping bags and cocked weapons. 'What the fuck?' someone shouted. Then we were laughing – uncontrollably, holding our bellies. By the silver light of the autumn moon, the leaping, howling, scrambling silhouettes of our comrades could be seen on the long spit of land as they ran, half-naked through a corridor of snapping splashing reptiles. None of the instructors had informed us that Ngezi Dam was used for crocodile research and reputedly had the biggest population of the reptiles per square mile in southern Africa. The rugged boys spent the rest of the night cowering down beside the canteen, their sleeping bags and tents now property of the monster crocs.

No wonder the thunder flashes. Losing a recuit to a croc would have been unfortunate.

The trainers would often become as proud of – and as close to – the recruits as we were to one another. They became father figures to us. I expect one or two recruits might have even had a secret liaison with an instructor, but never with an officer, to my knowledge. Of course, I was jealous as hell, green with envy, explosive with lust. One particular non-sporty recruit seemed to have taken a shine to one very handsome instructor from South Africa. The recruit would spend many an hour in his room 'polishing his boots'.

I was insane with anger, particularly when we were outside dragging our mattresses up and down the corridors to get that surreal shine on the floor. But lust was never on the menu. I knew that. I knew that a false move would and could kill me. Many of these guys had seen action both in our own bush war and also in Vietnam. I knew what they were capable of when shit-faced. Love was possible, I suppose, in an ethereal and intangible way. But lust was out. And so it confused us one night down at Ngezi when the instructors called us all out of our bivouacs and made us line up for parade in front of their fire, naked. We were instructed to go behind the canteen, remove every item of clothing, except our weapons, and return to the fireside, salute and stand at attention, in line, shouldering our semi-automatic rifles.

'134144 Trooper Wood, sir!'

The instructors sat in deck chairs, beers in their hands, watching as each recruit came before them, stamped their foot in the dust, dick flopping about, then shuffled into line with their comrades. It was like some seedy, weird, porn movie. After a brief inspection, they dismissed us. The confused, silent, naked parade returned to their bivvies and it was never mentioned again.

That night, I had my first wet dream.

The following morning, we were divided into groups of four and sent off on a 100-mile trek. There was little time to think beyond the next mile, the next pitstop, the next bully beef meal.

Of the 26 boys in the 3 Commando training troop, five of us

were singled out to do a medic course. This was done at a remote camp on the Zambezi River where we spent an utterly blissful ten days swimming in the river, lounging on the sandbanks, and, of course, learning about medical aid. We used one another as pin cushions for cannulas and Ringer's Lactate drips, learning the ABCs of first aid, how to staunch a gunshot wound, how to detect brain damage, how to save a life, and also how to allow a man to die with dignity.

The medic instructors were casual, fun and completely different from the trainers back at HQ. When they found out that my father was at a hunting camp only a few hundred yards down the river, they allowed my mates and me to wander over and surprise them. No one was in camp when we arrived, but having grown up with the cook boy, we settled down in the deck chairs and were fed snacks and beers.

By the time my dad returned from his day hunting, he found five rather inebriated and lively soldiers lounging around his camp. But the joy and happiness I saw in his face when he recognised me, his little boy, all grown up in camouflage and carrying a rifle was worth all the effort of leaving school and going into the army. It was the first time he had seen me since I left school.

That was the moment I knew my father loved me.

Being a medic had its advantages. I was in charge of the saline drips and would often administer them to hungover soldiers. There is nothing like a drip to get over a binge. I also had a small vial of morphine tied around my neck. If ever the morphine left my person, I would end up in the box.

Even if one was to break the vial, you were expected to scoop up the soil and bring it back. Of course these rules could become somewhat relaxed in times of stress. The chaps looked up to you if you were a medic. After all, you were in charge of saving their lives.

Unfortunately, the downside of being a medic was the kit. A medic was expected to carry his own pack (laden with bully beef, canned ham, revolting tinned curried eggs, margarine in a tube, jam in a tube, and the indestructible ration biscuits that could only be eaten after soaking them in water overnight). On top of the pack was the radio. All medics carried the field radio, a large brick the size of a car battery with a forgettable name such as AN/PRC-25 transceiver, attached to which was an aerial, bobbing around above you several feet high. It would have been comical had it not made you a complete sitting duck, not to mention extremely difficult when walking beneath low-hanging branches.

'Let's slot the medic,' was a common joke among the lads. Slot being slang for 'shoot'.

Following our passing-out parade and having been integrated into 3 Commando as fully-fledged troopers, we often found ourselves at a loose end. The action down at the sharp end did not materialise in the fashion that we had been led to believe. Yet with a battalion full of hard-arse soldiers back from the war, not to mention us young recruits raring to go, the officers quite rightly felt that it would be good policy to keep us all occupied. Weeks of training and preparation to fight were followed by days of idleness. Hurry-up-and-wait became the norm.

I now found myself rubbing shoulders with hardened veterans, many of whom were heroes. Being the youngest, they took me under their wing, teaching me both their good and bad habits. I was still able to drink many of them under the table, so my reputation as a party animal was kept intact. It was only natural that I would have platonic crushes on a few of the soldiers, but my desire to stay alive and in one piece was stronger than any form of puppy love.

One Sunday, after a day spent in Salisbury on R&R, we were instructed to gather on the parade ground for roll call. It had been a blazing hot autumn day and most, if not all, of 3 Commando, new recruits and hardened soldiers were dressed in boxer shorts, T-shirts and flip-flops, known as 'slip-slops'. Something was up. We could feel it. We now knew our instructors like we knew our own loved ones. We understood their moods and their movements, their twitches and their tics.

'What the hell is going on?' mumbled one troopie under his breath.

'Dunno,' whispered another, 'but it looks damn fishy.'

'Have you noticed the lorries over there?' said one chap. Across from the parade ground a few Bedford RLs[88] were sat idling.

'Shun!' shouted the colour sergeant. 'Brace up, men. Eyes forward.' The ramrod straight colour sarge marched past with his handlebar whiskers twitching nervously.

It is somewhat difficult to brace up in slip-slops, so not surprisingly there was a collective muffled shuffle as we came to attention. All eyes rolled sideways to catch the commanding officer of the battalion, lieutenant colonel Passaportis, walk on to the parade ground. We adored our CO. He was young, tough and extremely gifted. He was the kind of man needed to run a bunch of unruly soldiers often likened to those from the French Foreign Legion.

---

[88] The RL was the British military's main medium-sized lorry (truck), built in the 1950s to late 1960s by Vauxhall Motors' subsidiary Bedford.

'Take everything out of your pockets, soldiers,' he commanded.

'Everything!' shouted the colour sarge, just for the hell of it.

Quickly we emptied out our pockets; packets of Madison Toasted, Kingsgate, lighters, chewing gum, keys, Swiss Army knives, the odd rubber, wallets and loose change.

'And the watches, gentlemen.' By now a small pile of contraband had been piled up on a groundsheet on the concrete.

'Fuckers!' mumbled the chap beside me, 'it's hardly illegal stuff, is it?' We were confused by this sudden confiscation of our property.

Relieved of all our worldly goods, and having had a thorough pat-down, we were then instructed to get into the waiting truck. Without so much as a briefing, we departed, canvas sides of the lorry secured to prevent any of us seeing where we were going.

'Hey, guys. Check it out,' shouted one soldier. He had his dick out and was pulling back his foreskin in a weird way.

'Jesus, bugger. What are you playing at?' the man next to him said, moving away slightly.

'Voila!' he said, revealing a small, very tightly folded $20 bill.

'Sorted,' he said, buttoning up his fly and sitting back with a satisfied smirk.

'You fucker … how did you have time to do that?' We did not wait for an answer.

Like all good armies that have been taught to sleep at anytime, anywhere, we all soon drifted off. After an hour or more, the RL slowed down to about 10-miles-per-hour. We began hitting the odd bump in the road, which woke most of us up. By now it was dark outside.

'Right, lads' shouted a sergeant. 'I'm going to give you each a piece of paper. Then, when I call your names, you de-bus on the move.'

He began calling names in alphabetical order, in twos, or occasionally threes. The vehicle drove a few miles before another two names were called. Slowly, the lorry emptied of soldiers as they slipped over the back and out on to the dirt road, disappearing into the gloom. I was near the end. All the Vs and all the Ws, I thought: Van Zyl, Wood, Wessel. Not really guys I would normally mix with, one being a hard-nosed grease monkey and the other a slightly weedy admin man. My heart sank.

Silently, we de-bussed and stood on the lonely road as the dust settled. We looked at each other. Slip-slops, T-shirts, shorts, no wallets, no fags, no rifle. No nothing. Then we read the paper. It was brief, it was simple, and very clear:

THIS IS AN EXERCISE TO TEST BOTH YOUR ENDURANCE AND YOUR APTITUDE>YOU ARE TO MAKE YOUR WAY TO BEITBRIDGE> YOU WILL RECEIVE FURTHER INSTRUCTIONS FROM MR J.L. ANDERSON WHERE YOU WILL PROCEED TO CAMP 02. LAKE KYLE> YOU WILL RENDEZVOUS AT 1600HRS IN 3 DAYS FROM NOW>ANYONE CAUGHT TRYING TO SNEAK BACK INTO THE BARRACKS OR CAUGHT USING ANY FORM OF MILITARY TRANSPORT WILL BE SENT TO THE BOX.

It was signed by Lt Col Passaportis.

'Jeez, man,' groaned Van Zyl. 'Rendezvous in three days? Are they kidding?'

Beitbridge was on the border of Rhodesia and South Africa. That would mean a journey from the Midlands to Bulawayo then down to the South African border, hundreds of miles. Then, from Beitbridge, several hundred miles more to Lake Kyle in the lowveld. Some random chap called Anderson? It was certainly a part of the world quite unknown to me, being what I like to think of as a northerner.

'Any ideas, lads?' I said.

'Well let's at least get to the main road. We can hike from there,' said Wessel.

Unbeknown to us, each group had been given a different task, a different route, but all were to finally meet at the lake. Some were sent north to Kariba, others to the eastern highlands and a few to Victoria Falls.

And off we set, three rather dusty, forlorn-looking boys, penniless and without cigarettes or food. After a 10-mile walk, we finally made the main road to Bulawayo, where we were picked up by a clapped-out, crowded car full of Africans. Immediately, they took a shine to these odd white men they had found on the road to nowhere. It was not lost on us that the fast whizzing vehicles that had shot past without stopping had all been driven by whites, either with lives too busy to stop and pick up a hiker or else too wary of the many liberal Scandinavian social and health workers who seemed to have piled into the country.

I found myself squeezed tightly between a middle-aged woman with a loud, deep laugh and a shy teenage boy with an endearing smile. On my lap, the woman had deposited a bag of knitting that she happily clacked away at quite unfazed by the extra passengers. Occasionally, the car axle hit the tarmac with a worrying crunch, sending a shower of sparks behind us into the darkness. The driver was smoking a huge roll-up made of newspaper and tobacco scrap that he passed around together with some hot-roasted sweet potatoes followed by a bottle filled with Chibuku local beer. A rickety tape deck, bound to the dashboard with masking tape, was pumping out some upbeat marimba music. Soon we were all relaxed, if not somewhat smelly with Chibuku and sweat, but more importantly headed for Bulawayo.

It soon became apparent that I had landed with my bum in the butter. Both Van Zyl and Wessel spoke fluent Ndebele[89]. Both came from this part of the world. Both had a certain amount of street credibility, which I suspect I was lacking.

'My uncle lives in Bulawayo,' Wessel informed us. 'Let's go there and we can stay the night.' It was a grand plan of action. Indeed, it was our only plan of action.

By the time we farted our way up to Wessel's uncle's gate, it was late. I had hoped to find myself in a nice, middle-class white neighbourhood with sprinklers and alarm systems. Instead, I was surprised to see that street lights tended to be few and far between. The verges were hard dirt rather than the green, mowed variety I was more used to. The area looked downbeat, unkempt, poor and inhabited by a rougher variety of person than I was used to.

'This is the place, here,' said Wessel, indicating a square, whitewashed home.

---

[89] Ndebele is an African language belonging to the Nguni group of Bantu languages. It is spoken by the Ndebele or Matabele people of Zimbabwe.

Red mud from the rainy season had splattered the walls like a crime scene. We thanked our travelling companions who, eager to get to their own homes, sped off in a cloud of smoke and laughter. Creaking open an old, rusted chain-link fence, we entered the yard. The bungalow beyond was in total darkness, half hidden by a large, gnarled frangipani. There was no garden to speak of, just a couple of dilapidated cars, one without wheels, balanced on bricks. The porch was in deep shadow beneath the thin sliver of a moon.

Suddenly, to our horror, out of the darkness came a Beowulf-like creature that terrified the living daylights out of us. It was massive and hairy and was sprinting across the yard at a terrific speed, the long shadow cast by the moon threw a nightmarish shape across the dead lawn. And it was coming straight at us. To our horror, we realised it was an enormous male baboon. It let out a series of blood-curdling barks, baring its hideous fangs, its eyes white and terrifying as it bore down on us.

'A fucking baboon ... RUN!' we shouted, scrambling over each other to get away from the lethal fangs.

At the last second, the baboon lurched, then emitted a death-rattling choke as it was yanked back, falling on its hind legs like the slain Grendel. Then it was at us again, lunging against the chain clamped around its neck. Again and again. In the silence of the night the noise was enough to make the bowels loosen.

All three of us were on our backsides in the dirt, dumbstruck.

'What the fucking hell is that?' shouted Van Zyl.

'Wessel, you bastard, who has a baboon chained to their veranda?' It was a shock but soon we began to laugh. 'Jesus, who are your cousins anyway, don't they believe in mastiffs or Alsatians or axe-wielding murderers like normal fucking people?'

A light came on inside the house and soon the silhouette of a man appeared carrying a shotgun.

'Who's out there?' inquired this South African drawl.

'It's me, uncle. Your nephew, Terry. I'm here with some friends. Can you get rid of the bloody door bitch so we can come in?'

There was a snort from inside and a hard pull of the chain, followed by a good shout that sent the animal scurrying back to his half sawn-off tractor-tyre den. Tiptoeing past, I edged my way inside the sitting room and to relative safety.

Now, I don't like to look a gift horse in the mouth, but the place was a tip. Literally. A huge pile of unwashed clothes took pride of place in the middle of the sitting room floor. I mean huge, at least up to my shoulders in height. Perhaps we had arrived on laundry day. No one seemed to notice it. They simply made their way around it as if it was not there. Occasionally, a grunt and a chink of a chain from outside reminded me that being indoors was far more preferable to being made lunch of by a male baboon.

'Sheesh, you guys must be thirsty, hey?' said the woman emerging from a bedroom, curlers in her hair and fag hanging from her mouth.

'Ja, tant Anna,' said Wessel. 'And if you can find us some scoff, too, that would be mooshy.'

This eccentric man and his wife, who chose to keep a baboon as a guard dog, who chose not to care about personal hygiene or laundry, or the niceties of life such as decent furniture, could not have been kinder, feeding us at that late hour and gesturing for us to find a space to doss down for the night. I was grateful for the roof over my head and the fact that my face had not been torn off by a maddened ape.

Early next morning, we departed for the border and Beitbridge, where we were to find the elusive Mr Anderson. We clearly did not have the heart to ask Wessel's relations for money, but they were kind enough to push a greasy brown paper bag full of delicious-smelling biltong our way, and a couple of packs of much-needed tobacco.

Until now, everything had taken place under the cover of darkness. When I found myself once again in another car full of lively, kind black people, making our way the couple of hundred miles or so to the border town of Beitbridge, I was able for the first time to enjoy the beauty of the lowveld, the mountainous granite Matopos Hills off to the left where Cecil John Rhodes had been buried (with the help of my great granddad), the endless flat dry savannah off to the right, the shimmering ribbon of tarmac meandering into the distance, constantly avoiding small herds of goats or the odd antelope, and the big blue skies of Matabeleland.

Making it to Beitbridge with plenty of daylight to spare, we set off in search of Mr Anderson. Our first port of call: the railway station, where we met a charming, elderly station master. After we explained our situation, he shook his head and with a twinkle in his blue eyes, he pointed the way to the local Beitbridge Hotel.

'Mr Anderson owns the hotel. Good luck,' he said as he waved us away.

Just as we were turning to go, he motioned us back, taking in our slip-slops and dirty T-shirts and crew-cuts.

'So are you boys undercover, then?'

We looked at each other. I suppose we were, really. We nodded in unison.

'Bloody good show,' he said, 'you lads all deserve a damn medal.' We smiled.

'So you need to get to Lake Kyle, huh? Come back here tomorrow at 12. I might be able to help.'

He was rubbing the side of his nose like a James Bond villain. We shook hands and departed for the old colonial hotel up the hill.

True to the station master's word, Mr Anderson (and his wife) were not only the managers of the hotel, but had been expecting us. They greeted us like long-lost children, first pulling us to their bosoms and then showing us up to our room, where they insisted (rather politely) that we have a bath then come downstairs to eat and have a chat. This was all becoming rather easy and extremely enjoyable.

That evening, Mr Anderson gave us a letter to give to our CO and the following morning sent us clean, nourished and happy to the train station. A long, hissing cargo train was waiting at the platform. And we had a berth on it. Well, not quite a berth. The station master had spoken to the driver about these three undercover operators and asked if he could help out. And so that is how I found myself travelling on the very front of a train, on what they call the cowcatcher, for hundreds of miles all the way down to the sugar cane plantation town of Triangle. It was spectacular, and by far the best way to travel by train with the warm lowveld wind in our hair and the thunder and power of a massive locomotive behind us.

Triangle, we knew, was not quite on our route, although it was in the right direction, to a degree. But, as luck would have it,

Van Zyl's family came from Triangle. Having assured us that the best he could do in the way of household pets and exotic guard dogs were a long-haired Siamese and a pair of parakeets, we decided it was an opportunity we could not miss. How we were to get from there to Lake Kyle was quite something else, but we still had 48 hours to kill.

I was beginning to warm to my travelling companions. Thinking about it, I realised that I had done precious little to aid and abet our band of brothers along this journey. I was determined that this would end now.

Fortunately, I did just that.

That evening, the Triangle club had an outdoor movie. They were showing *The Return of the Pink Panther*. It was the highlight of the Triangle social scene and three strapping soldiers (undercover) were certainly not going to miss out. While Van Zyl and Wessel were on a bale of hay necking some girls, I was out trying to redeem my utterly poor reputation for having contributed bugger all to the trip. At the bar I saw my quarry and made my move. I had noticed a group of air force officers at the club, and after some inquiring discovered that there was an airbase nearby. Using all the charm in the world I hinted to one of the pilots that:

    A. My cousin, Mick Grier, was the air commodore of the Rhodesian Air Force *(true)*

    B. We were undercover and urgently needed to get to Fort Victoria near Lake Kyle *(half true)*

I felt that I had nothing to lose. 'Meet me at the base tomorrow morning,' he instructed. And that, so I thought, was that.

The following morning, the three of us found ourselves standing to attention in front of a desk manned by a Rhodesian Air Force officer. All I could see was lots of gold braid.

'I am told you are on some clandestine operation?' asked the man. His tone was sceptical.

'Yes, sir,' we answered together.

'I must say, I am surprised,' he went on shaking his head. 'I have not been told of any ops down in Operation Repulse. Normally we would be informed of this sort of thing.'

He frowned, then looking at me said, 'Who are you with, anyway? What outfit are you with? You say you want to commandeer a plane to take you to Fort Vic?'

Christ, I thought, it just seemed so easy last night over a beer.

'Yes, sir,' I said confidently. 'We are with the RLI sir, 3 Commando. Totally undercover you see, sir.'

'Well, you know we cannot just allow some brown-jobs (the derogatory name for soldiers, as opposed to blue-jobs for air force) to walk in out of the bush and expect us to lay on an aircraft. It is most odd, I must say. You do realise that I will need to call your base and get more details?'

'Yes, sir,' we said. My heart sank. It was the box for us for sure. We were going down. We had stayed with relatives. We had lied to an officer and now we were attempting to hijack a plane to take us a few hundred miles on the pretence that we were on clandestine operations.

Silently, we stood while the officer dialled the operator and got patched through to the RLI. Please, please don't answer. I eyed my mates. Wessel looked back at me – if only looks could kill. The phone kept ringing. Please be busy or something. Whatever happens, please do not get hold of any 3 Commando staff. We stood frozen, the whole while the officer looking back at us and waiting for us to crumble. We could hear the ringing, again and again, then the click and faint answer. He hmmm'd and nodded and said, 'Yes, no, hmm, yes, I see, I see, well thank you. You have been most helpful.'

Then looking up at us one more time, he called in his aide.

'Jones, get these men an aircraft. Now!'

And that was how I managed to get us flown in an RAF Douglas Dakota, just the three of us, to our rendezvous on Lake Kyle and with hours to spare.

By now, the war was winding down. In many ways these assignments were simply a way to kill time. A means of keeping the troops out of trouble. As Mugabe's ZANU and Nkomo's ZIPRA forces laid down their arms, the writing was on the wall. This assignment was soon followed by several anti-poaching operations and one extraordinary war game operation that involved the full might of the army and air force, hundreds and thousands of rounds of ammo, RPGs, missiles, grenades and troops.

It was a spectacular show of might from a dying army, and I expect a way to get rid of unwanted ammunition. After all, why give it over to Mugabe? I do remember mounting a machine gun and aiming it at a large tree and firing rounds until it finally toppled. We hurled grenades into rivers just to see how many fish we could kill, and once tied several claymore mines to a small baobab tree and blew it sky high. It was all very well, but it had to end.

I was never to see the action that had been promised. I have no idea how I would have reacted under actual fire. I expect my training, which was up there with the best, would have ensured that I did everything as ordered. The RLI was officially disbanded on 25 July 1980, with a final parade before a small crowd which included the outgoing prime minister, Ian Smith. The regimental colours were marched past for the last time, and three days later the Trooper statue, a bronze sculpture of a troopie leaning upon his weapon, was dismantled and spirited away to South Africa, and from there to Hatfield House in the UK, seat of the Marquis of Salisbury, a fitting resting place for a symbol of such pride.

Soon afterwards, the battalion became integrated with Mugabe's troops and became known as One Commando Battalion. It fascinated me to see how the soldiers, be they friend or foe, mixed quite happily. The men we were trying to kill last month were now eating with us in the same mess hall. It may have been because the RLI was made up of so many soldiers of fortune, men who cared little about the politics and more about the action. The wrangling and arguments of state were left to the suits in government.

Resentment and anger would follow many years later. For now though, we all just had a job to do. I remained in this hybrid army until Christmas, but the ghosts of the RLI were way too strong and civilian life beckoned. I departed proud, strong, fit and ready to face the world.

14

Lib and the Great Nehanda

My mother was well known for being slightly spooky. Most of the household staff were aware of this. Rural Africans are extremely superstitious and ghosts were a part of everyday life. At many a breakfast, Lib would come into the dining room and tell us about one of her dreams. They were never ordinary. Of course, she knew which dreams were safe dreams and which dreams were real.

On one occasion, in early June 1972, she came down to breakfast in tears. She had dreamed that night of a terrible disaster. She gave a detailed account of women crying. She described children, even their school uniforms. She knew many people had died, but she could not place where it was. Silently, we listened, as did the kitchen staff. Even my dad, for once, didn't tell her to belt up. Then, on 6 June, a series of underground explosions rocked the Wankie No 2 colliery, killing 426 men. Horrified, we all realised that the uniform Lib had described was from the local Wankie school. Her dream had come true.

Other dreams were closer to home. One was about a young boy who had died. Again she was not able to tell who it was, but we all knew a few months later when a friend of mine died of cancer. It didn't surprise any of us too much. My mother's maternal grandmother also had preminitory dreams and conducted numerous séances. Although back at the turn of the century these were à la mode, granny Adams' dreams often came true.

In the middle of the night on 15 April 1912 she sat bolt upright in bed and screamed, 'Tommy's drowning!'

Her wail woke the entire household.

'For god's sake, woman,' grumbled my long-suffering great-grandfather, also called Tom. 'I'm not drowning. I'm right here.'

'Not you, Thomas,' she moaned. 'Tommy! My brother Tommy is drowning...'

She could see him, her favourite brother, surrounded by ice-cold dark water.

'He is drowning. I just know it.' She clutched her husband's arm, her fingernails digging into his flesh.

'Tommy is safe in London, for heaven's sake. Now, shut up. I'm tired,' he said before blowing out the candle.

The next morning every newspaper in the world bore some version of the headline: 'Titanic Sinks. 1,500 Souls Drown'.

Tommy Weston, my great-grandmother's brother was on board, and had been having a torrid affair with a married woman. Thankfully, he was saved, plucked from the icy waters, but went on to America where he was shot dead by the cuckolded husband of his lover. You only get so many chances in life. Tommy's nine lives had run out.

For mum, this ominous gift would return one day to save her life.

This psychic precognition was not isolated to her alone. The Victory Block and Sipolilo district held a long and highly distinguished lineage of female soothsayers, witches and mediums. This was especially widespread in the late 19th century, but went much further back in time.

From the 15th century, the powerful Shona kingdom stretched from the mighty Zambezi River in the north down to the banks of the sluggish Limpopo in the south – essentially all of what became Rhodesia plus chunks of Zambia, Mozambique and South Africa. It was called Wena we Mutapa in the Shona language but is now more commonly known as Monomutapa. The seat of this once powerful kingdom was Sipolilo, only a few short miles from M'sitwe Farm.

Sipolilo was home to a famous Shona spirit-medium named Mbuya Nehanda. She must have had great authority even before the 1896-97 Matabele and Mashona rebellions, a powerful woman committed to upholding traditional Shona culture. In many ways, Mbuya Nehanda was a politician and was instrumental in organising the nationwide resistance to colonial rule during that first *chimurenga*. Even the Matabele king, Lobengula, recognised her power and influence.

Mbuya Nehanda came from a long line of female spirit-mediums stretching as far back as 1430. As white people, we were vaguely aware of the history surrounding this powerful woman, or family of women, and their kingdom of Monomutapa. The Mashona rebellion was initiated in Matabeleland in May 1896 and by that October had spread to Mashonaland. The driving force behind the uprising was Mbuya Nehanda.

The role and influence of this woman cannot be understated. As far as the people were concerned god, or Mwari, spoke through Myuba Nehanda. And she was telling them that Mwari blamed the white man for all the troubles that had come upon the land. They had brought the locusts and the rinderpest[90], and to crown it all the Mashona people, the owners of the cattle which had

---

[90]Rinderpest (also cattle-plague or steppe murrain) was a viral disease affecting cattle, buffaloes and other even-toed ungulates such as antelopes, giraffes, wildebeest and warthogs. It was finally eradicated in 2011.

died, were not allowed to eat the meat off the carcasses because they had to be burned and buried. Through Mbuya Nehanda, Mwari decreed that the white men were to be driven from the country. They, the natives, had nothing to fear, Mwari would turn the bullets of the white man into water.

Mbuya Nehanda and her spirit-medium husband, Kaguvi, were charged with murder. The husband for the death of an African policeman; the wife for the death of the native commissioner Pollard. Both were found guilty and sentenced to die by hanging. At Mbuya Nehanda's execution a drama unfolded, events which could have been interpreted as a display of her spiritual power. Two failed attempts were made to hang Mbuya Nehanda before an African prisoner advised the hangman to remove a tobacco pouch – and its contents – from the woman's belt. This was done immediately and the third attempt was successful.

A faded black-and-white photo shows Mbuya Nehanda dressed in a duiker *kaross*[91] standing by the gallows, her empty *dugs* hanging flat down to her waist, the noose around her neck. Her eyes eternally defiant.

The spirit-medium's dying words were, 'My bones will rise again.'

And rise they did ...

A century after her death, Mugabe ordered his war veterans to start occupying white-owned farms. He said it was time to take back the land that belonged to them. Farms all around the country were being occupied, many violently, and now it was our turn.

It was mid-morning on the farm. From the sitting-room radio,

---

[91] A cloak made from animal hide, usually sheepskin, with the hair left on.

the gentle notes from *Lillibullero*[92] played on the BBC World Service. Woody was out somewhere on the other side of the farm, several miles away. Lib was pottering, as always, from one side of the garden to the other, pulling weeds, dead-heading flowers and checking that the seedlings had been watered properly. It was best to keep occupied even though it meant walking past the freshly dug graves made ready for the dogs when the time came. Crackers, the Jack Russell, was sniffing out snakes and lizards, his wee tail vibrating with excitement.

In the distance Libby could hear a low drumming from the compound down by the river. It was unusual for the tom-toms to be going on a weekday, but not unheard of. It could have been a wedding, or funeral, or the birth of a child. Gradually, the drums got louder and louder, accompanied by several yowling women and chanting men. At first it reminded her of the *n'yau* who used to come every Christmas. But as the voices got louder, the bright morning began to take on a very sinister atmosphere.

Sensing trouble Lib dashed across the lawn back into the house. 'Konda!' she called. Konda emerged from the kitchen wringing a hand towel. His eyes white with fear. A sheen of sweat across his brow.

'It is the war vets, madam,' he whispered. She could smell the fear on him.

'Hurry, then. You must go and find the boss now, Konda, quickly. Checha, checha. Go down the back of the hill and see if he is at the sheds.' At that, Lib dashed across the house to the bedroom and got on the agric-alert.

But the time for that was over, the shouting and chanting by

---

[92] *Lillibulero* dates back to the English Civil War and is the BBC World Service's signature tune.

now had reached the bottom of the garden, and the hysteria in the voices was unmistakable. Any escape route was cut off. Lib could hear the voices from at least 300 people, screaming, all caught up in the pack mentality. She hurried across the lawn to try to lock the security gate. It was too late. The gang was already at the gate. Bile built up in her throat. She wanted to be sick. She could feel Crackers shivering against her leg. Now, suddenly surrounded by a sea of faces baying for blood, she realised the game was up. This was it. This was when it all happened – when you saw your life in slow motion. Raped, torn apart, and murdered by a mob.

Wafts of pungent *dagga*, the weed the locals smoked to get high, filled her nostrils. She recoiled from the sour smell of Chibuku beer and the eyes all around her yellow and bloodshot from cheap alcohol and smoke. The frenzied *toi toi* raised clouds of dust from their dancing bare feet and sent the dogs into frantic lunges and snarls. The gang surrounded her in a sea of hatred and bitterness.

She noticed Alec in the crowd and instinctively knew that he was the ring leader. Banished from the farm, now he was back to get his revenge. She thought back to when he was a tiny kid playing at the back of the house with Pete. An age of innocence. She snapped back to the present. Some people held *panga*[93]. Others axes. Many were carrying sticks. Others seemed possessed or in a drug-induced hypnotic state. Beside Alec was one of the most vitriolic of the gang, a surly man called Kanga Chepe. She had noticed him loitering around the compound and down at the sheds for several weeks.

'One look at him and all I could see was 'rape' written all over his face. Just pure evil. It was utterly terrifying,' Lib said later.

---

[93] A broad, heavy knife of east African origin.

Kanga Chepe reached out and with one long, filthy finger, stuck it up my mother's nose and tried to pull her towards him. Then the shoving and pushing began. First one tentative push, followed by another slightly bolder shove. Encouraged, they all began fighting to get at her, grabbing her dress, her hair, her arms squeezed by rough workers' hands. From one side to the other. Helpless. Pushed around like some rag doll.

'This is our land, now,' one of them screamed.

She recognised him as a teenager who had grown up on the farm. He had always been polite, shy even. She had given him his first job as a garden boy when he was no higher than a hoe. And now here he was screaming and swearing at her, the Shona language pouring out. She felt fortunate that she could not understand what was being screamed. Then they reverted to English and the true horror began to seep in.

'We're going to kill you, you white bitch,' Kanga Chepe growled into her ear. He had a crazed look that turned her blood cold.

'You deserve to die,' shouted one of the women. 'You fucking white whore.'

Where in god's name was John when you needed him, thought Lib.

Someone elbowed her from behind. They were all around her.

Another boy, a kid really, grabbed her hair and yanked. Utter loathing seethed in his eyes, again she knew him as one of the boys from the farm. A cattle boy. Usually timid. Now rabid as a jackal.

By now it seemed like everything was taking place under water, at a distance. Almost a silent throbbing, the drumming and clamouring muted as if her ears were blocked by cotton wool. Somewhere in the distance she could hear the hysterical barking of the dogs. Crackers the terrier snapping at something. The time for panic had come and gone. This was it. This was, she realised, her time to stand tall.

'Stop!' she shouted. Her voice sounded dry and brittle, but clearly had the desired effect.

All of a sudden, all around there was muffled silence, the scuffling of feet and a few inaudible voices, people shifting from foot to foot. Now every inch of amateur dramatics, every tiny bit of elocution training and education and stoicism and bravery came down to this one brief moment. Mess this up, missy, and you are done for. Slowly, dramatically and with as much height a five-feet-four woman could muster, she glared at the faces surrounding her, rotating like a woman possessed, gently prizing a pair of snotty hands from her torn sleeve. She faced a sea of eyes, dust-streaked faces, chapped and cracked lips drawn back into snarls. Many, she noticed, had spittle hanging in threads from their chins.

She knew these people. Most of them had grown up on this very farm. She noted some were wearing old clothes that once belonged to her kids, hand-me-downs. Some stolen. Was that Duncan's rugby jersey? Is that shirt one of Mandy's? She tried to focus. What was happening? How could it have come to this? One woman, still in her teens, a tiny baby bound tightly on her back, spat at her. The gob hit her neck and slid down her chest. The woman's undisguised loathing evident in her dark, opaque eyes.

'It was the women, always the women, who were the most vicious,' mum said later.

'They were responsible for this insanity. This pack madness.

Well, of course, Alec also. I could see him the whole time quietly standing to one side, like he was directing everything. The little sod. Of course it got me thinking. Incredible how I could think so clearly what with all the shoving and pushing. But I started wondering what I had ever done to them to deserve this.'

Her temples began to throb as an uncontrollable rage began to take hold, it was as if her head was in a vice. Drawing a deep breath, she slowly took in the scene and then pointed her finger:

'Now you listen here, you little shits...' she paused for effect.

'I am related to Mbuya Nehanda.'

Mbuya Nehanda? Where the hell did that come from, she thought. She must have been going gaga. She wanted to giggle with hysteria, but managed to continue.

'Oh, yes,' she went on. 'I am the white Mbuya Nehanda – and I know all of you. I know your faces,' she pointed to Alec.

'I know your parents. I saw you all grow up as piccannins,' she stuck her finger into the chest of Kanga Chepe.

'And remember this, my grandchildren learned to speak Shona before they could speak English. My grandfather carried Cecil John Rhodes' coffin up the hills of the Matopos. I have as much right to be here as any of you. I am a Zimbabwean. I am an African.'

She stopped, hesitated and then took a deep breath.

'I don't care what you do to me. You can do what you want with me. You can kill me. Do you hear me? I do not care what you do to me.'

Now she was turning around, slowly taking in each of their faces.

'But if just one of you harms any of my children, I will come back and haunt you.'

She let the statement sink in. You could have heard a pin drop.

Mbuya Nehanda's spiritualism was very real to them, after all she was born only a few miles away.

Libby now looked around her. Silence. Eyes darted furtively from person to the next. Unsure. Hesitant.

This was bad *muti*. Everyone had heard from the kitchen staff that Lib could be a bit eerie. In fact some even went as far as calling her a witch. And everyone believed that bad spirits and *tokoloshes*[94] roamed the land.

Someone shrugged. Another laughed nervously, but there was no conviction in it.

A few of the men smiled. 'Aaah, madam,' one voice said, 'you cannot scare us.'

Others looked to the orator. It was Alec. They were looking for guidance. For some form of bravery. It was not forthcoming. Then they shrugged. Resigned. Shook their heads. Backed away. Better to kill someone who is not a witch.

Almost as one, the group retreated. A pathway opened up behind Lib. Not taking her eyes off them, she edged away, knowing that a lion will always attack a running animal. She quietly walked back across the lawn. The blood-red anger before her

---

[94] A mischievous and lascivious water sprite from African folklore.

and the silent angry stares from behind bore into her body like knives. Holding herself erect, she walked slowly across the garden, like a soldier in no-man's land. Her instinct was to run, to scream, to escape as quickly as she could. Her head cleared. Her aural senses came rushing back. She gulped air as the feeling of suffocation lessened its grip. The dogs were going crazy. Had they been barking the entire time? She had no idea.

As soon as she was at the house, she collapsed on the veranda floor, gasping, exhausted and unable to move. The pips announcing the start of the BBC news played somewhere in the background.

It was over. They would be back, but for now she was safe.

And where the hell was Woody?

Crackers was licking her face. His little body trembling from the assault. She gave him a hug and, gathering herself, she stood up, walked across the veranda and lowered herself into the rattan chair. Her legs were barely able to support her small frame. In the distance, she heard the Land Rover labouring up the hill. There were no tom-toms. No ululating. No banging of drums. By now, the mob was long gone.

Woody strode on to the veranda.

'Konda. Bring tea,' he ordered, then glancing across at Lib, remarked in his dry, deep voice, 'Christ, woman, what the hell's wrong with you? You look like you've seen a bloody ghost.'

She looked across at him and shook her head. If only you knew, she thought. If only you knew.

Two weeks after the assault in October 2002, my parents were forced off the farm. Kanga Chepe took over the house and ended up sleeping in Lib's bed.

The dogs were put down. It was the end of my family's time on the farm.

THE END

This is a tribute to
M'sitwe Farm, Rhodesia
1949-2002

About the Author

Peter Wood was born in Salisbury, Rhodesia in 1962. He grew up on a farm called M'sitwe in the Lomagundi area of the country near Umvukwes, spending the best part of his childhood running barefoot through the untamed bushveld with his brother and sister Duncan and Mandy. It was a wild part of the world and the children were often gone from dusk to dawn, exploring the 13,000-acre property, climbing rocky *kopjes*, exploring caves and camping along the rivers. Despite a civil war that ravaged the land until the end of white rule in 1980, these were salad days and many of Peter's and his family's adventures are described in *Mud Between Your Toes.*

Peter went to Umvukwes Junior School and then Prince Edward High School in Salisbury (now Harare). After completing one year in the Rhodesian Light Infantry he left the country of his birth and moved to London, then on to Hong Kong where he now lives.

He has been granted Chinese nationality and a Hong Kong passport, but still considers himself African to the core.

Printed in Great Britain
by Amazon